EVERYTHING IS MOVING

BY CASSIE WALKER

To Jon, obviously.

A MAP OF THE
NICOYA PENINSULA, COSTA RICA

Contents

Departure

November 22nd, 2011...

I AWOKE TO AN ALARM at 5:15A.M. on my parent's couch. Mom was there, gently shaking my shoulder, cooing her favorite pet names to rouse me from my slumber. I sat up on my elbows to see Jon, lying perpendicular to me on the L-shaped couch, snoring contentedly. I poked him a few times with my toes and he woke up. He looked at me angrily, but my manic smile was infectious: tonight we would be in Costa Rica. We brushed our teeth, packed the paste and brushes, and wordlessly slipped into the clothes we had allocated for travel.

We pleaded with the animals to enter their crates, crammed our belongings into a van we borrowed from Dad's friend, and embraced Mom in a tearful, yet giddy goodbye. Jon and I piled into the passenger's seats, Dad climbed into the driver's, and we were off.

We left twenty minutes late, but still stopped to get coffee and bagels, munching slowly and quietly as we drove through the dark, suburban morning towards

Chicago-O'Hare Airport. The sun rose behind cold, gray clouds, and thick drops of rain splattered the windshield, a reminder of the coming winter, one of the reasons we were leaving our hometown. We pulled up to our terminal (on time!), shed our heavy coats, and found a large luggage cart to load everything and everyone on. We hugged Dad and he drove off, merging, then disappearing into the steady stream of cars. We headed inside to check-in.

Flying internationally with three animals requires a lot of paperwork, and the lady behind the counter did not seem too happy to find us in her queue. She warmed up in the thirty minutes we spent in her presence, mostly because our dog, Marley, has the unique ability to melt anyone's heart. Once his crate was checked and loaded onto a new luggage cart, we waved goodbye to him and watched as he was rolled away by a whistling airport employee. Our suitcases were whisked away at this point as well, so we gathered ourselves, our cats, and our carryons, and headed to security.

It was necessary to let the cats out of the bags to send their carriers, and not their cells, through the x-ray. I grabbed Dylan, his yellow eyes scanning the scenery, but his fluffy body as relaxed and bored as usual. Jon grabbed Clover, her claws cautiously clutching his forearm. We made it through the metal detectors without anyone escaping.

Aboard the airplane, a friendly flight attendant informed us that Marley was safely stowed, so I sat, Clover shoved under the seat in front of me, and thought about what I really wanted out of this trip; and out of my Life…

The flight to Miami was painless. Once electronic devices were approved, we used the iPad to watch *The Office*, play some *Solitaire*, and go over our traveling phrases en Español. The most exciting part was witnessing The Cats experience a plane landing for the first time. I was proud of them for taking it in stride.

We had a layover, so I took The Cats to a family restroom, and tried to convince them to pee on a pile of paper towels. Needless to say, I was unsuccessful. Clover hid in a cabinet. Dylan roamed the room shooting me disdainful looks about putting him on an airplane only to arrive in an airport bathroom. I shoved them both back into their carriers and crossed my fingers they could hold it for another few hours.

Returning to our gate, I sent Jon to find some coffee, then ate a peanut butter and jelly sandwich that we had packed the night before. I inhaled the warm comfort of the beverage and closed my eyes, letting my thoughts drift away...

This was certainly not my first flight to Florida. Beginning at the age of four, I had traveled to Orlando a few times a year to visit MomMom and PopPop. It wasn't Jon's first flight either. In fact, his amount of airport experience made my annual voyages seem totally insignificant...

I snapped out of my daydream at the announcement of our boarding and turned to Jon whose thumbs were moving wildly across the screen of his iPhone. He smiled without looking up and explained that he was just trying to send some last minute messages before we turned off our cell phones for six months. We dragged our belongings on board again, and this time I was able to snag the seat by the window.

The aerial view of the southern tip of Florida and its Keys was truly miraculous. Flying over sparse clouds made us feel like we were looking at the sky instead of the ocean: a swirly blue and green sky, like an exaggerated twilight in the middle of the day. We really do live on a beautiful planet. I thought back to the last time Jon and I were on a plane, eleven months ago, when we flew to Hawaii with his entire family.

The moment we stepped off the plane in Honolulu I felt different, something in the way the warm air smelled made me feel drunk. I could feel the circulation that my appendages had been missing all winter return with a vengeance at the sight of the sun. I was in love.

It was my first Walker family vacation. Jon and the rest of the Walker Brothers were all married or engaged to a couple of ladies known as the Sister Chicks. The plan was for everyone to start having kids in the near future, so we figured we might as well go on a vacation before it became a logistical nightmare. Throughout the week I watched each couple connect in a signature way, arms around shoulders, hands tucked into elbows, kisses stolen in the midst of conversation. I knew I was lucky to have fallen into such a great family.

At the time, Jon and I were recently "unemployed", and planning our wedding, so the trip felt like an irresponsible financial decision. However, once we saw Mother Nature in all of her beauty, something awoke inside of us that we had never realized we were missing. On day two of our vacation Jon and I sat on the beach, watching the sun sink below the water, and started discussing moving to the islands. Once The Townhouse was gone, we were going to have to start over, why not start over here? We kept our thoughts to ourselves, feeling completely crazy, but also completely sure that it was a possibility.

A record-breaking snow storm hit Chicago the day before our scheduled return, and the airlines had to cancel all the flights, stranding us in tropical Hawaii for a few extra days. They offered us any return ticket we liked, and while most of the Walkers got the earliest flight back, Jon and I decided to take the opportunity for a free vacation extension to enjoy a little pre-wedding honeymoon/taste of life in Hawaii. We spent the next few days doing a little sight seeing and a lot of apartment shopping. We talked to locals, got the neighborhood vibes, and walked away from our familiar strip to check out other urban island spots. Mostly what we found was that Hawaii was *incredibly* expensive.

In the following months, we planned and planned, trying to figure out how best to relocate ourselves from the suburbs to paradise. One day, we stumbled upon an Internet link comparing Hawaii to Costa Rica, and we both read on intently, chewing on our lower lips. We found out that Costa Rica has a very low cost of living, it is practically on the equator, tourist friendly, and considered the most ecologically conscious country in the world. Just like that, Hawaii was over, and the rest, well…

It was 5:30P.M. when we landed in San José, Costa Rica. The airport was like any airport I had been to, except everything was in Español with English subtitles instead of the reverse. We got through immigration easily, and then we were off to find Marley. His crate rolled out on a belt, accompanied by a few other canine friends, and although his tail was wagging uncontrollably, his eyes gave away his complete fatigue. We got him through customs and walked out the door.

I thought we had brought so few things until we accumulated all of our belongings again in San José. We had three suitcases, two cat carriers, one backpack, one dog crate, and one guitar. We piled everything on yet another luggage cart, and headed to the rental car station.

Despite having reserved an SUV weeks ago, the only car they had that night was a compact one that would not accommodate the two of us and all of our worldly possessions. Exhausted and starving, we decided to take a taxi to our hotel. We could pick up a car in the morning, when we would drive to Montezuma, our final destination.

We hopped in a taxi van and told the driver the name of our hotel. Either he couldn't understand us, or had never heard of it, so we flagged down a friendly, English-speaking airport attendant and explained the situation. He talked to our driver in rapid Español, the speed of the language a slap in the face despite my meticulous practice in the previous weeks with Rosetta Stone. As soon as they stopped talking, the car gunned forward without anytime for a *"gracias"*. Cell phone-less and completely unsure of what directions the driver was operating under, we entered wide-eyed onto the highways of San José.

It was nighttime and a nightmare. Traffic was lane-less, and the route full of u-turns. I was relieved we weren't driving, panicking just having to ride in the car. The Costa Rican capital reminded me of Los Angeles, except for the signs en Español and the hordes of scrawny dogs and children running around in the street. As the car jerked over the pot-holed pavement, the animals wedged in the backseat remained eerily quiet. Their silence set me on edge, having been caged since sunrise, I expected to hear them crying.

We arrived at a dead end and our driver started talking to us in Español. I explained that mi Español es malo and he slowed down enough for me to gather that we were lost. I nodded, but all we could do was point at the name of our hotel, tiny blue text on an illuminated but disconnected iPhone. The resourceful driver called the number listed on his own cell phone while I concentrated on listening, recognizing a few out of context words here and there. Soon, we sped off, back in the direction we had come from.

We hadn't ventured too far off route and soon we pulled up to the gate of our hotel. I took Marley to pee on his first Costa Rican tree, and by the time he was finished, Jon had paid the driver, and unloaded all of our bags.

The "hotel" was actually a small bed and breakfast, and its proprietors were a married couple that we had contacted many times via email, a sweet lady named Violeta, and her husband Daniel. Daniel's English was much better than my Español, so we were able to explain that we needed food and litter for our cats, food for our dog, and food for ourselves. He had never heard of cat litter, but gave us directions to a local supermercado, and offered to accompany Jon there. Jon graciously accepted. The men headed off on foot while I stayed behind with Violeta and our pets.

Violeta's English was just as good as my Español: a vocabulary of about forty words, most of them colors and numbers. With a joint effort, we were able to have a conversation. She assured me that Marley was free to run around. I asked her for water to give to him and the cats. She obliged, offering me a glass as well. We all drank deeply as Jon and Daniel returned with the bad news that the supermercado was closed. Our host offered to drive Jon to a different store, and again, we graciously accepted. Before they left, Daniel asked if we needed dinner and we nodded vigorously, explaining that we were vegetarianos. He seemed seriously shocked. With a hopeful expression he asked, *"peces?"*. My meager Español knew that meant fish and I was torn between hunger and idealism. I shrugged, we needed to eat.

The boys headed out again and I surveyed Marley as he ran around the property. Outside the gate, I could hear dogs barking, and he was having fun chiming in. I continued my conversation with Violeta, telling her the casa was bonita and that the food she was cooking smelled muy bien. She corrected me, explaining that it smelled muy rico, and I appreciated her help with my study of this new language. She asked where I was from and I said Chicago, where it was frío. As we acclimated to our language barrier we actually shared a few laughs, and she insisted that my pronunciation was good, despite how few words I actually knew.

I was able to get the Internet password and started compulsively Googling things. I learned about the limited availability of cat litter in Costa Rica, while simultaneously researching what products can serve as a replacement. I used Google Translate to look up anything that might aid in my conversation with Violeta, but time passed slowly, and I started to worry that I would never see Jon again.

Suddenly, Violeta appeared and handed me a receipt: our dinner was here. I went to our room, but realized before I got there that Jon had his wallet and I had zero cash (an ATM run, dinner, and cat litter shopping was part of our plan when we thought we would be driving our own SUV). I explained that my esposo had my dinero and she offered to pay for the food if I would pay her back. Sí, por favor. I went back to Googling. Only a few seconds later she appeared again. Her esposo had all of *her* dinero. Oops. She tried to teléfono her esposo, but he never answered.

Thankfully, it was only a few minutes before the esposos arrived at the hotel safe and sound (with litter!), and were able to buy us dinner. We poured the litter into a disposable roasting pan that Jon had ingeniously purchased in the absence of an actual litter box, and finally freed The Cats from their carriers. Dylan gave an appreciative grunt as he dug his paws into the pebbles. We apologized to him profusely, scratching both felines between the ears, before heading out to the front porch to eat. The fish was fried and greasy, and still had its face, but we were hungry, so it was muy rico.

As my belly filled I could feel the stress melting away, but my mind was still racing, trying to catch up with all the events of the day. I had expected to be exhausted, after all traveling was nothing new, but today had been so much more than traveling. I had never really thought about our stay in San José. It was simply a place to sleep before heading off to Montezuma in the morning. Now that we were here, I couldn't help but see how naive that oversight had been. The inability to rent a car and buy cat litter. Those details didn't even register as things to think about back when we were sitting in the suburbs of Chicago planning this trip.

And then there was the language barrier. One of my motivations for traveling to Central America had been to learn Español. Many times I had imagined disembarking from the plane six months from now, fluent in the beautiful language. Never once did I imagine the first night in the country, and the isolation of being on foreign soil without the ability to ask any pertinent questions. Back home I was excited to learn about a new culture, now here I was in the thick of it, and it was quite intimidating. In the past year I had felt so disconnected from my own culture, yet tonight I realized how much I *was* my culture. I was an overprivileged white girl, who had shown up on someone else's steps, with all of my stuff, demanding someplace warm to live. At least that's how I felt.

Luckily, the Costa Rican people, who refer to themselves as Ticos, are quite hospitable. Their benevolent attitudes were already being displayed to us. Not only did we not get murdered by our taxi driver, but he went above and beyond to help two lost and frazzled gringos. We didn't get ripped off by Violeta and Daniel either. They took us to two grocery stores, acquired our dinner, and helped us to learn things about ourselves that we might have never known otherwise. After dinner we were spent, so Jon and I, along with our pets, crowded into our room. Everyone stretched, yawned, piled on the bed, and instantly, fell asleep.

Our rest was fitful, constantly interrupted by barking dogs, and we woke up earlier than usual, to the unexpected sound of roosters crowing. Violeta made us café, and then we started to figure out how we were going to get to Montezuma without our rental car. Wary of driving after our experience the night before, we had recently decided to hire a car with a driver, an idea that had previously been our worst-case-scenario option.

We soon found out that finding someone willing to drive twenty hours (round-trip) with one hour of notice was not an easy feat. Especially with cargo that includes three animals, and when options are limited to companies that understand at least some English. We recruited Google Translate and Violeta to help us, and were eventually able to find a car that would fit our needs (although it did not fit our budget). Successful, we repacked the few belongings that had escaped from our suitcases, and sat down to a nice breakfast of toast and frutas with Violeta.

The taxi was our first tangible experience with the Costa Rican phrase, "Pura Vida". The words translate literally as "Pure Life" but from what we read on the Internet, they can mean anything from "Shit Happens" to "Absolutely", and also act as a greeting, similar to "Aloha", meaning "Hello", "Goodbye", and "I'm Fine". The taxi was an hour late (we had a ferry to catch at noon) and it was a compact car (zoom to the dog crate, two cat carriers, a guitar, our luggage, plus the now-empty roasting pan, animal food, and litter). Regardless, the driver was all smiles as he shoved all the animal accessories inside Marley's crate and secured said crate to the roof of his tiny automobile. When it held, he shrugged and smiled, *"Pura Vida"*.

We put The Cats and the guitar in the front seat, our luggage in the trunk, and Jon and I squeezed in the backseat with Marley. Within minutes, we were back on the streets of San José.

Driver spoke fantastic English and helped us gain a few useful phrases en Español. He informed us that Ticos refer to Montezuma as *"MonteFuma"* because it is full of pot-smoking hippies. It was obvious from our conversation that he took great pride in his country, and his friendly, laid-back demeanor was totally infectious.

Leaving the chaos of San José, Costa Rica became the insanely beautiful place that we saw during our Internet research. Green mountains gave depth to the horizon and the road was lined with trees taller than I ever imagined trees could grow. I watched the cows roaming the rolling countryside and wondered why I saw so few cows in Illinois… I attempted to read every sign, to soak in all the Español, and soon I realized that many of the streets we were turning down were unmarked. We would never have made it to Montezuma on our own, and we were officially glad for the mishap with our rental car. It was as if the universe knew we were unprepared for the trip and intentionally threw us off course. Pura Vida.

Driver stopped at a frutas stand run by his buddy, where we grabbed a few fresh papayas and some delicious mango ceviche made by Driver's buddy's mom. I devoured the dish, even though it wasn't vegetarian, figuring I could get back to my ideals when I wasn't trying to traverse across countries. We practiced our Español, learned how to identify ripeness of the exotic produce, converted our money, and then got back in the car to continue our journey. After a few hours we arrived at the ferry in Puntarenas. There, we, along with Driver and his compact car, would cross the Gulf de Nicoya.

For the first time since we landed we were completely aware of how *hot* it can be in Costa Rica. We stood sweating, in the chaos of busy Puntarenas, glad again to have accidentally found ourselves here with a guide. Driver bought our tickets while Jon and I retrieved the animals from the car. Driver returned, handed us our vouchers, then walked back towards his taxi (which would have been lost in the sea of identical taxis had Marley's crate not wobbled precariously above the swarm). We boarded the ferry and watched over the railing as the tiny car with the huge crate on top meandered aboard amongst trucks and other taxis. Once it was parked safely, we downed some bottled water, and shared some with our furry friends of course.

When the ferry started to move, the breeze alleviated the sweltering heat. We fell back in our seats, looked at each other, and started laughing hysterically. When we planned this trip we thought we were crazy for traveling with three animals for two straight days. Now that we sat here, we *knew* we were crazy. The look on Marley's face told us he was more exhausted than we were. We all settled down to watch Puntarenas disappear into the horizon, and wait for Paquera to solidify out of the mist ahead.

While we floated, we talked to Driver about his experience traversing this beautiful country with Tourists for a living. He told us that after twenty years of driving a taxi, he had enough stories to fill a book, like the time he saw President Clinton and Monica Lewinsky vacationing together weeks before their infamous affair became news. Whether that was true or not, we will never know, but nonetheless, he told a great story.

As we approached the Nicoya Peninsula, the view we were met with reminded us of *Jurassic Park*. Driver informed us that the aerial scenes from the movie were filmed here in Costa Rica, so Jon took a moment to whistle the theme song as we watched the mountainous landscape move closer. Once ashore, we put our animals and ourselves back in the car. Our journey was almost over and we were more than ready to be settled. We rolled down the windows and enjoyed the feel of the wind on our faces as we sped through the countryside.

The peninsula was significantly less populated than the other side of the Gulf had been. The towns we passed were small, and infrequent. We could actually feel the atmosphere shift as we went deeper into untouched territory. It was both exhilarating and formidable. We kept hearing the strangest noise, which we joked *had* to be a dinosaur, but Driver informed us that it was just a big monkey, *"very friendly"*, he added with a smile and a shrug.

As we continued, the roads got worse, the asphalt more infrequent, and Driver had to expertly navigate the car/crate to avoid potholes, like some real-life adaptation of *Frogger*. Our pace was eventually slowed to a few kilometers per hour, and we grew restless as we swerved and hobbled down the dusty, dirt roads.

Finally, we reached the small beach town of Montezuma, stopping outside an office building with a familiar logo. Jon ran in to inquire about our rental, then appeared moments later, dashing off towards an ATM. A young lady walked out of the office, straight to the taxi, and handed me the keys with a smile. Immediately, she turned to Driver and started to speak in muy rápido Español. After a few minutes, Jon had returned with her deposit, so she looked to us and said in English, *"He doesn't know the area very well, but you will be fine. I gave him my phone number"*. With that piece of confidence she turned away from the car and the taxi turned down another dirt road, even worse than the ones we had trespassed on previously.

Driver explained that Cabuya (our actual final destination) was only 7km away, but that distance could easily take us an hour on these terrible roads. Having thought our voyage was going to be over once we hit Montezuma, this came as a blow to morale inside the tiny taxi.

We pushed onward, weaving to avoid the rough terrain, crossing bridges that appeared to be made of wooden planks placed across rocks. At one point, the path was completely covered in water, and we all crossed our fingers as the taxi bravely plunged through it. I was stunned at the generosity of this person that we had met entirely by chance. Driver had no idea what he was getting himself into when he accepted our business this morning, yet here he was, sticking with us through an adventure I think any ordinary taxi driver would have quit hours ago. Without him, Jon and I would have been totally screwed. I ruminated on the kindness of strangers and allowed it to rattle my expectations about what it takes to be a part of a community.

We thought we were deep in the jungle when we were driving to Montezuma, but were now forced to admit that we had no idea how deep a jungle went. As we drove, we noticed there were no other cars. We saw a four-wheeler, the occasional bicycle, and a few pedestrians, but it seemed obvious that the wildlife outnumbered the humans in this particular part of the planet.

We stopped someone who was walking in our direction and asked if we were on the right path. She assured us that we were and that we just had to continue straight about 400 meters and we would be there! I had no clue how far 400 meters was (thanks to a USA education), and I am not good at estimating distance in feet and miles either (thanks to my brain), but it sounded close, so I got excited. We drove straight until we ran into another pedestrian who said, *Yes, go straight...400 meters.* This happened a few more times until we found ourselves in front The Café: the landmark given to us back in Montezuma that would help us to find The Cabina. The Café was undoubtably there, but what to do next was lost on all of us. Driver began talking to a man laboring on a nearby house and together the two of them went into The Café, leaving me, Jon, and our animal family waiting in the taxi. Driver emerged looking exasperated, and we drove past two houses before he pulled over and said, *"This should be it"*. Nervous, we exited the car. Right away we recognized the house from the pictures on Craigslist.

Two wild dogs and three gigantic horses watched from a farm across the dusty path as we gingerly opened the gate to enter our home for the next month. Driver and Builder were with us. We all thought there was a good chance someone was inside, since the porch light was on, the upstairs window open, and we all heard what we assumed was a dog scratching around up there somewhere. The four of us walked around the house shouting *"hola"*, but no one answered. Eventually, we decided just to go for it. We put our key in the door, and crossed the threshold.

The Cabina was dark and there was not a light switch to be found. Staying close, Jon and I walked up the rickety stairs, expecting to meet a human or animal at any moment. We entered the bedroom, walked through it, and opened the door at the other end. We stepped out on the balcony to investigate the scratching we had heard from below, but nothing was there. We laughed nervously, shrugged, and headed back downstairs. Driver had located a light switch, so we navigated our luggage safely inside. With that, Jon paid him, and he was gone.

We were scared. No doubt about it. We felt very far away from tiny Montezuma, which seemed like the Big Apple compared to isolated Cabuya. We sucked it up, we had already paid for the month, so this place was going to be our home, whether we liked it or not. We set the animals free, made sure they had food and water, opened the windows to illuminate the place a little better, and did some exploring. We found a sheet of instructions hung on the bathroom door, raising our eyebrows at the mention of not flushing toilet paper down the toilet, but smiling in relief as we read The Cabina's phone number and wi-fi password.

Immediately, we set about finding the phone to call our rental contact and ask her about getting some light bulbs. When we couldn't find the phone, we unpacked the laptop to email her, and to our surprise (well maybe not at this point) we found the wi-fi wasn't working. We returned the laptop to its safe haven in Jon's backpack and set out on foot for The Café, which advertised English and free wi-fi, and was much closer than it had seemed when we were lost in the taxi.

It was 4:00(or 5:00)P.M. From our research we had thought Costa Rica was on Eastern Time, but a map in the airline magazine informed us that it was on Central Time, just like Chicago. After 24 hours in the country we still hadn't figured out which was correct, but either way we knew we were hungry.

We were the only people in The Café, but we were soon greeted by Cocinera, the owner, who was very amiable and sat with us, striking up a conversation. She spoke only Español and prompted us to do the same, but filled in English words when our expressions became bewildered. She told us that we could come and use the Internet any time, even if The Café wasn't open, and we officially knew, even in the Midwest, we had never met anyone as amiable as the Ticos.

The only vegetarian item on the menu was a pizza, which didn't seem particularly authentic, but sounded great paired with two well-deserved cervezas. Cocinera excused herself and headed to the kitchen, while Jon sent an email to our rental contact, then another to both sets of our parents to let them know that we were safe. Unable to explain our journey thus far, we kept it short and sweet, and sent a picture with our beers, one where we didn't look quite as exhausted as we felt.

Cocinera's dog, Lobo, an oversized black Labrador with the wrinkly face of some mixed DNA, came to sit with us, and I scratched his ears. I figured he had a collar so he was okay to pet, and he seemed happy for the affection. As I scratched I flipped his floppy ear open and saw two huge ticks happily snacking on it. I froze, then regained my bravery, lifting the ear again to show Jon. As we looked, we actually found four ticks. We both felt so bad for the guy, but were definitely less tempted to touch him. My thoughts immediately jumped to Marley and The Cats. They all take preventative flea and tick medication, but I wasn't sure if the treatments were up to something like the infestation of Lobo. We vowed to each other to check the f-animal-y for vile critters each time they went outside.

I wasn't necessarily disgusted by Lobo's ticks, in fact I expected it, based on my research. In Costa Rica, pets don't live in the house, they live outside, with the ticks. We didn't really care if the Ticos judged us for letting Marley sleep in our bed, but we also weren't going to judge them for acting consistently with their cultural norms.

Our pizza came and was everything two hungry and tired travelers could want. After we finished, Cocinera brought us a piece of chocolate cake as a *"Welcome to Cabuya"* gift, and sat down to give us a quick Español lesson while we devoured the treat. The sun began to set, so we headed back to The Cabina, Marley's exuberant greeting making the place feel a little more like home.

Without wi-fi or light bulbs, our night appeared to be over. We showered and hopped into our little bed, quickly followed by both Dylan and Marley, who had managed to stay tick-free, so far. We turned off the light and immediately realized that after twenty-six years on this planet, neither of us had ever really been engulfed in darkness. It was pitch black to the point where I couldn't even see Jon, who was close enough to touch. We laid there, hoping our eyes would adjust. They never did.

We closed our eyes to make the darkness less disconcerting, and fell asleep listening to the baritone wails of the "very friendly" monkeys.

We awoke some time later to the sound of Marley pacing. It was still so dark we couldn't see him, so we feared his vision was also occluded and that he was bound to fall down the treacherous stairs. We could also hear him panting and concluded that he had to pee, his poor little body knocked off of its normal rhythms. I was convinced that it had to be close to sunrise, but when we opened the laptop to use it as a flashlight, we saw that it was only 1:00(or 2:00)A.M. We stuck close together as we climbed slowly down the stairs and out the front door.

The sight that awaited us took our breath away. Stars, stars, stars, and more stars. It was an experience more intense than I would have ever considered stargazing. There were more stars in this sky than I ever remember seeing, even at the Planetarium! I never realized I hadn't seen the entire Orion constellation before, but there he stood, belt, sword, head and arrow, and I finally understood the depiction, now that he was more than just three bright dots. Jon and I squeezed each others palms in the darkness.

It was so overwhelming, paired with the sound of nothing but animals and insects. It was just too much for our exhausted brains to handle. We took it in for one more moment, whistled for Marley, headed back into the house, up the scary stairs, and fell into bed. The encompassing darkness seemed almost welcome after all that intense beauty. We both lay awake trying to come to grips with why the stars had affected us so powerfully. I dreamed of trying to explain the vision to my family back home and realized, even in my unconscious state, that some things simply can't be explained.

La Zona Azule

THE NEXT TIME WE AWOKE it was 6:00(or 7:00)A.M., and the sun was out. We couldn't wait to see the beach so we put Marley on his leash and headed down the road. What we saw was both beautiful and sad, but mostly sad. The scene was solid rock. The water was miles away. There was no sand, only sharp pebbles that morphed into slimy boulders. We turned north and started walking in the direction of Montezuma hoping to find something that resembled the sandy beaches we had seen online. Totally secluded, we let Marley off his leash to explore.

The first sign of life that we ran into was a pack of vultures. In the early morning calm, they were feeding on dead fish and eels that had washed up on the rocks. It was a little creepy, but also glorious in the way that it brought our attention to the circle of life. I found them to be immense and magnificent birds, and even if I would have found them repulsive, I still would have to admit that they were doing a better job cleaning up the beach than most human efforts. I felt genuinely bad for interrupting their breakfast.

After walking for a bit, we decided to head back, but when we reached the little path where we should have turned to go to The Cabina, we continued south, exploring a little more. Soon, we realized that the rocky expanse extended out to a small tuft of green. From our research, we recognized this as Isla Cementerio, an island burial ground accessible by foot during low tide.

Totally uplifted that the lack of ocean was due to low tide and not just a lack of ocean, we decided to walk to the island. Two wild dogs joined us, and when we looked back towards the shore, we saw our first human of the day: a skinny Tico climbing straight up a palm tree to grab a coconut. About half way to our destination, we noticed the purr of the waves and wondered if the tide was coming or going. Unsure of how quickly our walkway would be underwater, we decided not to go any farther. We sat down where we were, on a flat rock, and devoured two apples that Jon had picked up in San José.

We were melancholy as we listened to the incoming tide. We had left behind so much to take a six month sabbatical on the beach, and this rocky expanse was just not what we had expected. It seemed that even in high tide this basin would be too rocky and shallow to swim, and no matter what the water did, there still wouldn't be any sand to relax on. Pura Vida? So what if this wasn't what we expected? It was still a beautiful place to spend a month. No matter the lack of swimming, it still beat winter in Chicago...

And to be fair, the beach *wasn't* the only reason we had come here. The Nicoya Peninsula (which encompasses Cabuya and Montezuma) is one of Earth's five

Blue Zones: spots on the globe with especially high rates of centenarians and especially low rates of disease. Studies of Blue Zones have shown the common factors of: a semi-vegetarian diet (heavy in legumes), paired with constant, moderate physical activity, and plenty of social engagement. When Jon and I found ourselves confused about the meaning of our own lives, we figured we should go somewhere that seemed to have Life figured out.

In general, Costa Rica has a higher life expectancy than most developed countries. They also boast a lower healthcare budget than their counterparts, despite their socialized system. In Nicoya, that life expectancy increases, and Ticos from this region are more than twice as likely to reach a healthy 90 than people from The States. Researchers studying the area found that the variables that seem to make this difference (in addition to those listed above) are a focus on family and faith, and a "plan de vida" or "reason to live", which keeps Nicoyans active, even in their old age. Furthermore, it is rumored that the water in the region is loaded with healthy minerals.

Apples finished, we headed back. Jon pointed out a few, small fishing boats balanced on the rocks, reinforcing our hypothesis that where we were walking would be ocean floor in just a few hours. We were excited to return at high tide, but for now we moved on to our next adventure: finding The Supermercado.

We found a path that led us away from the ocean and back to the dusty road, but instead of turning towards The Cabina and The Café, we continued in a new direction, based on directions Cocinera had given to us the previous evening. We walked through the beautiful farm land, taking in the open space, and eventually we saw our second and third humans of the day, chatting outside a cabina. We asked them where to find The Supermercado, and from their hand gestures, I gained that we had to go straight. I understood only one word of their explanation, *"panadería"* (Español for bakery), and when I repeated *"panadería"*, one of the humans responded with a *"sí "* and gestured to his left. We continued on, hoping I had correctly translated that we were to head straight until we hit the bakery, and the super would be on our left.

We didn't have to go far to see the sign for La Panadería, and from there, to our delight, we saw The Supermercado! Excited, we headed in, looking for some healthy, unprocessed, Blue Zone food.

Unfortunately, the small, disorganized store was filled mostly with chips, sweets, and frozen burritos. After a few laps we were able to find a few fresh vegetables, some rice, black beans, general seasonings, and tortillas. We also grabbed some beer, red wine, and two 5-gallon jugs of water. Every time we have poured water from the tap it has been cloudy, and we have heard the phrase *"don't drink the water"* too many times to take any risks. So instead of trusting the maybe magical water of Nicoya, we chose to walk twenty hot minutes carrying eighty pounds of Ice Mountain's finest. I made a mental note to talk to Cocinera about the water next time that I saw her. We left The Supermercado feeling prepared enough to cook tonight's Thanksgiving meal, which was definitely not going to be the traditional turkey and mashed potatoes…

We stopped quickly at The Café to check our email, but still hadn't been contacted about our lack of wi-fi and lightbulbs. Cocinera laughed at us when we asked her about the water and the time zone, but helpfully assured us that it was perfectly safe to drink from the tap, and that it was, in fact, 4:00P.M. Armed with this information we headed back to The Cabina, where Jon set about figuring out our kitchen situation. While he worked, I grabbed a copy of Ernest Hemingway's *For Whom the Bell Tolls* that lie abandoned on a shelf. I retreated to a hammock on the porch for a reading session that immediately turned into a nap.

The next day, we wanted to settle in to our new jungle abode, but life was fraught with the anxiety of finding a place to live the following month. "Holy Week" (Christmas-New Years Day) is hands down the busiest and most expensive time to be in Nicoya, and of course our lease of The Cabina ends on December 23rd. Pura Vida. We were in contact with someone who had a place available in Cabuya for $250/month, but we were wary of how cheap it was, having thought The Cabina was cheap at $450/month. At this point, we didn't have a lot of options, so we figured out where it was located and decided to try and find it. We walked in the same direction as the day before, stopping at La Panadería for some breakfast.

We weren't ready for beans so we ordered a bebida de frutas (smoothie) and in the name of social engagement, struck up a conversation with two gringos sitting at the table behind us. They were from Utah and had walked here from Montezuma. The lady owned a house there, and was a dual citizen, a Tica-Gringa, as she referred to herself. They told us about the organic farmers market in Montezuma Centro on Saturday mornings, and they gushed about Cabuya and its many assets, helping us feel more confident about our choice of destinations. Out of nowhere they mentioned the delicious water, the he-gringo explaining that there is so much calcium in the agua that it is cloudy when poured, but crystal clear moments later. Now, assured that the water from our tap was plenty safe to drink, we raised a glass to not having to cart anymore giant water bottles home from The Supermercado.

When they left, the conversation continued with a young woman, a yoga teacher, who had also walked here from Montezuma. She reinforced the idea that we needed to focus on locking down a place for Holy Week, adding that most people have their reservations by October. We were officially worried we would be homeless in Costa Rica. For Christmas. No bueno.

Seeing our distress, the young woman gave us the number of Granjero, the man she rents from, and suggested we ask the waitress at La Panadería if she had any leads as well. We got another number, for a landlady named Konstnär, and we thanked everyone, anxious to get home and start searching.

But first, we saw the cheap cabina. Jon loved the place and the price, but I had my reservations. It was tucked back in a seriously local part of town, far from the main road, and its bathroom was outside. Jon insisted that it wasn't creepy, but it looked an awful lot like an outhouse, and I pee like clockwork every night around 1:00(or

2:00)A.M. As we walked home I let the fact that it was half the price of The Cabina sink into my mind. We did come here on a tight budget, and I knew that would require some sacrifices. I was determined to be brave. I was determined not to be an overprivileged white girl.

At the cheap-and-maybe-creepy cabina, we were very close to Cabo Blanco, the first national park of Costa Rica, a destination we were determined to appreciate during our stay. To find the entrance we had to walk a little deeper into the jungle, and we both felt the intimidating sense that we were infringing on local territory. The wild dogs barked with more hostility as we moved on, and even the cattle seemed to be glaring at us as they munched tropical grasses from behind fences that didn't seem solid enough to discourage them from trampling us.

Thankfully, the uneasy feeling dissipated as soon as we approached the park. A beautiful white-blue stream welcomed us, and we crouched over it to wash the sweat from our faces. We cupped our hands and drank the calcium rich water, Marley lapping happily at our sides. To hike the preserve would take a few hours, and we were both too exhausted to undertake that now, so we headed back, past the angry dogs and cows, and to The Cabina, excited to return to Cabo Blanco soon.

When we got home, we had a phone, and the Internet! But it wasn't wi-fi, it was an ethernet cord about a foot long that stretched taut across the kitchen, impeding the only path to the bathroom. We had to stand awkwardly between the front door and kitchen counter to use it, but we no longer had to buy something at The

Café every time we wanted to check our email. As soon as we closed the laptop, we reapplied our sunscreen, and headed out to see the high tide. The beach was a completely different scene from the last time we had been there. Waves crashed onto the shore, and although the floor was rocky, we were able to wade into the water. We hugged each other tightly and jumped for joy. We had the Internet and a beach. Our little adventure was going to work out after all!!!

That night, back at The Cabina, Jon made dinner while I used Google Translate to prepare a speech for calling potential landlords. So far my Español had been somewhat useful when I could use hand gestures to help express myself, but talking on the phone would be a different kind of experience. I called both Konstnär and Granjero, and no one answered, so I was forced to leave voicemail messages, which I am not good at, even in my native tongue. I spoke in an awkward staccato, fingers crossed, hoping they would call me back.

Jon and I busted into our six-pack and sat on the porch, trying to soak in how wonderful and terrible our trip had been thus far. We thought about how we had talked with every single human we had seen that day, a feat that would have been impossible in our lives back home. The experience felt like a game, clicking on characters to reveal information, trying to find the answers to a quest one happened to find oneself upon...

Soon, Konstnär returned my call, but was sad to inform us that she did not have any properties in our price range. She had a strong European accent, but spoke English perfectly, so the transaction was quick and easy.

Granjero called too, and that was not as simple. We could communicate in one another's language just enough to set up a meeting, which would be held Sunday evening, at The Café.

We woke up early on Saturday and immediately headed out on foot for Montezuma Centro and the organic farmers market. Still in Cabuya, we were amazed to see a dog that looked exactly like Marley, except, not nearly as skinny, and with red fur, like a fox. Soon after, a woman approached us on her bicycle followed by the doppelgänger dog. She wanted to meet us because she had never before seen another dog that looked so much like hers. I recognized her accent and after a short exchange I realized that she was Konstnär, the woman with the expensive rentals. We introduced ourselves and found out that she worked at the farmers market. We told her we would see her soon as she headed off ahead on her bicycle.

Not far from the exchange, we came upon Rio Lajas, and the river's beauty took my breath away. Blue, green, and crystal-clear, the agua sparkled throughout, bathing the rocks below in sunlight. The other worldly colors must have come from the extra calcium in the water and I wondered if the fish here lived longer lives too, or if the Blue Zone thing was specific to humans. Konstnär was there, swimming with her dogs, and a young mother and her tot were splashing around nearby. My flushed body desperately wanted to jump into the cool, sparkling water, but we had walked so long and only come so far, if we didn't press on we could miss the market, which supposedly sold out in minutes.

We continued our trek towards Montezuma Centro, completely in awe of the beautiful landscape around us. The beach and the trees were like some amplified painting: the colors and sounds more vibrant than our wildest expectations. It was so hot, and the ocean sparkled nearby, peeking at us through the trees, tempting us to jump and play in her rippling waves.

We trudged on towards the market...

It was over an hour later that we arrived in Montezuma Centro. We collapsed onto an uprooted tree, located in the spray of the sea, and half-joked about how constant, moderate exercise was killing us. We drank water from the bottles we brought along, and attempted to eat breakfast, only to realize we had left our apples at The Cabina. We asked a passerby what time it was, and found we still had about half an hour before the market opened.

Despite being only a cross section of two dirt roads, Montezuma Centro seemed so busy compared to sleepy Cabuya. There were people shopping, eating, and conversing, a familiar bustle in an unfamiliar setting. We thought back to Chicago and its suburbs, and found their size and population hard to fathom in comparison. Hungry, we grabbed a bebida de frutas from a bright orange cafe.

While looking for the market, we ran into our amigos from Utah. They offered to walk us through the jungle to La Cascada de Montezuma (a waterfall) that afternoon, and we agreed, the four of us (plus Marley) joining the rest of the town at the park, gathered around a vegetable truck.

The farmers market was crowded, and hectic. People were waiting by their favorite veggies, anxious to start grabbing them up. We hadn't even come with a shopping list. We tied Marley to a tree and went about shopping. Much of the harvest was unrecognizable to us, and what we did recognize wasn't labeled with a price. I had been craving a salad so I grabbed some delicious looking lettuce. Jon grabbed his staples. We paid a little over 6mil (~$12) in the chaos, and waved to Konstnär before heading back to the streets of Montezuma.

Quickly, to my dismay, I was reminded that lettuce hates the heat. I clutched my already wilting bounty, knowing it was going to take at least an hour to walk home, in the middle of the afternoon, in the tropics. We also realized we would not be able to hike to a waterfall with our bags heavy with a week's worth of produce. Pura Vida. We checked the bus schedule, found a bus to Cabuya in an hour and a half, and decided to grab some lunch in the shade.

We popped into a restaurant called Bar Restaurante Moctezuma. It was recommended by the Utahnians for its cheap fare and fantastic view of the Gulf de Nicoya, and appreciated by Jon for its to-the-point nomenclature. We ordered a vegetable sandwich, a plate of fruit, and asked the waitress to bring us some ice for our lettuce. She obliged and brought the ice quickly, helping me pour it into the plastic bag containing the delicate leaves. The lettuce perked up a bit, but the ice started melting immediately.

The food was satisfying but we were full and out of the restaurant way before bus time. Jon did some calculations and realized that the bus really wouldn't get us home any faster than walking, since we still had to wait an hour. Plus, there was a good chance Marley wouldn't be allowed on the bus, meaning the inevitable walk would only be delayed another hour. Pura Vida. We headed back to Cabuya on foot, just a little miserable in the heat, anxious that our entire trip would be in vain, and disappointed we couldn't spend the day in Montezuma.

A few minutes into our journey, a French woman and her two young sons stopped and asked if we needed a ride. Thankful, we threw Marley in the back of her SUV, and I sat up front while Jon squeezed himself in back with the boys. This was my first time hitchhiking, and I was glad it was with an outgoing mother. I took a deep breath, shook the water out of my lettuce bag, and we were off! Pura Vida!

Our ride was a scene from a movie. The woman drove fast and recklessly over the dusty, pock-marked, road, the bumps so large and unexpected that I was bouncing off my seat every few seconds, grasping tight to my bag of leaking lettuce. While she drove, the woman recounted her life story in very broken English, about her ten years in Cabuya, her Italian ex-husband, and the monkey she had adopted, who was like her baby until it was killed, not long ago, by a bigger monkey. She talked quickly, and with wild gestures of her hands that seemed never to touch the steering wheel, as we skidded along. I kept my eyes on the road, but she seemed content to look at me while she roughly translated her stories and the philosophies that they had endowed upon her. Finally, the little

SUV slammed to a halt beside Rio Lajas. This was her stop, we would have to walk the rest of the way. We got out, even Marley flustered from the bumpy ride, and thanked her before heading down the road.

We stopped in front of Konstnär's place to memorize the email address attached to a sign outside of her property. After meeting us this morning, she wanted us to inquire again about renting. I suppose there really is truth to the idea that who you know goes a long way in a small town.

When we arrived home, there was wi-fi! But the phone was gone, along with the instruction page that contained the wi-fi password. So actually, we were worse off than before. We trekked back to The Café to send a very nasty email to our rental contact, but found one from her instead explaining that there had been severe drama with the phone company and that she would personally be returning to Cabuya later today to deliver our tools for communication. Sufficed, we returned home where I settled into the hammock for another attempt at reading that turned into a nap.

Soon Lessor arrived. She had no phone, but she did have our wi-fi password, and as Millennials we were totally fine with that. We were grateful to her for helping us, we knew first hand what a hassle it was traveling between Montezuma and Cabuya, and she had come from farther away, in Cobano. We felt bad that we had started our relationship having to complain so much, and she felt bad we had started our relationship having to complain so much. Pura Vida. Before she left, she wanted us to come with her to meet another one of her lessees, our neighbor to the right, Joe.

Cabuya Joe, as he claims the locals call him, is a retired cop from the West Coast. The first words out of his mouth were complaints about the IRS and from there the words just kept flowing. It was refreshing to be around someone who spoke English, and comforting that someone could tell stories as entertaining and as everlasting as Mom. He gave Jon a machete to aid in the opening of coconuts and the killing of boa constrictors, and warned us about which Ticos to be on the look out for as fellow Tourists. He talked until we were starving hungry and had to excuse ourselves. On our way out he told us to come by anytime his gate was open, and drooling at his gorgeous swimming pool, we knew this was an offer we would definitely take him up on.

Our holiday rental situation, or lack there of, was still a source of extreme stress. It turned out that the cheap-and-maybe-creepy cabina was not the one we would actually be able to rent... *that* would be a *"similar"* one, just a little farther down the road to Cabo Blanco. We were invited to see the "similar" cabina on Sunday, the same day we were meeting Granjero and Konstnär...

We started with Konstnär's place. Her houses were rented over Holy Week, but she informed us that if we rented her property, we could stay in the guest room at her casa during the holiday. Her casa (which was not for rent) was huge and gorgeous and beach front, yet somehow still embodied the humble nature of Cabuyan architecture. She was an artist and her studio was full of upcycled masterpieces crafted from items she found strolling the beaches of Nicoya with her dogs. The guest room doubled as a workspace, and although entirely livable, it was full of loose jewelry making supplies. We knew living there with so many cat toys would be a disaster, so as of now, we were still homeless for Christmas.

We hopped in her car and drove to the property that would be available in January. It was a hip, private cabina near La Panadería, and it had an indoor bathroom! We left Konstnär's happy to have a living option, even if it was out of our price range.

Close to the "similar" cabina, we headed there next. If the cabina we had seen before was sketchy, this one was terrifying. It resembled a poorly built tree-house, sans tree, its foundation instead supported by four wooden stilts. Even from the ground it was possible to see through the cracks between the panels of wood that composed the structure, and I couldn't help but think they looked quite inviting for the oversized spiders and snakes that Cabuya Joe had warned us about the night before. Walking up the stairs shook the whole place, and here, the bathroom *and* the kitchen were outside. Jon and I both agreed that the house was scary, but currently, it was our only option for Holy Week. We crossed our fingers that our meeting with Granjero would offer us something with enclosed walls.

We walked hand in hand back to The Cabina, waving to Joe who was approaching on his ATV. He was headed into Cobano, but told us his gate was open and we should go swimming. Gracious for the invitation, we jumped in.

The afternoon passed with another hammock read / nap, and soon it was time to head to The Café to meet with Granjero. When we got to The Café, Granjero was already waiting for us, chatting, apparently peacefully, with Cocinera. We sat down all smiles, but quickly the language barrier made the situation awkward and tense. Luckily, and obviously, The Café was vacant except for our meeting, and Cocinera was happy to help translate. We found out Granjero had a house on the beach available from January until May, and a house on his farm where we could stay over Holy Week. Cocinera, who was evidently on our side, convinced him to offer us a wonderfully cheap rate if we rented with him for the entire five months we were here. Then, she seamlessly switched sides, and negotiated Granjero a hefty down payment. In the end we all smiled and shook hands, agreeing to meet him at his farm the following morning to see the properties. With that, Granjero became friendly, offering to help watch Marley if we ever had to leave the property, and explaining that his houses were the best in Cabuya. With a smile and a *"Pura Vida"* he stood abruptly, and left with a wave.

We stayed, ate, and chatted with Cocinera, practicing our Español, hoping that as of tomorrow we would no longer be homeless for the holidays. Our meal was a delicious fresh snapper, caught by a local fisherman, and I kept thinking about a conversation I had months ago with Mom, when she was wondering why I wouldn't eat fish. I told her that my enemy was processed, poisoned foods, not meat. In a perfect world, where the fish were ocean-caught at a rate that does not hijack every food chain in the sea, and the meat, milk, and eggs are drug, hormone, cage, and torture-free, from farms where relationships are symbiotic, I would totally eat it. In fact, I would much rather eat those things than over-processed soy. However, it was cheaper to be vegetarian than to support ethical farming, so for me, the choice seemed clear... But now here we were in Costa Rica, with the tables turned completely. It was easier to eat ocean-caught, ecologically sustainable, organic, drug-free fish than it was to supplement a vegetarian diet.

We heard the approaching roar of an ATV and were soon joined by Cabuya Joe. The four of us got lost in a wonderful conversation, laughing, and getting to know one another a little bit better. We learned that Joe's wife would be joining him in Cabuya tomorrow, and I also found out that it was kind of racist to say *"Yo soy Americano"*, because Central America is America too. Well duh, you silly white girl. I blushed and practiced the phrase, *"I am from The States"*. We walked home relaxed, and a little buzzed, and Jon lit a small fire in our yard to keep the bugs away while we watched the stars. Again, we were taken aback by how magnificent the unpolluted night sky looked. We sat out there, staring, until I dozed off in my chair.

We woke up the next morning and headed out to meet Granjero. He was waiting for us in the middle of the dusty road, and guided us the rest of the way to his farm. He had an expansive property, and before we could even see the house he took us to a tree and picked little apples for us to snack on. He explained, *"Es natural"* and I nodded, chomping into the pesticide-free fruit. When we entered his farm house we were immediately relieved. We wouldn't have to stay in a scary place for Christmas. It boasted an indoor bathroom, plus a kitchen with an oven and a stove, not just hot plate burners. It had fans, a pillow top mattress, and a most incredible view of the farm with the mountains looming behind it. We told him, with what little Español we knew, that we loved it and wanted to live here. He was glad and wanted to show us the whole farm, we excitedly obliged.

The farm was separated into a few segments by barbed wires, and as we ducked under the first fence, he explained that his family has lived on this land for over a hundred years. We crossed under, over, and through the spiky wire, beckoned by his *"Come, I show you."* Awestruck, we strolled through his seemingly endless land, Marley trotting along at our heels.

Suddenly, three practically identical blonde labs began circling Granjero's ankles, and he began yelling at them in Español. When we asked about the pups Granjero simply responded, *"Come, I show you."* He walked to a tree, yanked off a long skinny branch, and swiftly removed its smaller branches with his machete. He raised the stick as if to hit the dogs with it, but only screamed *"Va! (Go!)"* All three perros responded to the gesture by turning away, tails between their legs, and trotting off. He handed me the stick and explained in his hybrid of Español, English, and pantomime, that only Tigra is his dog. Oso and Rosa are her son and daughter, respectively. They have other owners, but like to spend most of their time with their mom (awww). Granjero explained that Oso and Tigra are harmless, but that Rosa has a reputation for aggression and violence. He pointed to the stick weapon he had just constructed as the answer to Rosa's behavioral issues.

Granjero named every tree we passed, pulling ripe fruit from the branches, which he shoved into our already overflowing arms. We were stunned to find that we were not only no longer homeless, but that we had somehow found ourselves living on an organic farm. A scenario from our wildest dreams. Pura Vida. Before we could thank him for his generosity, he had run off in a new direction with a *"Come, I show you!"* This time we came to a lemon tree and he showed us how to choose the ripest fruit, even making us pick some to ensure that we were listening to his explanations. *"Good for sto-mack"* he repeated a few times as he happily rubbed his belly. *"Eat in morning, good for sto-mack, before even café."* That sounded like some solid Blue Zone advice...

We piled our goodies into our backpack and followed him across the dusty road to his house on the beach, where we could be staying from January-May. We turned down a hidden driveway, encircled by a natural arbor of drooping palm trees, and we could hear the ocean as we walked passed one house and towards another. We crossed through another natural archway and met a woman, about our age, who invited us to wander around and see the property. Indoor bathroom/kitchen: check. Sturdy woodwork: check. Extra bedroom for guests: bonus! The ocean as a backyard: priceless! Once again, we were in love. We would take it. The property was more than we could ask for, and apparently, it even came with an adorable "wild" dog, Luna.

We stood at the edge of the property, looking out over the sea at high tide. Granjero explained that when we moved in, he would take us out on his fishing boat to catch our dinners and watch for whales. He said we could also ride his horses up into the mountains to find perfect, private waterfalls. He smiled and gestured all around him with his arms, *"Es a pair-a-dice."* The words sounded almost like a plea. I nodded vigorously, yes, this was a paradise, and yes, Granjero, I could see it all around me. He smiled, nodded, and shrugged, *"We have time."* With another abrupt wave, he went back to the farm to go about his day.

We decided to pop in and talk to the current tenant again, to make sure there was nothing we were missing. This deal simply seemed too good to be true. She told us the property was amazing, Granjero was always this nice, and that this was a great deal for Cabuya. Excited to finally have a place, we decided to go for swim in nearby Rio Lajas, a very short walk from our soon-to-be beach house. Stress free, we sunbathed, and even lured Marley into the water with his favorite squeaky toy. We figured out that he could swim, he just didn't really want to.

The view of the Gulf from within the lagoon was breathtaking, and we were both so overjoyed with our future lodgings that we splashed and played like a couple of toddlers. We saw Konstnär again and timidly explained that we found a cheaper place to live and she seemed genuinely happy for us. Her dogs were swimming, and that seemed to relieve Marley's fears just slightly, although he still preferred to watch us, safely, from dry land.

We stayed at Rio Lajas until the water that had accumulated in my ears was making me crazy and we had to head home. On our walk, a shuttle van stopped beside us and Cabuya Joe leaned out the window to introduce us to the driver, Cocinera's husband, who everyone called Pájaro. He explained that they were off to Tambor to pick up Joe's wife at the airport. Resourcefully, Jon asked if he could jump in the back of the shuttle and take advantage of the free ride to the ATM in Montezuma Centro, where he could acquire Granjero's hefty down payment. The boys welcomed him in, and slightly nervous that we would never see each other again, we parted ways for the first time on Costa Rican soil since his grocery run in San José.

The shuttle lurched off towards Montezuma as Marley and I continued down the road to The Cabina. Along the way I helped some very lost looking gringos find Cabo Blanco, and recommended that they eat at La Panadería along the way. It was strange to realize these people didn't see me as a tourist, especially after such a short time in the country. This feeling seeped into a joyous confidence as I settled into my hammock to read/nap.

Before long, I heard the roar of a motorcycle come to a halt nearby, and a familiar shout of *"muchas gracias!"* come from my favorite voice. Jon was home, he had hitchhiked back from Montezuma, with our deposit, and brought cookies and cervezas to help celebrate our good fortune.

The following morning, we headed out to meet Granjero at Rio Lajas. We paid him and then talked with him about moving out of The Cabina and into La Hacienda sooner than December 23rd. He agreed, the three of us negotiating a move-in date by writing prospective numbers in the sand. Afterwards, he told us about traditional Costa Rican casados, the meal typically eaten by Ticos twice a day. Curious and hungry we headed off to find one, stopping at a soda across from The Supermercado, and ordering the meal of rice, beans, avocado, egg, veggies (or meat), salad, and plátanos. It was totally congruous with the Blue Zone diet, delicious, and very inspirational to Jon, who immediately wanted to try cooking one himself.

We stopped at The Supermercado, got the ingredients we didn't already have, and headed home. I spent a few hours writing, a few studying with Rosetta Stone, and a few reading in the hammock with Ernest Hemingway. Jon kept himself busy, and must have spent at least a little of his time in the kitchen, because as soon as I was hungry, my first homemade casado was waiting for me.

That night, I was reminded that Jon is an incredible cook, with a knack for using limited ingredients and only one pan. I decided in that moment I wanted to eat that meal everyday of my life, especially if it would help me live to be 100.

Then I wondered how I would feel about it in May.

The Culture

TWO WEEKS INTO OUR ADVENTURE, and we have officially established a routine. The days begin when an iguana, who we call Roofie, wakes up to run circles in the ceiling above our bed. Roofie was the source of the scratching we had been unable to identify on our first day at the Cabina. The flurry of activity is quickly followed by loud, wailing cries from The Cats, who have been up since dawn, pacing in front of the door, waiting to get outside. Marley is the first one out of bed, and his lazy stretch through down and upward dog reminds me that I need to do more yoga. We head downstairs, let the animals out, and quarter two of Granjero's "good-for-stomack" limones. Once outside, we sit at the picnic table digging the fruit out of the pulp and silently munching. Always through with his limón in record time, Jon is usually still chewing while he pours the café.

The Cats have been outside since we woke up, but in an effort to outdoor potty train them, we move their litter box (which is still just a roasting pan, now filled with sand from the beach) to its designated outdoor corner. Situated and caffeinated, we go about our day.

Marley takes to his role as a Tico guard dog: frequently combing the perimeter, nose and ears alert, ready to greet anything from roaming horses to our neighbors with his ferocious bark.

I first met Marley in 2008, just after we moved into The Big House. We were on our way to pick up a drum set Jon found on Craigslist, but en route we turned into the local animal shelter. As much as I wanted to visit the homeless kitties, I knew our newly nested emotional states wouldn't leave there without adopting one, and I told Jon so. He responded that it was a dog, he had already picked him out, and there was never even a drum set. Surprise! I was elated and the moment I met Marley I knew that we all needed each other...

The Cats have also come to enjoy the tropical atmosphere taking every opportunity to escape The Cabina and frolic in the wilderness of the yard. Our fat, suburban house cat, Dylan, is unrecognizable as a jungle feline who runs at top speed through the tall grasses, catching geckos, and dashing up trees. He crouches low, his big yellow eyes surveying each and every insect, as he prepares to leap into the air, for an unsuspecting swat at his prey.

Dylan I met at a no-kill shelter in downtown Chicago, in the summer of 2005. Jon and I poked and cooed at all the cages until he looked up at us, all eyes, massive orbs floating above a lanky skeleton, everything encased in a layer of white and gray fluff. He was clumsy, yet confident, and when we took him back to Jon's apartment, we found out he loved to play fetch with peanut shells...

Clover parades around Costa Rica like a socialite on vacation. She spends her days stretching, sleeping, and basking in the sunshine. She is often found surrounded by recently murdered bugs.

Clover and I met in a small suburban home that was substituting as a zoo. It was summer of 2007, I had just graduated from Northwestern, Jon had just bought The Townhouse, and Dylan and I had just moved in. Mom called to tell me that her friend had found a litter of tiny orange tabbies whose mother had recently been eaten by coyotes. Mom wished she could adopt one, so she decided to tempt me to do so instead. Jon's birthday was coming up, and a little orange tabby named Rajah (his favorite Disney movie is *Aladdin*) seemed like the perfect gift. I approached him about the idea and he was stunned, insisting that he had been contemplating getting me a kitten for my birthday (the dates are less than a month apart). We decided to go see the kittens, and it was the runt, the only gray tabby, that stole our hearts. Her tiny body seemed unfit for life, yet she bravely climbed towards us, smacked us with her paw, and meowed with a sound much too large for her small mouth...

As for me, I spend most of my days on the equator at our picnic table, staring unblinkingly at a computer screen (I am here to write after all). Jon spends much of his time in the hammock, strumming his guitar (he is here to write after all).

Jon I met in 2002. The first time I saw him was at a show in someone's parent's basement, where he was on "stage" tuning his guitar. My boyfriend at the time introduced him to me as the coolest person I would ever meet.

The second time I saw him he was also on the stage, this time performing at his high school's "Battle of the Bands". An entirely different boyfriend had accompanied me to this show, and when he leaned over to ask me how we knew this band again, I pointed to each member in turn, expanding upon our friendship, until my finger pointed to Jon, and I shrugged, *"I don't really know that guy."* My boyfriend slumped back into his seat and teased, *"I bet you marry him."*

The next time I saw Jon, he asked me to dance, and I agreed. My date was unhappy that I spent all night flirting with some other guy, but I didn't care. When I got home, I gushed to Mom all about the cutest boy I had ever met. About a month later, he asked me to be his girlfriend.

On that fateful night, Jon's high school band was playing a show. A friend behind the merch table misidentified me as his girlfriend, and Jon responded, *"She isn't my girlfriend"*, and then turned to me with a mischievous smile, *"unless you want to be"*. I was charmed and said, *"I do."* He then drew a ring on my finger with a Sharpie to make it official...

Nine years later, our fingers both sport actual wedding rings. His glinting in the light as he makes an ever-more delicious casado, mine covered in bubbles as I stand two feet away scrubbing at the dishes. By the time dinner is over, the sky is pale, and the bats are flying around in the twilight. We lug the roasting pan back up the stairs to its designated indoor corner, and each grab a squirmy cat from their favorite outdoor sleeping spot. Systematically, we run our fingers through their coats, checking every inch of them for ticks. We squelch their escape attempts by luring them upstairs with food. From there it is a rush to perform the tick check on Marley before The Cats realize it is their final opportunity to run down the stairs and out into the darkening yard. Everyone tick-free and accounted for, we bolt the door, successfully keeping the jungle out and the f-animal-y in.

As beautiful as the days are in Costa Rica, the nights are equally as frightening. The pitch darkness is still disconcerting, and sundown happens around 6:00P.M., everyday. Bugs are attracted to lights and computer screens, so we are forced to turn in early. Having been night owls for our entire lives, we often find ourselves suspended in the darkness, wondering aloud what nocturnal jungle insects are crawling around nearby, and whether or not the dead scorpion we found Clover playing with earlier had died before of after they met.

On one of the first nights here, in the middle of the night, a crash from downstairs woke us both. From the darkness of our room we could see the faint glow of a light illuminating our kitchen, and we knew neither of us had turned it on. Jon raced for the machete, fearing the worst, but halfway down the stairs we realized Dylan had simply knocked my book light (which flips open and automatically turns on) off of the kitchen counter. We were relieved it wasn't a burglar, but that relief was short lived because we soon found out just what Dylan had been chasing when he catapulted the book light. A huge spider, the size of my palm, was in the middle of our kitchen. In a joint effort (in which I am sure I was of no help) we (Jon) successfully swept the spider out into the night (my hero). During the eviction we counted its legs and realized it wasn't a spider, but some other bizarro creepy crawly. Either way we were glad to be rid of it.

One morning, when our legs had adjusted to all the constant, moderate exercise, we agreed that we should finally hike through Cabo Blanco. We packed our bag with some fruit and water, and wound down the path lined with dogs and cattle, until we arrived at the white-blue stream. Forging onward this time we passed through giant trees that hung like willows, providing much appreciated shade. The hike would end at the tip of the peninsula, which is known for its white sand beach. Already, we were dreaming of the cool splash into the ocean's water.

A few minutes into the ancient jungle, we approached a service desk to pay for entry into the park. It was then, to our great disappointment, we found out Marley would not be allowed in. We begged to no avail. Disappointed, and still hot, we headed home. Pura Vida.

We pulled over at a familiar stretch of beach to re-deem our adventurous spirit, but it was the low tide, rocky, time of day, so instead of swimming we took to exploring the driftwood.

By now, we were used to fish and lobster carcasses washed ashore, but today we had the pleasure of finding a giant sea turtle carcass. I know it sounds strange to say that seeing a dead animal was a pleasure, but in this peaceful setting, the observation of death only reinforced the beauty of life. This turtle had been decomposing for some time, but was easily recognizable, even as only a shell and skeleton. My inner anatomy geek was delighted to see the phalanges that were normally hidden, encased in their webbing. I wanted a picture to show to the next person who disregarded evolution by saying, *"You think things just crawled out of the ocean and started growing fingers and toes?"*

Anatomy and Biology were always my favorite subjects, despite the fact that I majored in Psychology. I chose Psychology because I loved the scientific rationale behind behaviors that seemed like common sense. I often made the joke that I studied Psychology to treat my own neuroses, but seriously, the more I studied the brain and the body together, the more I began to realize they were fundamentally linked to one another. During my collegiate career it was my intention to pursue medical school and become a psychiatrist, but towards the end, Jon started touring the world, and my priorities shifted.

After graduation, I enrolled in a program which would allow me to achieve a second Bachelor's Degree in Nursing in only one year, hoping I could continue my passion for healthcare without dedicating so much of my life to my career. Unfortunately, I hated it. Every day I felt as though I was taking steps down someone else's path. I was sick of appeasing system abusers, and ignoring the ill yet uninsured. I was sick of stifling my instinct and intellect in order to stifle the symptoms of a society refusing to care for itself. I was sick of being overworked and underpaid. I was sick of working for third party insurance and pharmaceutical companies...

Back in Cabuya, I couldn't help but wonder if the turtle had died a violent and exciting death, or if one day while swimming he had simply ceased to be. I will never know, but I felt certain it wasn't due to work-related stress. A Tico couple that had been collecting shells along the shore came to gaze at the turtle with us and the emotion of the silent vigil overcame any language barrier. Before they left, the man turned to us and said *"Vida es Vida"* and the translation was clear and beautiful, *"Life is Life"*.

As we strolled the beach, we had a very serious conversation about how to do our laundry. In the heat we found ourselves changing clothes a few times a day, and we were antsy to get the sand and sweat out of his gray teeshirts and my sundresses. However, we hadn't passed anything that resembled a laundromat, except for a tiny house with *"lavandería"* handwritten on a cardboard sign. It seemed too far to trek on foot with two week's worth of clothes and towels, so we decided to ask our favorite neighbor, Cabuya Joe, how he does his laundry.

Well, he has a washing machine. He told us we could give his housekeeper a few mil colones (about $5) and that she would take care of it for us. It was weird having someone other than myself or Mom doing my laundry, but I was glad I didn't have to walk a few kilometers with a heavy bag of soiled clothes, just to pay a different Tica to do my laundry.

When we handed over our clothes and colones, we met Joe's wife, Dolly. She was a happy lady with an infectious laugh who appeared to be addicted to giving Marley dog treats. She was an ER nurse and a Reiki practitioner, so the two of us found a lot of common ground talking about the schism and inevitable marriage between conventional and holistic medicine. It had been at least a week since I had really thought about teaching, about the power of healing, and about our society's disconnect from wellness. I couldn't believe how much I missed talking to someone who really spoke my language (and I don't mean English.) Dolly and I planned to meet later that evening for a personalized Pilates session, and with that, the friendly neighbors headed to Montezuma, while Jon and I headed back to the beach. I stretched on the sand and tried to remember my favorite sequences for Dolly's Introduction to Pilates session.

I had my Introduction to Pilates session a few weeks after my departure from nursing school, and during the class I was instantly transported back to my seven year stint as a ballerina. I was happy to find that my flexibility and technique had remained relatively in tact, and I reveled in the act of challenging my mind and my body, reminded of the joy that can be found when one can simply appreciate being alive in a present moment. I was hooked. I started taking two classes in a row, sometimes twice a day. In no time I was beginning the training and certification process to become a Pilates Instructor. In less than six months, the same amount of time I studied nursing, practicing Pilates had made me healthy again- in my mind, my body, and my soul.

Pilates came naturally to me because I was able to pool knowledge from my studies of anatomy, psychology, and ballet, furthering an even deeper belief in the idea of MindBody wellness.

What exactly do I mean by MindBody? Well, I want the term to describe the human experience when the mind is fully engaged in the present pursuit of the physical body (pilates, yoga, sports), or the physical body is fully engaged in the present pursuit of the mind (writing, music, meditation). These activities, and many more, allow us to unite our mind and body, to balance their exertion and relaxation, and they have proven to bring joy and peace to millions of humans throughout history.

Why? Often our bodies do things on "autopilot" while our minds are occupied elsewhere, and vice versa. Even if they are fundamentally codependent on one another (mind can not exist without body, body can not exist without mind) it is not necessary for them to always work together. In this way they are one, but also two. Not mind and body, not mindbody, but MindBody. And also BodyMind, because neither is more important than the other, they are simply two facets of the same consciousness.

As a teacher, I loved working with my students. I truly enjoyed seeing the effect that engaging their MindBodies had on their various lives. It was invigorating to see their interest and progress, and my thoughts about the corruption of the healthcare system were often validated by their dramatic results. I had cured low back pain, shoulder tendonitis, chronic body image disorders, and more, simply by teaching people how to stand up straight and breathe.

I learned so much more about the spine and brain seeing those things in action, than I had in countless hours of lectures. Now, don't get me wrong, I am grateful for my education, obviously, without it I would have never attained such a great understanding of the human Mind-Body. Despite my complaints about The System, I know that I am a product of The System, that I owe everything I am to The System, and that The System isn't all bad. I believe it is because I care about The System that I feel the need to critique it. Nothing is perfect, but everything could always be better.

I snapped to the present moment and I looked around at the jungle. It seemed as though geographic movement was proving to be as good for the human experience as physical movement had been all those years ago. Pura Vida.

Returning to Cabuya Joe's, I rolled out two mats near the pool while Joe convinced Jon to join him for a ride on his ATV. As soon as Dolly's class began I found the rhythm of my teaching groove, talking about the importance of alignment and breathing, as if I had never left the studios in the suburbs. Dolly enjoyed the class and afterwards we sat and giggled through what Mom has adequately termed the "yoga buzz": the abundance of positive energy that immediately follows a good workout. After the men returned, we passed the night talking and enjoying a night swim in their pool, watching the infinite stars from the cool oasis. It was hours past our usual bedtime when Jon and I sleepily walked home, phalanges intertwined, Marley leading the way, back to The Cabina and The Cats.

The following afternoon, we returned to the beach, but upon arrival the water was still passed the rocks, the tide caught between high and low. We decided it was close enough to get in, so we climbed over the slippery stones that our feet were starting to acclimate too, and sunk into the warm océano. We found some boulders to sit on and talked as the tide gently nudged at the base of our spines.

As much as we were loving our jungle adventure, we were also feeling a little lonely. We missed our community: our parents, our siblings, our friends. We hadn't even realized how connected to them we had been until we were here with no phones, and practically no one who spoke English.

I thought back to our wedding night, a time when we should have been alone, but instead found ourselves amidst our community...

After the formal celebrations, we headed upstairs with a small crew of friends and picked up a few lost-looking, far-from-sober, guests along the way. We entered our hotel room, opened a bottle of champagne and poured shots into plastic cups to pass around. Mom and Dad showed up with a bottle of whiskey, Jon's brother with a guitar, his dad with a plastic shrub he had borrowed from the hotel lobby, my East Coast cousins brought a cooler of beer, and Jon's aunties brought the wine and snack food. About forty people graced our wedding suite, and we proceeded to have a bodacious party.

Jon and I sat on our nuptial bed with my sorority sisters. A joint or two was passed around as the music turned into a sing-a-long: a room full of people belting out The Beatles' "Don't Let Me Down", unaware that it was 3:00A.M. After that, we received a warning knock from hotel management, but it did little to stifle our spirits. A second knock scared most of the guests away, and the third, asked for the groom specifically and explained to Jon that the hotel really didn't want to kick us out of here on our wedding night, but....

Our wedding that had lasted until 5:00A.M. seemed like a lifetime away. At home we had more friends than we could keep up with. Here, our best friends are animals, and they don't speak English either. I guess the old adage *"the grass is always greener"*, isn't quite right... Sometimes the grass is green, and sometimes it is dead and brown, sometimes it is filled with spiky weeds, sometimes it is crawling with ants, sometimes it is covered in snow, and sometimes it is sand instead. The grass has the potential to be many things, it just can't be everything at once.

We continued talking, splashing our faces with the salty water, until the tide pushed at our shoulder blades, jostling us from our reverie. We stood up, navigated back over the now underwater rocks, and found a sandy spot lined with fallen trees. Jon quickly built a little campfire to dry us off.

While I read, Jon began attempting to dislodge coconuts from nearby palm trees. We both love drinking coconut water and were dying to try it fresh from the source. A friendly Tico appeared out of nowhere, offered to help, and proceeded to shimmy up the tree with his bare hands and feet to cut down a branch full of heavy coconuts.

When he returned to the ground, he handed it to us explaining they were pipas: the young, green, coconuts, with the best water. We thanked him and the three of us sat on the rocks while he showed us with his knife how to hack up the pipa. He unveiled a tiny circle of white flesh and pierced it before handing it to me. We sat and happily drank the delicious juice while he showed us some other coconut techniques, like opening the pipa into two halves and eating the meat with a "spoon" he made from a slice of its shell.

He didn't speak English, which gave us an ample opportunity to practice our Español, and we found out that he lived in Cabuya his entire life, that he is a carpenter, and that his favorite place to hang out is at the Only Bar in Cabuya. His final coconut trick was to grab a long narrow leaf from the pipa tree and roll it in a spiral fashion. He showed us the final product, a small green cone, *"pipa para fumar"*, he smiled, and we both gave him a strange look. *"Young coconut for to smoke?"* I asked. He laughed and shook his head, *"Pipa, Pipe"* he explained and proceeded to fill the rolled up leaf with our favorite green smokey treat. We partook and watched the tide inch toward us.

Because we are facing east, the sun does not set over the sea. However, the transformation of the sky as day slips into her nightgown and crawls under her blanket of stars is spine-tingling. The hues tint the water a fantastical shade of silver-blue as the pelicans dive bravely between the rocks for their last chance at dinner. Glints of dying sunlight make the whole scene sparkle. When the color is gone, the sky becomes a shade of gray, and the sand becomes suddenly animated by the scurrying of hermit crabs. We grabbed our backpack and headed to check out the Only Bar in Cabuya.

The place was deserted but for the bartender and a table full of her friends who were watching the nightly news en Español on the television in the corner. As both strangers and gringos in a small town, we were ogled by the table while we ordered our cervezas. We settled into a well-lit corner with a deck of cards and played some of our favorite games from back home, reminiscing about poker nights and bars full of people we knew.

Jon and I missed our friends now. Don't get me wrong, it was fun to play together. But we had been together every moment of every day for weeks now, with no one else to talk to. Even with our passion for long-winded philosophical chats, we still found ourselves low on things to talk about. A romantic relationship can be many things, but it can't be everything at once.

To our delight we were soon joined by our new amigo from the beach, I will call him Pipa. He sat with us and we played "Ron" which sounded very fancy with the dramatic roll of his "R'", and was easy enough to teach two gringos, even if the direction of play did move clockwise. While we played, a skinny, biker-looking gentleman with crazy gray hair and stoned looking eyes came and introduced himself.

It was a most intense introduction, where he proceeded to tell us that he was from The States, but has been here in Cabuya for years writing a book about the decades he spent incarcerated for his dodgy financial pursuits. Unsure of how to react, we listened politely as he sat and told us what had to be the entire story. He explained his situation as *"the movie Catch Me if You Can times one hundred"*, and afterwards showed us a gnarly magic trick with our own deck of cards that won him a beer bought by Jon.

The three of us talked (mostly about Moneybags) and his accent reminded me of my East Coast family. While he talked I found myself daydreaming about a scenario where they were all hanging out together.

The rest of the bar had loosened up by now, its inhabitants singing and dancing, and we found out from Pipa that there is a fiesta here every Sunday where we can definitely learn to salsa dance. Over-served and quite sleepy we told Pipa and Moneybags we would see them Sunday, and we wandered home in the dark on the now familiar dusty path. On the way we wondered aloud how much of Moneybag's story could possibly be true, and whether it was legal or not for me to write about these crazy characters.

We awoke early and abruptly on Monday to Marley barking like a maniac. Shaking off his sleepy fog, Jon momentarily wrestled with the bolts on the porch door before throwing it open and following our rowdy dog onto the balcony to identify the cause of the ruckus.

There, standing in front of The Cabina, was our soon-to-be-landlord, Granjero, accompanied by his dogs. *"'S-coos-me"* he shouted, *"You come to my house! I have it limones, bananas, plántanos..."* and he continued listing fruit, counting each new one off on one of his fingers.

Perhaps we should have been annoyed that he woke us up, but Granjero's booming attempts at English were refreshing. Also, we could use some plantains. We told him we would come by in a bit, and he left with a smile and a wave. We headed downstairs, and as I entered the bathroom (drum roll please...) I saw my first scorpion! In the shower. Shudder.

December is scorpion season in Costa Rica. Winter here means the clawed critters are searching for ways out of the ocean's breeze (which they consider "cold"), and into one's cabina, specifically one's towels. No worries, the Ticos inform us, if you get bit by one, just hack it open with a machete and rub its poop (which contains an antidote) all over the bite. Right. No worries.

This particular scorpion looked a little worse for the wear, so we assumed that it had already met Clover, and our fears were muted. Both cats were happily playing in the yard, so it seemed unlikely that they had been stung. Jon grabbed the big blue cup that we have been using to trap the insects we find in The Cabina, and swept the injured scorpion inside it. As he was walking towards the door, a big brown spider with a white racing stripe scurried across his path. We had already met this spider's siblings, and learned from Google that they weren't dangerous, so without hesitation Jon scooped the spider into the cup as well. We figured the creepy crawlies could duke it out if they wanted to, but they simply ignored each other for the entire journey across the yard, keeping their distance in the bottom of the cup until Jon unceremoniously dumped them both into a bush at the edge of the property. When he came back inside we said in unison, *"Let's clean the house."*

We attacked the place with a washrag and a broom, and it was actually nice to admire the now shiny woodwork adorning The Cabina.

I am not exactly sure when my OCD about cleaning surfaced in my personality. To be clear, I am not OCD clean, but OCD about cleaning. As a creative type, I can accidentally get involved in a few projects at once, leaving my living space a complete and utter disaster for days at a time. When I do decide to clean up though, I clean deeply, leaving everything meticulously organized, often alphabetized, and scrubbed shiny. Its a habit I picked up from MomMom, who it is rumored, ironed her pajamas. After years of practice, cleaning is like meditation for me. I lose myself in the rhythm and allow my mind to wander while my body rejoices in the monotonous, physical task.

Today, I let my mind wander to the idea of culture. An idea that I have been simultaneously chasing and running away from. The thing I want most to remove myself from, and to immerse myself in.

In biology, a culture is a group of cells grown in a controlled environment. I guess that is reminiscent of the social terminology, our "cultures" are simply groups that grew out of humans reproducing in different environments. I thought of myself as a little bacterium, suddenly transplanted into an unfamiliar Petri dish. As if Jon and I and our f-animal-y were scratched off the cheek of the Midwest, placed in a sample of salt water and sand, and observed under heated conditions...

I plunged bravely into every corner and under every shadowy surface, ridding the place of any good, dusty, hiding places. I found a few tiny spiders, and let them flee to other corners because I do enjoy the free insect killing service they provide. I laughed to myself. In this particular Petri dish, I have spiders for roommates.

I didn't unearth anything else nearly as exciting as the scorpion, but Jon did. The next time I saw him, his face was paler than usual, and he was holding a piece of paper over the now infamous blue cup. He was pretty sure the spider he had found (in our bedroom) was the very poisonous brown recluse, and he was wondering if I wanted to see it. Um, no. No, I did not. The pictures online of its menacing eyeballs and the necrotic ulcers its venom produces were enough for me, thank you.

Jon sat down and started snapping photos of the critter who was aggressively dashing around the cup trying to figure out how best to bite him. The recluse was eventually deposited in another bush, even farther away than the scorpion/spider duo, and with the consolation of a clean cabina, we headed down the dusty road to visit Granjero at his farm.

Granjero was glad to see us, and immediately forced a bag into each of our hands. *"Come, I show you!"*, he declared with a wave of his arm, and headed into his farmland with more exuberance than even Marley could muster. We ducked through a barbed-wire fence and followed him to the nearest lemon tree. Granjero picked us a few giant lemons and explained, *"No dulce, not for eat"*. When I asked him what we were supposed to do with them if not eat them, he responded with a quick, *"ensalada"* and mimed pouring dressing over a salad.

Next, we stopped at a palm tree full of pipas and we were excited to explain (in our broken Español) that we knew what they were. He gave an excited jump, yanked a few from the tree, and with a *"Come, I show you!"* we were off again. We picked corn, apples, and starfruit, and saw where the avocados would grow in the spring. He showed us how to identify ripe fruit, and warned us about which plants had thorns to watch out for. The crash course in agriculture was fascinating, especially with so much foreign produce.

Back at the farm house, Granjero bounced away and returned with a giant, black, plastic trash bag that was filled to the brim. Like a warrior freeing his sword from its sheath, he reached into the bag and pulled out a massive branch of bananas. He picked two for each of us to snack on, then hacked off a bunch of yellow bananas, followed by a bunch of green ones for us to take home. He discarded the peels of the bananas under a nearby tree, explaining that it was *"Good for.."*, and vigorously pointing to the ground. We assumed that he meant the soil, but really, it could have been good for anything below our knees. Before we could ask, he was off again.

We stopped at a tree and Granjero stood, left hand on his hip, right pointer finger on his pursed lips, and stared at it. *"Es medicina"* he said to us seriously. *"Medicine for what?"* I asked. *"For everything!"* he exclaimed, his hands wildly darting from their resting places to draw an all-encompassing arc in the air. He searched in the branches of the tree and pulled out what looked like a spongy, waxy, ashen, potato. He held it to his nose, smelled it, and then held it out for us to sniff as well. If this thing looked gross, that was nothing compared to its stench of strong cheese and rotting citrus. He crinkled his nose and nodded at our disgusted expressions, then dumped the lumpy, smelly, miracle fruit into our bag.

We returned again to the farm house where he finally sat down, hacked open a pipa, and drank deeply. He told us to come see him whenever we needed more fruit, and we started home, bags heavy, unable to imagine ever needing more fruit. In the heat of the afternoon sun, the aroma of the mystery medicine soon became unbearable. Since neither one of us were sure what to do with it anyway, we tossed it on the side of the road, hoping it would be found by a sick monkey.

On our way home, we ran into Joe and Dolly who invited us over for dinner that night. We agreed, and then found out that they were barbecuing ribs. Joe explained that it was okay, that he had gotten these ribs from the local pig butcher, who was also the local pig farmer, and I wasn't against eating meat, just against eating tortured, poisoned meat, right? Surprised that he had actually listened to my vegetarian rationale, I was persuaded by his argument, and told him we would think about it. He grinned and told us he would see us at 5:00P.M.

Although recently well stocked with fruit from Granjero, we were lacking any other type of groceries, including beer, and we had just been invited to a dinner party. We headed out on foot to gather some grains and vegetables before we headed to Joe's to eat pork for the first time in a long time.

We were welcomed by the scent of wonderfully cooked food and the taste of good tequila. Soon, we were joined by Lessor and one of her colleagues, both of whom were Tica-Gringas that have lived in Cabuya for many years. They entertained us all with a plethora of stories about the area.

When we sat down for dinner, Joe put a slab of ribs on my plate and I had to admit they smelled damn good. It took only a few bites to realize that I missed barbecue sauce more than ribs, and I smiled internally, reaffirming my conviction to a plant-based diet, but glad my idealism had been challenged.

I looked around at these people I barely knew and realized that they were now part of my life, part of my culture, my community. They had helped me grow and learn. I enjoyed the wonderful, local, meal, but only had a second helping of the veggies.

Turning Left

WE WERE 21 YEARS OLD when Jon became our bread-winner. Despite my years in college pursuing a medical degree, it was his ability to write and play music (and look good while doing it) that landed us a six-figure income. At 22, we bought our first house. Well, he bought it, Dylan and I simply lived in it, while Jon resided on a tour bus. It had been over a year since Jon had been home for more than a week, but he was frustrated that he was financially successful, yet technically still living with his parents. We were told for as long as we could remember that money should be invested, and that real estate was a solid investment, so…

We found The Townhouse, well within our means, situated within walking distance to a Walker Brother and a few minutes away from the site of a brand new hospital (I would be starting nursing school in a few months). It was close enough to our parents, friends, and good Mexican food to seal the deal. Jon was on tour when we closed, so he gave me power of attorney. I signed both of our names to the staggering stack of papers that I hoped our lawyer had read through more closely.

Once we unpacked, Jon and I officially lived together for the first time in our six year relationship...but remember, Jon lived on a bus. So there I was, a recent graduate from Northwestern, with a few months to kill before school started again, decorating a house that my famous boyfriend had recently bought for me to live in. This was the American Dream.

The following summer, the whole "being a nurse" thing fell apart. Then, via TV and the Internet, I watched the downward spiral of the financial crisis of 2008. I learned everything I could about subprime mortgages and predatory banking, because the more I learned the more I realized this crazy news story was happening to us. We were angry. The Townhouse was only supposed to be an investment, a place to live while we saved for our real house. Now our investment was a big flop, and it wasn't even in our control. Despite our modest purchase, hefty down payment, and consistent mortgage payments, The Townhouse was still, very suddenly, underwater.

Even though the crisis effected the music industry, Jon's "job" was still relatively secure, so we wondered if we could use the situation to our advantage. Homes were cheaper now than ever before, we could buy our dream home for pennies on the dollar, rent out The Townhouse, and sell everything at a profit once the market recovered. We did the financials over and over in our heads, and decided to purchase the dream home, but still try to be frugal about it.

Of course we found it. On Craigslist. Ten minutes from The Townhouse, 5 bedrooms, 3.5 baths, and an epically beautiful great room: walls of windows overlooking a private half-acre that backed up to a stream and wooded area. It cost less than half of what The Bank had approved for us to borrow. We had fallen so hard we didn't even look at any other properties.

It was like we had hit a BOGO deal, overpaying for The Townhouse only to steal The Big House. It wasn't new or perfect, in fact it had very vintage bathrooms and a distinctly haunted vibe, but we wanted it, so we bought it. We were 23.

The month we moved in, I also voted for the first time, for President Obama. I had been legally able to vote in 2004, but I was simply too disenfranchised with the idea of politics to even care about voting. Mom worked in local government, so she had quite a bit of zeal for the topic, but she was a Republican, and I had more Democratic leanings. Unable to identify with the point of view of someone I loved so completely made me feel hopeless that punching a hole near someone's name was going to make any difference about anything.

Over the years, the more Mom and I would talk about it, the less I saw my beliefs represented by The System. Republicans preach small government, which is a great idea! Yet, it is they who have sold us to an overreaching corporate dictatorship and attempt to legislate our morality. On the other side, Democrats preach social justice, which is a great idea! Yet, it is they who chose bureaucracy over efficiency to create programs that keep people in their places. The hypocrisy was maddening, but Obama promised to Change all that…

The Townhouse rented quickly to a friend's brother, and by December we had adopted Marley and thrown our first Christmas and New Year's Eve parties. This was the American Dream, but even *BIGGER*.

I had everything that could ever be wanted. Yet, all of it, the money, the leisure, the glamour, I would have given it all away just to *be* with Jon for more than a few days in months. I was lonely and uninspired, this new suburban bliss no match for my busy days on campus.

And Jon. Jon felt overworked and out of control of his life. He had reached a level of success that his middle-class community envied. He was constantly being told that his dreams were coming true, when in fact, his happiness and creativity felt more oppressed than ever. Exhausted, he could no longer be sure if he was contradicting his love for music by quitting the band, or by sticking with it. Eventually, he had to quit.

I planned a trip to New Orleans to see him play during that final tour. It was bittersweet to see him on stage, performing like crazy, hearing songs that I knew had been the source of his greatest happiness, as well as his greatest unhappiness. I searched for the right things to say to him, until I realized he had said them already: "*Do not be afraid, for the wind it doesn't stay, it blows and goes away…*"

I thought… do not be afraid to move on. Do not be afraid to stand up for happiness, art, or truth. Do not be afraid to be multi-dimensional. Do not be afraid to make decisions that are difficult. Do not be afraid to make mistakes. Do not be afraid to lose, or to win. Do not be afraid to see the things in life that others spend lifetimes refusing to see. Do not be afraid to fight for what you are, because you have the qualities that turn heads, open minds, and move people to dance, to sing, and to laugh. These are qualities that make life worth living, that make art worth making, that make love worth learning. These are the qualities that will propel you towards success no matter what you choose to do. Do not be afraid of the chaotic winds of life, because they do not stay. They blow away.

Jon wanted to pursue life in his own way, to make his career only part of his multi-dimensional self. I was proud of him. It felt like was the right decision. However, it did leave us two "unemployed" 25-year olds with two mortgages.

We walked Marley through a wintery bird sanctuary near The Big House, brainstorming about what our life was going to be like now. We could no longer afford either of our houses. We both knew we had the potential to create our best work yet, but something had to give. We looked at each other open and honestly, what did we want to do? We found out that neither one of us really cared about The Big House, the TV's that lined each of its floors, or the BMW in its garage. We would sell it all, move back into The Townhouse, and brace ourselves for whatever would happen next. We purged everything but the animals, and burned the things that felt too significant to sell, using the autumn air and the epic flames as an excuse to throw a few final parties.

As the rooms around me emptied, I read *Atlas Shrugged,* and felt as though Ayn Rand was talking to me through the years. She had this idea that the corruption of the dollar occurred when people's motivation and production were no longer for knowledge and innovation, but simply *for* money. In her fictional society, it was no longer the goal to learn, develop, and share work with others; rather, it was to put in hours and leave with a paycheck. It felt so familiar.

The Bank used to exist to invest in productive members of society. When The Bank's intention became to make money instead of financing innovation, it became corrupt. When the The Healthcare System's intention became to make money instead of produce health, it became corrupt. When the The Music Industry's intention became to make money instead of cultivating art, it became corrupt.

So what is the solution? Slip out on society, just like so many characters in her novel, in the hopes of building something with a little more truth and integrity? For me, that would mean retreating from the capitalist economic system, the one thing Rand seemed to find so infallible. How could we agree on so much, yet disagree on something so fundamental?

I didn't know, but I guessed Rand would be throwing a tantrum in her grave if she knew the socially-backwards, ultra-corporate Tea Party was quoting her work and that some Hollywood movie producer had made a profit by misinterpreting it. The politicians and the media miss her biggest point: the *love* of money is the root of all evil. Money as a symbol is not evil, but money as a passion most certainly is.

When The Big House finally sold, it was for less than we paid for it, but more than we owed on it, and our living expenses were quartered. With that success, we moved back into The Townhouse. We couldn't afford the mortgage on our new salaries, and neither of us wanted Jon to pour the savings he did have into an underwater townhome, so our lawyer suggested we "strategically default" in hopes of obtaining a "short sale". We researched the options, agreed it was our best bet, stopped paying The Bank, put the house up for sale, then waited, wondering what would happen next.

It was during this time that we went to Hawaii with the Walkers and decided to seriously *move*. We had lived in the suburbs of Chicago for our entire lives, even if Jon was traveling the last few years. We were ready to start over.

Then we started watching what some might consider "conspiracy theory" documentaries. The first documentary we watched together was called *Collapse* where an ex-CIA agent chain-smoked through an hour or so worth of material explaining how the world as we know it is coming to an end, sooner than we think, because the financial system is just a game that most of us are pawns in, the housing crisis was inevitable and whatever bubble bursts next will burst with a greater ferocity, and all this will lead to the collapse of modern industrial civilization.

It was then that I really began losing faith in American Democracy. It suddenly seemed so obvious that hard working people everywhere were being systematically taken advantage of. Instead of solving the problem, American Party Politics simply narrated the argument of who was doing the taking: The Rich or The Poor. In the past few years I had come to think of us as The Rich, but now I saw we were always The Poor. Well, we were so much richer than most of The Poor, but that only made how rich The Rich were more atrocious.

We replaced our cable with YouTube and Netflix, spending our TV time searching for good documentaries. We studied up on a variety of subjects, notably the exposures of environmental damage, inequality, and the corruption of Industry. We soaked in all the mind-numbing information.

We felt hopeless, scared that we were going to soon be fist fighting to feed our f-animal-y. All of this solidified our decision to move. We wanted to find a place where we could play music, stretch, learn, read, and live happily ever after, away from the winter, at least until the human-induced climate catastrophe took us out. If the world was about to end, we wanted to spend whatever time we had left in a paradise.

We reduced our spending significantly, so our salaries as a Pilates Instructor and Independent Musician were currently covering our expenses, but barely. Neither of us wanted to dedicate our time or talent to The Man, who seemed to be letting the entire world around him down, but we couldn't escape the fact that we needed jobs if we wanted to eat.

We discovered the *Zeitgeist* documentary series, detailed visual lectures focused on the idea that the majority of the social problems that plague the human species are not solely the result of corruption or flaws of human nature, rather, they are "symptoms" born out of an out-dated social structure.

We listened carefully to the inevitable fate of our cur-rent systems, and excitedly to the prospect of a more sus-tainable, resource-based economy. For the first time since our foray into documentaries, we felt hope. It wasn't all over, it was simply beginning. We knew now that we weren't alone in our thoughts and that we couldn't sacri-fice our quest and live falsely. We had to follow our hearts.

After several months of filing redundant paper work, The Bank declined our short-sale offer and foreclosed on us. Then, they set a sale date for The Townhouse: No-vember 15th. After that, we would have thirty days to leave the property. We would be gone before Christmas.

We were ready to go to Costa Rica, having narrowed our search down to the Nicoya Peninsula and finding a couple available rentals in our price range. We made vet appointments to prepare the animals for their in-ternational journey and sat down to finalize our flight. Airfare was very expensive around Thanksgiving, so our options were to leave the week before, or the second week of December.

Our plant-based diet really didn't fit in with modern Thanksgiving, and we both now associated the holiday with the genocide of the Native Americans, however we agreed it would be a great way to say adiós to our fami-lies. Thanksgiving was only a month away, we still had so much to plan before we could leave the country...

On November 16th, we returned from a brisk walk with Marley to find a large, black BMW SUV parked in front of The Townhouse's garage. The man within it introduced himself, explained that his company had just bought the property from The Bank, and that he was hoping he could take a look. We figured he didn't even have to ask, so we invited him in. He commented on how empty the house was and we told him our story of the past year of elimination. We asked him what exactly his company owned and what we could take with us, and he winked, explaining the dishwasher and microwave were built into the cabinets, but everything else was ours to do with as we pleased...

Before he left, he asked how soon we could be out of the property. We assured him we wanted out A.S.A.P. and he offered to pay us a few hundred dollars to be out in two weeks. We told him if he doubled it we could be out by Sunday. He agreed. When he left, we high-fived, who would have thought we would have gotten paid to leave this place?!

We sold the appliances that weren't built into the cabinets, and packed everything we would be bringing to Costa Rica into two suitcases. A third suitcase was packed for the few nights we would spend at my parent's house before our flight would depart the following Tuesday. We looked at our joint checking account, added the amount we had received for the appliances and our hasty move, and decided our funds would allow us to travel until May. We called our friends and families and made plans to see them all one last time before we left.

Almost exactly a year to the day since we had left The Big House we were finally moving on from the lives of our past. We both felt a gigantic wave of relief as we

handed our new friend the keys and he handed us a fat
wad of cash in return. We put the two squishy cat carriers
inside Marley's travel crate, put it in the flatbed of my
pickup truck, and covered it with a blanket to keep them
warm in the autumn air. Three suitcases and one guitar
went in as well, and Jon and I sat up front, Marley curling up on my lap. We pulled away from The Townhouse
and turned right, driving away from suburban home
ownership, and out into the gusty morning...

A few weeks later, here we are in Cabuya, and everywhere we have gone has required us to turn right out of
The Cabina. The Café, The Supermercado, Rio Lajas, The
Only Bar, the ocean, Montezuma, even Granjero's farm:
all are a la derecha. We are leaving The Cabina in a few
days, and wanted to see what lies to the left before we go.
We awoke early on Monday morning, excited to make a
ton of terrible *Zoolander* jokes about spending our day
turning to the left.

The Cabina is on The Road to Mal Pais, which when
traveled towards the left (or west if you're getting techni-
cal) crosses the peninsula, ending at the small surfing village of Mal Pais (which is frequented by Mel Gibson, according to Cabuya Joe). We knew from talking to Cocinera that this road was somewhat treacherous, because it
consists of very steep hills, giant potholes, and the occasional stream that covers the road. Many a Tourist has
been hurt trying to trespass it on an ATV, so we decided
the safest way to travel would be on our feet. That way,
we figured, we couldn't accumulate enough momentum

to kill ourselves. We left The Cats outside to frolic, locked up The Cabina, and turned left.

The first thing we noticed was that The Cabina sat on the edge of civilization. Within minutes, houses became nonexistent, and soon, even the power lines had to disperse to make room for thickening leaves. As we walked the trees became taller and the cries of birds, primates, and insects began to close in on us. The second thing we noticed was a towering hill ahead.

Staring at what appeared to be a vertical drop, we probably would have turned back if Marley hadn't started straight up the middle of the daunting slope. We looked to each other and shrugged, we needed to get in some cardio anyway, and luckily, albeit uncharacteristically, we had both worn shoes. We leaned our body weight forward, placing careful steps, one in front of the other, and started up the rocky incline.

A quarter of the way up, I started to sweat profusely. Heat was escaping my body via the salty liquid and mixing with the sunscreen and bug spray I had liberally applied, achieving a perfect sting as it dripped rhythmically past my eyelashes. Half way up my ears started to pop, and I could hear my labored breathing echoing inside my now clogged head. Three quarters of the way up Jon stopped. He was looking back, mouth open in awe. I caught up to him and turned too, witnessing a most spectacular view of Cabuya: the blue-green of the gulf shone in the sun, and Isla Cementerio was visible in its entirety from this aerial view: a tuft of gnarled greenery with sandy appendages stretching out into the dazzling sea.

Regaining the breath that the climb and the view had taken away from us (and of course forgetting to snap a picture), we continued on, determined now to make it to the top. Standing at the peak we were able to look down on Cabo Blanco to our left, see the mountains to our right, and turn around to see Cabuya below us. When we looked ahead, all we could see was Marley, trotting happily, unaffected by the steep climb. Now that my heart rate had calmed a bit, the endorphins enticed us to continue further.

The hill fell almost as steeply as it rose, but this time with serpentine curves that hid the trail ahead from view. We started down, walking in zig-zags to slow our momentum, calling out to Marley whenever he got too far ahead for us to see. At the bottom we ran into our first obstacle: a small waterfall that covered the road.

We contemplated turning back at this point, but decided to go on since we had only hiked for about forty-five minutes and already dedicated our entire day to this journey. Plus, Marley had already crossed the stream. We hopped across on protruding stones, Jon leaping bravely across in a matter of seconds, while I stalled and wobbled awkwardly on each and every stone, calculating the force I would need to exert through my calves in order to make it dryly to the next one.

After the waterfall-crossing, the road was much flatter, and the shade provided by the colossal trees was welcome. We continued on in silence, listening to the birds and the monkeys chattering loudly in the treetops. We reached another hill, easily as steep as the last; but prepared and refreshed, we started up without hesitation.

The sweating and ear-popping occurred again, but this time my body seemed accustomed to the stress, the muscles of my legs feeling more confident as they pushed me up the hill, to the top, down again, and across another stream. This pattern occurred a few times and on a stretch of flat land we stopped to sip some water, gave some to Marley, and wondered if we were going to have the energy to make it back. Figuring we had to be at least half way to Mal Pais, we didn't want to turn around just yet. We had come way too far to not make it to our destination, and worst case scenario we could always hitchhike home. Although so far, we had only been passed by one ATV...

Screwing the cap back on our water, Jon readjusted his backpack high on his shoulders, and we were off again. A few more climbs, descents, and stream-hops later, we started to see evidence of civilization again. Power lines occurred first, then the quietening of the wildlife, and finally a hotel, followed closely by a few Tico homes. We had made it to Mal Pais! Now all we had to do was find the beach. We kept walking, rejuvenated by the reaching of our destination, and I started to dream about food while my aching feet continued to push me forward.

We reached an intersection with a handprinted sign: "Fish Market to the left, Montezuma to the right". Figuring the Fish Market would probably be on the ocean, and that Montezuma was back across the peninsula, we turned left again. This took us to the literal edge of Mal Pais, a rocky and isolated beach bordering Cabo Blanco, and crowded with fishing boats. This did not seem like a surf haven at all.

We turned around and headed back in the direction we had come from. Luckily, we soon ran into an English speaking couple that informed us that Mal Pais Centro was a few kilometers away, down The Road to Montezuma.

Okay, so we hadn't reached our destination. We wrapped our brains around that disappointing news and reasoned that a few kilometers, especially if it was flat, was nothing compared to turning around and hiking back on an empty stomach. So we turned down The Road to Montezuma and continued walking.

The terrain was much more manageable, but the elements were not. The sun reflected off the water and the sandy path, blinding us, and we could feel our pale skin burning in the inescapable glare. On this road, we were often passed by ATV's. They projected lingering clouds of dust into the air, which eventually settled in my nose, lungs, and on my skin, meeting the sweat-sunscreen-bugspray mix, and forming a thin film which I hoped would protect me from more sunburn. We walked on and on, our moods worsening in direct correlation with the swelling of our feet and the emptiness of our stomachs.

Finally, we turned a corner and saw Mal Pais Centro, a downtown slightly larger than Montezuma but absolutely swarming with people. Music blared and people bustled around the surf shops and eateries. People here seemed much younger, and much whiter, than we had previously encountered, and although it was comforting to see so many signs in English, it felt like we had somehow walked all the way to southern California.

We walked up to a souvenir shop and asked a group of girls sitting outside if there was a bus to Montezuma. They told us there was a bus that left at 2:00P.M., but they had no idea what time it currently was. Delighted that there was a bus, we asked the first person wearing a watch, *"qué hora es?"* and found out that it was 1:41P.M. I guess the timing was perfect, but we had wanted to see the beach and eat some food. Explaining to Jon that I was hangry (a wonderful term Mom and the rest of the Internet uses to explain the bitch that one can become on an empty stomach) we set out to find the quickest thing to eat, so that we wouldn't miss the bus. Spotting a nearby bebida de frutas shop, I popped in and ordered us a mango-pineapple-orange bebida. It was delicious, and filling enough to restore my temperament to benign.

We sat on the curb, waiting for the bus, and Jon struck up a conversation with a 20-something who appeared to be a rapper (he had big gold chains, no shirt, a lopsided baseball cap, sunglasses, and a plethora of violent tattoos). He spoke in Español except for the word "fuck" and tried to convince us to ride in his taxi while simultaneously drinking a beer. We explained that we were broke so we would have to wait for the bus, and he shrugged, continuing to talk to us despite our disinterest in his business. Neither one of us were really sure if he was being friendly or not, but he did tell us that the bus was at 2:30P.M., not 2:00P.M., and that it went to Cobano, not Montezuma; but we could catch a bus in Cobano that would take us to Montezuma.

We felt uneasy sitting on the curb with this strange yet informative man, but seeing as we were in no shape to walk anywhere else, we simply scooted closer together and sipped our bebida de frutas.

A few minutes later, an older Tico that we had seen outside the bebida de frutas shop sat down behind us and started selling ceviche out of his cooler. Realizing that someone showing up to sell cheap food at our bus stop was too good to pass up, we got a cup and happily munched on the tangy snack, washing it down with our fruity treat. The rapper seemed impressed that we had bought the cooler ceviche instead of going to a restaurant, and we were relieved that we had given this man reason to like us and not dislike us.

The bus pulled up and everyone on the curb slowly rose, gathered their belongings, and formed a line. We watched friends make tearful goodbyes, and surfers pack huge boards into the cargo underneath, but when we started to step aboard we were abruptly stopped. "No perro" the driver said motioning sharply at Marley. "Por favor" we begged, "We can pay for his fare", "He will sit with us", "He is a good boy." It was useless. "No, no perro." Well, shit.

Seeing our despair, the driver informed us that a local bus would get in at 4:30P.M., and that they might take the dog. We thanked him and walked away, now with two hours to kill in Mal Pais, and the nerve wracking feeling that we might be stuck here forever. If we couldn't get on the 4:30P.M. bus, we wouldn't be able to make the treacherous walk home before dark, even if we wanted to. Deciding to be optimistic about the bus, we went to the store, grabbed two tall boys, and headed towards the ocean.

The beach here really was amazing. The waves were powerful and picturesque and dotted with both professional and novice surfers. The sound of the downtown was drowned out by the consistent rhythm of the waves, and we were glad we had gotten to experience this, even if the experience had caused some severe mental, physical, and emotional stress.

Beers finished, and the waves too daunting to swim, we headed back to Mal Pais Centro to find out what time it was. We walked through the town and found that it extended into little villages, each with its own unique flair. The playful, surfer vibe had permeated every establishment, and although it was lively, it felt somehow disconcerting after weeks in isolated Cabuya. We had contemplated staying in Mal Pais when we planned this trip, and we wondered what it would have been like if we had, and whether we would have enjoyed this crazy walk had it ended at The Café...

Seriously sick of walking, we grabbed some water and went to sit back by our bus stop. It was only 3:15P.M. We brainstormed and decided that we would try hitchhiking to Cobano to catch the bus to Montezuma. If no one picked us up within the hour, we could always try the 4:30P.M. bus. We shook the dust off of Marley to make him more presentable, and waited patiently, extending our thumbs whenever an SUV or pick-up truck passed our way.

After multiple tries, we realized that hitchhiking from Mal Pais was more difficult than hitchhiking from Montezuma had ever been, and we started to think that our only hope was for Mel Gibson to drive by, recognize us as fellow Statesmen, whisk us away in a private helicopter, and drop us back at The Cabina. You know it has been a long day when you genuinely think that accidentally running into a celebrity in a foreign country is your most likely chance for survival.

A worn-down brown (or maybe just dusty) SUV eventually pulled over to our side of the road. It wasn't Mel, but it was a nice man who would take us, and our dog, to Cobano. We settled into his car and expressed our gratitude, explaining how far we had walked, and how far we still had left to go. He was on his way to the dentist in Cobano and seemed glad to help, and to have the company. His timing couldn't have been better, as soon as we left Mal Pais Centro, it began to rain.

The rain was welcome. It cooled the air and settled the dust and spritzed playfully at my face and arm through the open window. We found out our driver was from Argentina, and had just gotten married and had welcomed his first baby here in Costa Rica. He was an avid surfer and loved living in Mal Pais. He explained the major intersections, since this would be our first time in Cobano, and helped me practice asking *"Where is the bus to Montezuma?"* and *"What time does it leave?"* in Español. At 4:00P.M. we pulled into his dentist's office, thanked him again, and started walking.

If Cabuya was rural farmland, and Montezuma a small suburb, then Mal Pais was only a larger, hipper suburb, and Cobano was the big city. There was traffic here, and policemen! We were overwhelmed and held

Marley close on his leash. How were we supposed to find the bus? Even if we did successfully ask for directions, there was no guarantee we would understand them. And even if we did find the bus, what if it wouldn't take Marley?

As we were voicing our concerns, we literally bumped into Lessor. She stopped walking with her friend and wondered what we were doing out here. We explained the story about our walk and our subsequent bus drama, and she told us not to worry, that she was leaving Cobano soon and could take us back to Montezuma. She told us where her office was and that we should meet her there in thirty minutes. Shocked at our luck, we headed to kill some time at the Mega Super: a grocery store that seemed huge compared to those in Cabuya and Montezuma, but would have been dwarfed by any grocer in the Chicago suburbs. We figured we would see if their prices were any cheaper than Cabuya's, since we had a backpack and a ride and all.

I stayed outside with Marley while Jon went inside to shop, and almost immediately I saw Lessor jump in her car and drive away. I calmed myself by repeating in my head *"She wouldn't have just left without us…"*

After awhile, Jon came sprinting out of the Mega Super. He found the prices mostly the same as Cabuya, but with one exception: liquor! He smiled as he showed me the six-pack he had picked up and then proudly produced a $12 bottle of scotch from his bag. Although I was glad to see my man reunited with whiskey, I was still a little petrified that we had been left here, and that we hadn't done any research into taking the bus. Jon insisted that she would be back, she said a half an hour and it had only been ten minutes, we decided to stay as close to the office as possible. There was a "fast food" place on the corner so I ran inside, ordered a casado, and returned to sit with Jon and Marley on a concrete planter that had a good view of the whole street.

After we ate, Jon ran into a different large grocery store that was also across the street from Lessor's office, and this time he came out with peanut butter, bread, and another six-pack! At first I was amazed at his seemingly compulsive alcohol shopping, but when he got closer I saw that he had found our favorite beer from back home, Bohemia, and he was practically skipping across the street to explain to me that it had been the cheapest beer of all!

Unfortunately, this happy distraction didn't do much to lift my mood. I was nervous that we were missing all of our opportunities to get back to The Cabina, and that The Cats were going to be spending the night outside in the dark, and that we would be stuck in Cobano, which felt seedy and dangerous compared to Cabuya, which all of a sudden felt like home.

At the thirty minute mark, Lessor pulled up in her car and waved us over. Turns out, the friend she had been walking with earlier actually lives in Cabuya, and if we didn't mind waiting for her to go to the Mega Super, we could hitch a ride with her all the way back to The Cabina. We were overjoyed at the offer and said we didn't mind waiting at all. We sat back on our planter, split a beer, each ate a slice of bread, and watched the town get darker.

The friend emerged from the Mega Super and unlocked her obnoxiously teal colored car. After hellos, she immediately warned us, "*I am not that great at driving stick.*". Hooray. Oh well, there was no turning back now. We jumped in the car, it lurched forward, and we were on our way.

Again, as soon as we started to move it started to rain, the droplets illuminated by the headlights as we bounced along the road. I ruminated on how I had sacrificed an entire day's worth of mental and physical energy only to make it 7km; and even then, I only made it home thanks to the unflinching generosity of strangers.

We found out that our driver, Chrissy, had just purchased a house in Cabuya and had moved in two weeks ago with her thirteen dogs and eight cats (and here we thought we were animal lovers). She explained that it had cost her a small fortune to bring all of her rescues here, that she didn't speak Español, and that she was seriously aggravated to find out Hulu did not work internationally. It was refreshing to meet another traveler in over her head and we relaxed completely as we passed through the now familiar town of Montezuma, and down the dusty road, which after today, seemed so flat and inviting.

She screeched to a halt in front of The Cabina, and we promised to come and see her menagerie soon. Sprinting through the cool rain we arrived at our front door, never happier to see it, only to find it guarded by two wet and cranky cats.

Rituals

LAYING IN BED, EYES STILL closed, I could feel my feet throbbing from our walk the day before. I mentally checked in with the rest of my body to find that my back and hips were sore as well. I threw a heavy arm and leg over Jon and let the cool breeze slowly flit across my messily-braided hair....wait, what?! A cool breeze?! I became fully alert and raised my head towards our open window.

Mornings here are sunny and muggy. Usually, I peel my damp self out from under the covers at sunrise in an attempt to quickly get downstairs and outside. In contrast, today there was a beautiful breeze and it was making Cabuya feel lazy. The birds were squawking slowly, and even Roofie seemed to be tiptoeing around.

Eventually, we dragged ourselves out of bed, motivated only by café, and headed downstairs to take care of business. We were moving tomorrow and had to find a car that would take us, and our stuff, to Granjero's farm house.

I was jostled by the early morning teléfono Español immersion, but I found us a ride, and also called

Granjero to ensure that he remembered our move-in date. He told us he was ready, and that he had some papayas for us.

The overexertion of the day before mixed with the sleepy gloom of the present day made us feel lazy, so we took to the porch to watch The Cats creep through the grass. Without warning, it started to rain.

The rain was a soft hum, accompanied by another atmospheric drop in temperature. The droplets tickled the rooftop and exposed the fresh scent of each and every bright green leaf. Something about the drizzle made me feel completely at peace.

The Cats were not as happy. They dashed under the shelter of the picnic table, grumbling, sporadically bathing themselves and one another. Marley doesn't like the rain either, so he curled up with Jon in the hammock, and quivered. I used the tranquil atmosphere to mentally prepare to move the next day. There really wasn't much to prepare, we are pretty efficient movers.

Jon has basically been living out of a suitcase since high school, and I have moved annually since I left my parent's house almost a decade ago...

The first time I moved was to Michigan, on crutches and in a cast, about to be a Dance Major with a broken ankle. I was of little help to Jon and my parents who loaded my possessions into Dad's pickup truck, which had been gifted to me as a going- away-to-college present.

The following year, I moved to the transfer dorm at Northwestern University, a place where sophomores who had hated their freshman year at other colleges had come to start over. I met plenty of like-minded people on campus quickly, and thanks to a new website called Facebook, I could keep up with happenings at school, even if I spent most weekends at Jon's apartment in Chicago.

As a third year, I lived in my first apartment with a friend who was studying astrophysics. I cleaned the bathrooms, he helped me through statistics.

For my next move, Jon was touring, so I was forced to beg my parents, my best friend Bella, and Jon's friend Brogan, to help me move to the apartment where I would spend my senior year living with one sorority sister, and the three or four others that were constantly around.

This move was a memorable one. While I was busily packing up kitchen appliances, Mom gingerly entered the room behind me. With an awkward cough she informed me that Dad had found a roach under my bed. When I squealed in disgust she shrugged, squinted, and admitted that it was *"not that kind of a roach."* I was relieved and then immediately terrified to have to admit to Dad that I smoked weed. Luckily, he was a teen in the 1960's and was therefore understanding. He claimed that as long as my grades were good he didn't care how I spent my free time; but added that maybe next time, I could have more ganja on hand for my movers.

From there, Jon and I moved into The Townhouse and bought a huge bed, a huge TV, a huge poker/dinner table, and really, nothing else.

With Jon involved, moving was never an issue. Each Walker Brother has at least one, what I like to call, Significant Brother. A Significant Brother is a friend, who unlike most friends, attends family parties, and is generally a nonnegotiable part of the extended Walker family. Jon's closest Significant Brother was Brogan, but he had others, and his older brothers also had Significant Brothers. We recruited these brothers to help with the move into The Townhouse, and to The Big House, and then back into The Townhouse.

In hindsight, each of my moves was so obviously a rite of passage, a literal shift from one part of my life to the next. I couldn't help but wonder what part of me this next move would represent. I thought about my moving as a bizarre ritual, a tradition I kept to remind myself that it is sometimes essential to throw away your comforts and experience something new.

In Costa Rica, we moved alone. No brothers or sisters, significant or otherwise, to help us. We worked silently, listening to the rain, which had muted the sounds of the wildlife. I packed toiletries and first aid supplies. Jon condensed our kitchen into a few plastic bags. Our clothes were already in their suitcases, so all we had to do was shake out our shoes, and gather the roasting/litter pan, leashes, brushes, and bowls we needed for our furry counterparts. Done in record time, The Cabina was empty and clean, all of our possessions stacked neatly on its porch.

We sat at the picnic table, Jon's foot tapping out the rhythm of our nervous energy. While we waited, Dylan jumped onto the table in an attempt to get his belly scratched. As he flopped down onto his side, we noticed a big, black mark on his face. I looked closer, tried to rub it off, and then realized that it was actually a cluster of minuscule ticks.

Grossed out, I grabbed a cup of water (the only way to kill them is to drown them) and started picking them out of his whiskers with my nails then flinging them into the cup. The more I pulled out, the more there seemed to be, and Dylan. was. pissed. He had come over here for a nice, relaxing scratch and here I was poking and pulling at his face. Jon helped hold him down while I grabbed my tweezers.

I couldn't just brush them off because their little teeth were below his skin, and soon I was pulling out just as much fluffy white hair as I was little black ticks. By the time we had finished, there must have been fifty of them floating dead in the water. Nervous that there might be more ticks than we had previously noticed, we tried to sift through the rest of his coat to assure ourselves. Unfortunately, other than the now bald spot on his face, his fur was so thick that getting all the way down to his skin was impossible in most places. We couldn't uncover any more creepy crawlies, so we stuffed him into his carrier to recuperate. He stared daggers at us as he rubbed his now exposed flesh with a pink paw.

The car came and we piled everything in. Clover was on my lap, Marley on Jon's, and Dylan got a seat all to himself. We threw our luggage on the roof, and then set off down the rickety road, traveling only a few minutes before pulling in to La Hacienda.

On the dusty Road to Montezuma, La Hacienda cannot be seen. The only chance of finding it is to remember to turn near a small gate that is hidden from view by a large palm tree. The gate is memorable, however, once you notice it. It has a sign nailed to one of its posts, hand-painted, with only the word "perros".

The leaves of the palm dangle low enough to require a duck-and-weave upon entrance, and as the gate closes, one spies a primate skull nestled at the base of the palm, surrounded by decaying coconut shells. Past the gate, there is a path up a hill: two lines worn in the grass by the occasional pressure of car tires. Up that path, La Hacienda will come into view on the left, shaded and concealed by the enormous leaves of its surrounding trees.

Granjero was waiting for us amongst said trees and helped us unload our bags onto the beautiful mint-colored tile of La Hacienda's patio. With a *"Come, I show you!"*, he gave us a quick tour of the cozy two bedroom, showing us where all the light switches and garbage cans were. He performed a most spectacular Spanglish mime explaining how we should dispose of any natural food products over the back fence for his horses. Afterwards, he showed us how to use the washing machine, which was way more complicated than it sounds, because the dials consisted of Español words I don't know. Then, explaining he had to work, he smiled, waved, and walked to the house next door.

The Other Farmhouse is built in the treeless treehouse fashion of the creepy cabinas, but with an obviously more experienced hand. Overall, the appearance is one of sturdiness: a solid set of stairs that lead to a second story dormitorio, an open loft with no screens or bars to protect it from the elements. Below, the kitchen and porch are open to the air but distorted from view by drying laundry hanging around the perimeter. This seems to be the blueprint for the standard Cabuyan dwelling, and this one (like many), is currently in a state of partially lived-in (by Granjero) and partially under construction (also by Granjero).

We were so happy to finally be here. The Cabina was dark and full of hidden corners, but La Hacienda was open and bright. The walls were the energizing shade of spring daffodils, and the glossy tiles shone through the entire structure, making it impossible for any bugs to sneak by unnoticed. Every window was simply a screen, strongly reinforced with decorative metal bars, to let in the breeze, but not the bugs and burglars. Beyond them, we could see the expansive farmland that Granjero's family had tilled for over a century. Trees dripped with fruit as far as the eye could see, large exotic birds sang from their tallest branches, patches of vegetables and herbs excitedly reached for the sunlight, filling in any unoccupied soil. We let the animals free, and started unpacking.

Needing to take advantage of the daylight, I headed out to the washing machine in an attempt to put a dent in the laundry that we had accumulated since the last time we had washed our clothes at Cabuya Joe's. Granjero had been very firm that we were only to put four shirts in the washing machine at a time, but this seemed like a waste of water to me, so I improvised. I separated our mountain of laundry into about eight piles. Each consisted of a few small items like socks, underwear, or swimsuits, one pair of shorts or pants, and exactly four shirts. This way he couldn't say I didn't follow his rule…

I manually filled the washing machine by dumping four heavy buckets of water into it. Then, I sprinkled in some soap, and put the first pile of clothes inside. When it finished sloshing around, the hard work actually began. I reached into the now black water and pulled out the first item, rinsing it in the sink and wringing out the excess water. I stuck it in the tiny dryer and turned the dial to one minute, just like Granjero had shown me.

Immediately, the machine sprung to life. A loud and rapid banging noise accompanied its dramatic wobbling and I jumped back, eyes wide, as Jon ran from La Hacienda, and Granjero from The Other Farmhouse. Granjero flung open the dryer, stopping the commotion, and then rearranged the item of clothing inside. He smiled to show he knew it was a mistake, and then explained, *"Es centrifuge, you understanding?"*

Okay. Sure, Granjero. I understand centrifuge. What a word to have in common just as I was starting to decipher the pantomimes.

The now well-balanced shirt hummed quietly inside the dryer, and when its minute was up, I hung the damp garment on the clothesline that hung around the perimeter of the porch tiles. Then I turned and reached into the murky water to repeat the process for the rest of the articles inside. Needless to say, this was not the quickest I had ever done the laundry, and while I was wringing and hanging, Jon followed Granjero around the farm.

He returned with an armful of fruits and vegetables just as I finished a second load. We were out of hanging space, and everything was drying poorly in the damp air anyways, so the rest of the laundry would have to wait for tomorrow. Pura Vida.

At this point, we were hungry and hadn't moved in with a lot of groceries. We now had a ton of fruits and veggies, but thought we might need more than that to make both lunch and dinner. We locked up, walked down the car-tire path, through the gate, and went to explore our new neighborhood.

We found a small hotel which housed a famous (in Cabuya) little restaurant by its pool. We wandered in, sat down, and ordered an afternoon shot of tequila to celebrate our move. We were the only patrons at the establishment, but a family staying at the hotel was enticing a little dog to jump in the pool after a toy, and the paddling of his tiny legs was great entertainment for everyone. The owner, a Tica-Europa, chatted with us while we perused the menu. They had pancakes, with honey instead of maple syrup, and we hadn't even realized we missed pancakes until we read the words. We ordered two.

While we were eating, it started to pour. A sheet of rain pounded the pool and the ocean which was visible behind it. It sounded like hail on the metallic roof.

Stuck for the time being, we ordered dessert to follow our pancakes (ice cream with fresh papaya, watermelon, and pineapple) and enjoyed the sugar and tequila buzz while we watched a group of monkeys crawl through the trees, looking for dry shelter.

When the weather finally cleared, we headed back out on the Road to Montezuma. We had heard there was a fish market across from La Hacienda, and we wanted to check it out, even if we were both still unsure exactly how we felt about eating fish.

We both felt great being vegetarians, but the diet here in Cabuya does not offer a lot of vegetarian variety. Mostly because Cabuya is a fishing village. The whole town eats fish, and its economy depends upon people eating fish. We wanted to be part of the local culture, and we felt strongly that our purchase of peces would be supporting the right kind of agriculture; but still, somewhere deep inside we felt conflicted. Tonight, in this time of transition, the choice came down to eating fish because the fish market was closer than the grocery store.

We walked up to the open door of the market (which was actually someone's house), and were greeted by a skinny, shirtless man with hair longer than my own. I asked in Español if he had fish and with a nod he walked us through the kitchen and living room, and outside to a gigantic freezer. He whipped it open and it was filled with a variety of (thankfully, already de-boned and de-headed) fish. I asked what everything was and the only one we recognized was mahi-mahi, so we asked how much that cost. It was $8 a kilo, so we told him we would take a half-kilo. He plopped the fish onto a scale, sawed it in half with a knife he had brandished from his belt, wrapped it, and handed us the larger half. We paid him and asked if he could recommend anything else. With another nod he led us deeper onto the property and to another large cooler. He opened it and said, *"Camarones y Atun"*.

Looking inside, we saw plump bags filled with blue shrimp, still in their exoskeletons, sitting on top of a pile of dead and frozen tunas. The fish were larger than I had imagined them to be, as long as the cooler, and half as wide. The gigantic eye of the tuna on top gazed blankly at me from its frozen slumber, and I was glad I didn't have this humbling moment with the mahi-mahi. The shrimp was expensive, and we already had more fish than we would eat in a week, so with a gracias we walked back through the house, across the road, and to La Hacienda.

After a long day of moving (and after the lackluster water pressure at The Cabina), I was really looking forward to bathing in this clean, and well-equipped house. I entered the baño, turned on the faucet, and watched as a strong jet burst forth from a thin piece of PVC pipe hanging from the bathroom ceiling. I think I knew when I looked at the gushing water that it was going to be cold, but nothing could have prepared me for the shock of the pounding, freezing water as I stepped under it. I jumped back, bracing myself against the wall of the shower, staring at the offensive flood of H_2O. Okay, I thought to myself, the pressure is great. Your hair already feels cleaner just from getting hit with three seconds of that torrent, and…think about it… on a 90 degree-plus day this would be refreshing…

Shivering slightly, I scrubbed up my hair, soaped up my body, and gathered all of my courage to stand back under the spout. I focused on my breathing, like a good yogi, rinsed, and quickly turned the water off. From the other room, Jon commented on how that was easily the fastest shower I had ever taken. My teeth were still chattering too much to tell him why.

In the morning, Jon borrowed Granjero's bike and went to the grocery store. It was amazing how efficient this task became as soon as wheels got involved. He was back and forth in half the time (even though the store was farther from La Hacienda than The Cabina) and he was able to carry, on his own, the same amount of stuff that had previously required both of us. Thanks Technology.

Furthermore, the bike turned out to be a great toy for Marley. Marley's favorite game is to run as fast as he possibly can. To achieve this on our walks, he usually stops at a peculiar smelling bush and contemplates for a few minutes about how best to pee on it while we continue ahead. Then, when we are just far enough away, he runs at top speed to catch up to us, overestimates his speed, and runs twenty feet ahead of us while trying to slow down his momentum. As soon as Jon rode down the path on the bike, Marley had to sprint to catch up with him, and was able to chase him happily, never slowing down, pink tongue flapping against a blur of black fur, all the way, at least two miles, to The Supermercado and back. While they were gone, I went out back to feed the horses, and just like that, feeding these horses became one of my favorite rituals on the farm...

Every morning, after café, I grab a bucket of discarded food scraps for the two majestic beasts. As they happily munch, they peer down at Marley with a vague curiosity, while he barks and growls at their hooves. I stare past them, out across pastures, into the mountains and thank them for their free composting service. Before I leave, I gently swat the flies from their cheekbones, and contemplate the subtle harmonies of existence.

I head back with an empty compost bucket, passed sprouts in little pots that line the porch tiles, their border interrupted only by a single stone step. There, I discard my dusty flip flops next to Jon's, identical in style, the smaller ones a faded shade of black, the larger a dingy shade of brown. Stepping barefoot onto the gleaming patio, I see Jon, sunk into an indigo hammock that hovers just above the tiles, an arm outstretched and swinging him back and forth. He is watching The Cats, who are studying the fluttering speed of a herd of tiny white butterflies, who are encircling a crop of baby banana trees, who are poking their leafy heads out of the soil.

Each day is accompanied by a few more skimpy loads of laundry, and I develop a rhythm to my hanging and wringing. While the laundry swirls, I sweep the dust and bugs out of the house and off of the patio, proudly reclaiming the perfect shimmer of the tile. I laughed to myself when I realized how much comfort these mundane, adult acts bring me. Cleaning and settling into a space is really all I need to feel at home. So what if I live in the suburbs or on a jungle farm? The reality is, there is laundry to be done.

Afterwards, I grab the laptop and return to the patio to sit at its table: a small plastic circle, covered in a light blue cloth, threaded with images of tropical flowers. Atop the table is an old wine bottle that has been converted into a centerpiece by having a long, ivory candle forced down its neck. The tablecloth billows in the wind, revealing four black paws stretched towards the sun, and a sleepy sigh from Marley answers the breeze contentedly. I write, clicking away at the keys.

Behind me is a small shack, the size of an outhouse, with only three walls and a long tin roof shaded by a leafy tree. Inside the shack is a homemade grill, a metal grate atop a few bricks, the ground beneath covered in ashes, evidence of past cooks. The grill is usually smoking with a fire that Jon has been tending, but on this special day the metal grate was encumbered by a big pot that Granjero filled with black beans and a bunch of other things he found in his lawn, including culantro, peppers, onions, and green plantains.

On the day Granjero made us lunch, we placed a third chair around the patio table and sat down to a delicious meal of rice, beans, yucca, and fish...at 11:30A.M. We knew Ticos typically ate their casados as the first meal of the day instead of the last, but Jon and I simply are not hungry enough that early in the day. It amazes me that even when we eat and cook like the locals, we still don't eat and cook like the locals.

For Granjero, we stretched our tummies and ate every bite, praising the wonderful flavor of the slow cooked beans, and trying to hold a conversation en Español. It was easy to see that the human ritual of dining together was so natural, that it surpassed language and other cultural barriers. After the meal, he poured us each a frosty glass of fresh-squeezed limonada, digested for a few seconds, and jumped up with a wave. He immediately started busily wandering around the farm, collecting new vegetables. We were so full and exhausted from eating so early, we just watched him, in awe of his abundant energy.

In the afternoons, we return to our work, typing furiously and strumming languidly, along to the sounds of hammering and sawing that erupt every once in awhile from The Other Farmhouse. After a couple of cold showers, Jon does his thing in the kitchen, and then we eat again.

We calculated that our gourmet dinners were costing costing us about $1, and usually went something like: a thick piece of perfectly grilled mahi-mahi atop a mound of culantro infused rice, paired with roasted zucchini and chayote (think taste of celery with the texture of a potato). Jon was simply ecstatic to have a real stove again, and seemed to be showing off just what he could do with it. He would artfully chop watermelons and papaya for dessert and toss their skins into the bucket of waste that I would take to the horses in the morning.

After dinner, we retire to La Hacienda's beautiful bedroom. It is not beautiful in its lavishness, but rather in its calm tranquility. There is no furniture but for the bed itself, and the two handmade wooden tables that flank it. The bright white linens match the curtains that swirl in the wind, reminding me of two hypnotic dancers, attempting to draw the attention away from the unimaginable beauty of Mother Nature that lies between them. The insects provide the soundtrack as we end our days talking, watching something on the laptop, or taking on a more sultry adventure.

Okay. I will invite you into our bed, just for a moment...When Jon and I moved to The Townhouse, the first thing we did was buy a gigantic pillow-top mattress, paired with a few sets of fluffy white pillows, and a puffy white synthetic down blanket. We jokingly called it "Bed Island", since we spent days at a time rearranging ourselves on its surface to write, read, watch movies, and hang out together.

When we moved to The Big House, Bed Island moved with us, and when we returned again to The Townhouse, so did Bed Island. As we slowly got rid of our stuff, we knew we would someday have to part with it, seeing as it was too large to fit in an apartment, let alone a suitcase.

We stalled and stalled, elongating our time on this earth with Bed Island, soon realizing that we were not the only ones attached. Marley and Dylan slept each night nestled between our feet, and let's be honest, they spent their days in Bed Island too. Marley would snuggle himself under the covers and lay his little head upon the pillows. Dylan would stretch out on his back, fluffy tummy exposed to the ceiling fan. Clover only enjoyed Bed Island when she could have it to herself. When we finally sold the thing, the animals were forced to fight for sleeping space on its replacement: a futon mattress we had found in The Walker's basement.

Weeks later, at La Hacienda, we have a full size bed, and it is barely enough room for us two humans, let alone the f-animal-y. Furthermore, the little critters that want to curl up with us have just spent the day in the jungle, and are covered in the dirt, sand, and other unidentifiable filth that we have recently showered off. Finally, I understood Tico pet sleeping arrangements.

Sleeping has become torture as we spend the night trying to find space for our legs and keep our sheets clean. Finally, being the hard-hearted one, I declared:

"No more animals in the bed." I needed peace. I was sick of the coat of fur stuck to my sweaty shins and the dreams of ticks wandering off The Cats and into my hair.

So, we began closing our bedroom door and giving the menagerie free rein of the rest of La Hacienda. I knew from my nightly bathroom breaks that Marley kept his post, curled in a ball, in front of our door. The Cats were slightly more creative: Dylan usually stretched out on the blankets in Marley's traveling crate, Clover often on top of my suitcase, paws tucked under her chin. I woke up mornings feeling refreshed and well-rested, but Jon pouted, he missed sleeping with the animals.

Unfortunately, when we move to the house on the beach in a little over a week, all of the common living space will be outdoors. So, if we don't want to lock the animals inside our bedroom, they will have to sleep outside. Not just outside the door, but outside in the wilderness. We defer stressing about the details, and in this way, the days on the farm pass in a haze of peace and productivity.

After only a week at La Hacienda, I barely remember what daily life was like back at The Cabina, let alone back home in The States. All I knew was that it was blowing my mind that it was December. In my mind, December is a stressful time full of shopping, scraping windshields, and packing on layers of clothes to attend multitudes of holiday parties where I pack on layers of fat. 'Tis the season. Here in Cabuya there are no commercialized shopping deals or parties, and it's too hot even when my only layer of clothing is a bikini. 'Tis the season?

I wanted to make it a point to celebrate The Holidays this year in ways that we never had before, and probably never would again: to steal away to the lonely parts of the farm for stargazing bonfires, to take beach hikes, etc., to see how this season compared to Christmases past.

We even went so far as to frame that sleeping outside was an opportunity for a "new tradition" for the animals. So, on Christmas Eve, we decided to experiment with having them stay outside La Hacienda, a yard they were familiar with, before it was their only option at the beach.

Marley's eyes got big and sad as he watched the door slowly swing shut, and he gave a little whimper as he heard the click of the lock. We both felt lonely that night as we crawled under the sheets and stretched out our legs. When we awoke around 3:00A.M., to the sound of thunder, we immediately raced to the door. There, we saw our three favorite critters looking up at us, and we caved. No one should have to spend their first night outside in the rain. We kept them out of the bedroom again, but allowed them the shelter of La Hacienda for one more night.

The next night was Christmas, which also happens to be both Dylan and Marley's birthday, as well as Clover's half birthday (we did a lot of estimation about their birthdates). We decided to let Marley stay inside as a Birthday/Christmas present, but to leave The Cats outside as a Birthday/Christmas present, since they seemed to prefer it out there (assuming it wasn't raining).

After a bonfire, we again closed La Hacienda's door. We were watching *Home Alone* when we were interrupted by a ferocious cat growl. We ran out with our flashlights to look for the green glint of nocturnal eyes, and counted one, two, THREE sets of cat eyes! Marley chased after the third, which his nose did not recognize, and the other two darted off in opposite directions. We found Dylan quickly, crouching in the grass, bathing, evidently having forgotten about the recent commotion. Clover was trickier to find, and when we did locate her, it was fifteen feet up in a tree. She clung to a thick branch with all four sets of claws, emitting a low growl at the night around her. Jon found a handmade ladder near The Other Farmhouse and he wedged it up against the tree, climbing its precarious steps. I shined the flashlight towards Clover, eerily reflecting her eyes.

I was a terrible light-holder, jumpy, and constantly whipping the flashlight in the direction of any sound, or the slightest brush of tall grass on my ankles. While I was concentrating on staying steady, Jon was trying to grasp the agitated feline. She growled and hissed, long claws digging deeper into the tree bark, but eventually he was able to grab her around the middle and lift her struggling body off of the branch. I illuminated the ladder rungs as Jon carefully climbed down, Clover relaxing into his chest. We were just as scared as she was and on the walk back to our shiny tiles, we decided that the animals would again be sleeping in the house.

Jon looked at me with with eyes rounder and larger than those of the frightened kitten he held in his arms, *"Can't they sleep in bed? Since it's Christmas?"* Well, fine. How am I supposed to say no to that?

They each got a tick test and we were off to sleep, Marley's head hitting the pillow with a sigh of relief. So much for new traditions.

The next night we tried again, cats out, dog in. This time we were watching Carl Sagan's *The Cosmos*. Before long, we heard a mysterious banging noise. A rhythmic hammering that seemed to be coming from our porch. We turned on the light and saw The Cats staring hungrily at one of the eaves, so we turned the light off, and shone a flashlight where their eyes led us. We saw something flying around that was the source of the racket, but figuring they had it covered, we resumed our cosmic documentary.

When the banging picked up again, we ran to the door to try and catch a glimpse of whatever this thing was. It was flying around now, hitting its head on the tin roof, searching for something. I guessed it was a bat, but Jon thought it was a lost hummingbird. We illuminated the flashlight again and saw that its eyes reflected, so we knew it was something with night vision. As we contemplated, it started flying vigorously at our flashlight. Instantly and simultaneously we came to the jarring conclusion that this was a *massive* (I mean, we thought it was a bat/bird!) moth.

Dylan was trying to sneak inside with the same tenacity that he usually reserved for sneaking outside, so we decided to let him in. Clover seemed to want to continue the hunt, but we were afraid to leave her out there alone, so Jon ducked out and swept up both cat and roasting pan in one motion, sliding back into the house and bolting the door in the next. We shrugged at our inability to keep our animals outside, and when we sat to start our documentary again, we heard a horrible growl and hiss from another cat. We were relieved that ours were inside, and hoped that the house on the beach would have some sort of indoor alternative for the f-animal-y.

Casa Playa

WE CELEBRATED NEW YEAR'S EVE in Montezuma Centro with Granjero's extended family, and a majority of the rest of the town. When we awoke at La Hacienda in 2012, we had new neighbors, about ten of them, from Peru, all of whom showed up in a vintage van and set up tents around The Other Farmhouse. Luckily for us, great music (Español and English alike) constantly blasted from the speakers of that van, and we danced across our patio to Barry White fondly remembering the playlist Jon had meticulously constructed for our wedding. We lounged around, wrote, listened to the tunes, and cleaned until January 3rd, our day to move out. That morning, we piled all of our belongings back onto the porch and Jon sat amongst them, entertaining a tiny Peruvian neighbor boy, teaching him to chase The Cats, and play the piano on the iPad.

Soon, Granjero and his youngest daughter arrived with a car that was already bursting with luggage. She was on her way back to school (she was studying to be a pharmacist) but had generously offered to drop us off on her way out of town. We managed to squeeze our cats and our things into the remaining corner of the backseat, then I hopped into the front seat before the car headed down the hill. Jon, Granjero, and Marley all followed the car on foot, the men burdened with multiple plastic bags filled with our groceries, the dog excited for the challenge of chasing a more sophisticated set of wheels.

Marley proved to be as fast as the car, and when he started jumping up periodically to see in the windows, I started yelling at him in English while Granjero's daughter shouted in Español. Thankfully, we made the short journey without running him over, and as soon as we we parked, he spun on his paws and bolted back in the direction of Jon and Granjero. The three of them arrived by the time I had unloaded all of our belongings onto the sand, and with hugs, kisses, and bilingual goodbyes, we watched Granjero's family drive away, the promise to become Facebook friends lingering in the dusty air.

We looked at each other and smiled. This was it. The Beach House. La Casa de la Playa. Home until our flight back to Chicago. In five months, we return for a Walker Brother wedding, and the beginning of whatever is next, but for now, we are here. The crash of the waves and the birds in the trees were an epic welcoming chorus.

We did a quick inventory of the lot before putting the key in the kitchen door, intending to start the unpacking process with our perishable food items. As the heavy wooden door cracked open we were both hit with the strong odor of fried fish. The scent was enough to make me gag, and Jon scrunched up his face, gingerly pushing the door open with the tip of his finger. The kitchen was a dirty disaster.

There were open containers of food and spices everywhere, shelves piled high with grimy, indiscernible kitchen accessories, a case full of musty blankets, and counters and shelves that were alive with the scurrying of ants. The cleaning switch flipped on in both of us and we started pulling everything we could out of the room. Every counter and shelf was vacated and we made many interesting discoveries along the way: gecko traps filled with tiny skeletons, a jumbo rainbow-colored crab (now deceased) that had been living inside of a stock pot, a half a bottle of tequila, an Internet router, so on and so forth.

A rickety table covered in a Scooby Doo blanket and topped with a large electric burner was taking up much of the floor space, so we evicted it and placed it in the bodega. We piled everything we didn't want, but didn't want to throw away, on to this table and locked the door. It was refreshing to be rid of the clutter, but we knew many ants were still living where we hoped to (sooner rather than later) prepare our lunch.

Jon dumped buckets of soapy water over every surface and set to scrubbing. I swept the floors then meandered off to start the scrubbing process in the baño. We reconvened what seemed like hours later, sweaty with dirt streaked faces, and scarfed down a casado that Jon had miraculously created. We ate outside at a picnic table situated between the house and the ocean, Bob Marley emanating from the laptop's speakers, Luna curled up at our feet.

Luna is the full-figured, all-white, German Shepherd who calls this stretch of beach her home. Technically, she has no master, but she manages to stay well-fed by Ticos and Tourists alike by batting her honey eyes and swinging her flirtatious tail. To the locals, she is known as Luna Llena, Full Moon, a pun referring to her orb like mid-section. She and Marley have been sniffing at each other since our arrival, but whether or not they are aware of their adorable compatibility will never be known.

In some ways, they are perfect opposites: one is black, the other white, one is scrawny, the other round, one is guarded, the other playful, but in other ways they are strikingly similar. Both sport "attack mohawks", sympathetic brown eyes, curly tails, and a wandering spirit; they were yet another representation of the Yin and the Yang that continues to permeate our journey.

We were proud of our accomplishments, but knew there was still much to do. The now disinfected kitchen and baño were only a small portion of the property- the upstairs bedrooms remained uninspected, and the entire grounds were littered with dead leaves, rotting wood, and miscellaneous human possessions. We certainly weren't innocent in that respect. Besides what had gone into the kitchen, our luggage still remained sprawled out on the unfamiliar matte brown tiles of Casa Playa's patio.

Full, and eager to get back to work, Jon swung his legs over the bench and stood swiftly. I felt the earth shift, the picnic table tipping under its now unbalanced weight. My arms flung forward as my plate, still halfway full of rice and beans, slid on to my lap and crashed into my chest. Beside me, I was vaguely aware that the laptop was heading for a similar fate, and I knew that I had to reach to save it, but my instinct was intent on using my arms to break my fall. I hit the ground at the same moment as the machine and squeezed my eyes shut imagining the rolling table about to smush us both into the sand. I braced myself for the impact, but all that came was the sound of Jon's laughter.

He picked up the table, then me, then the laptop, and asked if I was okay. I was. I was more worried about the computer. He shrugged, it was still playing Bob Marley, so it couldn't be that broken. He brushed the sand off of it, and I brushed the sand off of myself, and Luna snatched a tiny plastic bag of dog treats that had been left for her on the table. She ran off and buried them under a tree while we examined the very uneven fourth leg of the picnic table. We decided the table was too great a risk and moved it out of sight behind some tall palm trees.

We brought our suitcases upstairs and stood, backs to the ocean, looking at three identical wooden doors. On each "Come I show you" tour, Granjero insisted that the bedroom all the way to the left was the "best bedroom", so we entered it first. It was a small, square room with a small square bed, adorned by a small square table with a small round lamp. The wooden planks that made up the walls, combined with the foliage of the palms directly outside each window, gave me the feeling that we were in fact living amongst the trees. Fabric decorated the space: the window draped with a white mesh mosquito net, the table covered in an antique crochet, and an emerald blanket woven with a jade pattern lay heavy on the bed. We placed a flashlight on the nightstand, propped open the heavy wooden door, slid the screen door shut, and continued down the hall.

The other two rooms were similar, but smaller, and didn't have screened doors, so we agreed with Granjero and decided on the first bedroom as our sleeping quarters. We were anticipating guests, in the form of my parents, at some point during our stay, but until someone actually showed up, one bedroom could be our closet. We dumped our suitcases in the furthest bedroom and went to examine the middle room.

We had brainstormed about where the f-animal-y would sleep once we got here, and our best idea so far had been to give them a room. We decided to tie the wooden door open, leaving the room accessible to the animals, never locking them in, or out. We put their bowls and bedding in the room, and found Clover already curled up in a corner, her striated fur completely camouflaged in the shadowy wood, yellow eyes twitching with excitement.

Back on the patio, I organized my books on a shelf that was conveniently located near a hammock while Jon squatted and started rearranging stones on a patch of sharp grey rocks. When I inquired about his project, he explained that he was making a path of large, flat rocks, so that we could walk to the baño barefooted. I sat beside him and started placing stones along the path in a bizarre form of nature *Tetris*. We ventured to the beach, combing the property for the flattest slabs and eventually we connected the brown tile to the white tile with an artfully curvaceous gray path. We each walked across it a few times, delighting in its luxury and beauty, and having accomplished quite enough for one day, decided it was time for dinner.

We placed Marley and Luna's food bowls on either side of the water bucket they had shared all day. Marley ignored his food, and Luna guarded hers with so much intensity, we decided to separate them at mealtimes. We sat at a table on the patio, finishing our supper as the sun went down, celebrating our new home with a fruity rum drink.

Exhausted, we rinsed the sand and dirt from ourselves in an outdoor shower, then turned in early. A quick shine of the flashlight into the animal's room found two familiar sets of sleepy cat eyes, surrounded by shadows that were stretched out contentedly. Marley was curled up at the top of the stairs, where he could see Luna in the same position on the stair landing. We entered our room and closed the screened door with a sigh. We crawled under the covers, anxious to lie in the dark and listen to the ocean. In minutes, it's rhythmic splash, accompanied by the chirp of the insects, had lulled us all into dreamland. We officially lived on the beach.

Often during the night, we were harshly awoken by eruptions of dog barking. It seemed every dog in Cabuya had come over to welcome Marley to the world of outdoor sleeping. Each new pack would engage him (and Luna) in a vicious howling match, and while he appeared to be having a marvelous time, we were miserable. Our tired bodies would relax deeply with the drone of the wind and the waves, only to be snapped awake moments later, our hearts racing and our heads throbbing.

A final explosion at daybreak was enough to wrench us out of our slumber for good, so we threw our blankets aside and sleepily trounced down the stairs, making twice the usual amount of café.

We sat at the patio table, and let the caffeine erase the scowls from our faces. As soon as our cups were empty we immediately sprang into action, continuing the excavation of Casa Playa. I started unearthing the laundry room, which was also outdoors. Jon headed wordlessly, deep into an entanglement of trees, gigantic brown palm leaves raining around him as he pruned a path to the sea with graceful swings of his machete.

The laundry was tucked away on the side of Casa Playa, near the tall trees that bordered the property. A slab of concrete supported a small washing machine, another temperamental centrifugal dryer, and a utility sink, full of mildewy mops, but promising for its aid in hand-rinsing and wringing. There was also a shelf, full of cleaning supplies whose identities were hidden in Español, but I guessed at their uses according to color and Googled anything I couldn't figure out. I was glad to have a couple of chemicals on my side, so I sprayed everything down and walked away, intending to return to scrub and rinse after the soapy molecules had soaked through the worst of the dirt.

I walked the sands of Casa Playa and began pulling left over sheets off of the clotheslines, which hung haphazardly at forehead height, in the sunniest parts of the yard. I shook the ants off the linens, folded them, and separated them into two piles: one clean, the other ripped or stained. Setting the unblemished pile on top of the other, I stashed them in The Closet, and got to raking. I was able to clear the decomposing leaves from the sand underneath the clotheslines, but not without evicting a number of crab families. Whenever my rake hit just the right collection of leaves, thirty of the creatures, identical in their colorful markings, but remarkably varied in size, would burst into action, like water boiling over a pot, scurrying under another leaf pile before I even had time to be startled.

Considering my fear of spiders, their spindly legs and quick speed should have chilled me to the bone, but for some reason I found them kind of cute, and set an intention for myself to create leaf piles around the perimeter of our property that would be to their liking.

I always pictured the wilderness as a violent chaos, but standing here amongst the crabs and ants and birds and lizards, it was obvious that wilderness is really widespread tolerance. Sure, there is a food chain; but for the most part, everyone seems more than able to exist to do their own things in their own spaces.

As I finished raking what in my imagination were savvy apartment complexes for crabs, I turned to watch Jon, who was marching silently around the well-groomed yard trying to determine the locations of the best beach views. All of a sudden, I realized that from where I was standing, I could see the ocean through the thinned palm leaves. Forgetting for a moment the sleepless night, the onslaught of dirty, physical labor, and the all consuming woes of humanity, I was instantly transported to paradise. My eyes watered at the beauty, and I inhaled deeply, my sinuses swelling with the scent of the salt.

I am unsure how long I stood there, absorbed in the moment, but I eventually snapped out of my reverie and returned to my work, filling a bucket with clean water, grabbing a new rag, and heading back to the washing machine.

We worked through lunch, and when I was finally finished, Jon was itching to give me a tour of the outdoor living room he had constructed. We started on the patio, just outside the kitchen, and walked to the left of the stairs that led to the bedrooms. There, a thick, exposed tree root created a natural enclave that would serve nicely as a compost pile, a perfect place to dump any unused foodstuff where it would decompose naturally as crab fare. A few more paces and we had reached the breakfast nook, a table made of a tree stump snuggled between two smaller tree-stump seats. Sitting on my stump, I enjoyed a clear view of the ocean as I relaxed beneath the shade of a nearby palm tree.

I stood, and we continued on through the soft sand until we reached two hammocks Jon hung in a V-formation, so that our heads could be close together but our feet were not in the way of the ocean view. Between them was another artful stump placed perfectly at arms distance, to rest a drink or a book, and to use to rock oneself into a relaxing swing. Between the trees that supported the feet-end was a flat wooden bench built into the sand, offering a closer view of the sea. We alternated between the hammocks and the bench as we watched daytime disappear into the clouds.

Returning down the sandy path back to the patio, Jon made dinner while I followed him with a sponge, discouraging any ant-ics. We ate by candlelight, the fluorescent bulbs attracting too many moths, and full bellies took our exhaustion to the next level. We soon pulled ourselves up the stairs and begged the dogs to be quiet as we crawled under the covers.

Sometime in the middle of the night, the dogs erupted in simultaneous, aggressive growling that was enough to make both of us sit straight up in bed. Before we were conscious enough to wonder what had happened, the putrid smell of skunk began to permeate the bedroom. Disgusted, we buried our noses in our pillows and coughed every time we emerged. Eventually we were able to communicate to one another that, maybe, one of the dogs had gotten sprayed by a skunk. Knowing the problem would still be there in the morning, we buried our faces again, and fell asleep breathing shallowly through our mouths.

The dogs had been much quieter, but our sleep still hadn't been sound, and our first fully conscious moment was drenched in the scent of skunk. We exited the room and cautiously whiffed both Marley and Luna, rejoicing in our luck that neither of them seemed to be the source of the smell. We proceeded to check The Cats, who seemed insulted by the mere question that they could harbor such an odor. Grateful that animal-bathing was no longer in the near future, we started down the stairs, our elation short lived as we realized the skunk must have sprayed directly in front of the kitchen door. We gagged slightly, joked that it didn't smell like fish anymore, and held our breath as we quickly gathered breakfast supplies and headed out to the nook.

The limones tasted sour, our nostrils full of skunk pheromones, but the view of low tide in the early morning sun made up for it. Our toes dug into the sand that stretched forward, turned into rock, and disappeared under a sheath of mysterious sea. The water created a shallow pool, clear blue, its white froth drifting across shadows of boulders that jut up to cradle the delicate feet of long-legged, longer-necked birds, who bent gracefully to pluck breakfast from the crevices. Farther out, the deeper water adopts a green opacity, shrouding all but the very tips of the stones, creating the illusion of the birds perched weightlessly on the water, wings outstretched as they bathe in the sun. Past the serene pools, the tide breaks, creating a white ruffle hem on an aquamarine skirt that extends, fluttering in the breeze, to the horizon.

Over breakfast, we discussed our living situation. We missed the clean and secluded aura of La Hacienda, but something about Casa Playa was magical. We concluded that if we just accepted that we were camping on the beach, the situation took on a much more positive light. If I were camping, I would be grateful for an indoor toilet, instead of bummed that I had to walk outside to use it. This mindset made everything seem like a luxury and we both relaxed slightly...we love camping!

When we moved back into The Townhouse, and were pondering a move to Hawaii, camping came to have a deeper meaning for us. We found a beautiful spot nearby and would set up our tent and lay under the stars taking in the beauty of Mother Nature, trying to redefine what it meant to have a home. My favorite thing about living outside was getting away from it all, breathing in the essence of the planet, reveling in the separation from stress, jobs, and money…

Well, that and Jon tending a fire. For me, this is one of his most attractive qualities. The reflection of heat off his forearms as he arranges the perfect pyramid amongst the flames does something to me that must be embedded in my DNA from prehistoric times. The more conspiracy theory documentaries we watch, the more this invaluable skill deepens my confidence in my choice of mate.

I would lie back, look up at the universe, and imagine I could feel the planet moving beneath me. It was as though I could see the galaxy expanding away from me and feel the Earth spinning below me, hurling itself around the sun, whose presence I could somehow feel at my back. It would make me laugh and I would think: Everything is Moving.

Literally. Everything is Moving. The planet, the stars, the universe itself. All is in constant motion. Every cell in my body, in the grass, in the rocks, in the trees, in the whole of Nature, all are sophisticated mechanisms with many moving parts. The blood in my veins, the crackle of the fire, time itself…

Everything is Moving. The things we think we know are being replaced daily with new information and technology. Our world is unrecognizable to that of a decade ago, and will be unrecognizable again in another decade.

Everything is Moving. When we look consciously at our world, anything can produce a strong emotional response. To look at the stars, at the hands of someone you love doing something they love, to view the ocean at sunset, to make a mistake and laugh, to feel the swell in your chest as joy moves in and anger moves out.

Everything is Moving. I had come to realize the key to a healthy body is to move it around, and the key to a healthy mind is to allow it to move and grow and experience new things. Maybe the key to a healthy soul is letting go of everything you believe in and moving forward to create something that you believe in more.

Of course, at the time I thought moving to paradise would change *everything* because, obviously, everything is *moving*. And now, as I type from my hammock on the beach, I am thinking I was only half right.

Everything is Moving. Being here in this unfamiliar situation did force me to grow, but the act of moving didn't wipe my slate clean, it simply transplanted my life to another corner of the Petri dish. Moving wasn't an answer, it was simply a next step, because, well, Everything is Moving. Everything. The spinning of the Earth, the emotions whirling within me, the trajectory of the fate of humanity, all of those things are still moving, even after I moved…

After dinner at Casa Playa, we sat at the outdoor patio table in reverie, until we were distracted by a rustling hum in the air. We shone our flashlights into the yard, trying to determine the source the scuttling, and in the circle of illuminated light, the ground came alive. What appeared to be rocks were actually hermit crabs of all sizes, tinkling along the sand and the tile. We walked over and shone our lights into the compost pile, watching in awe as hundreds of crabs scrambled over one another for a chance at the feast. From that moment, our compost was known as Crab City. We were moved by the sheer number of crabs, which immediately led us to become perplexed by their virtual nonexistence during daylight hours.

Watching this flurry of activity during a time when the atmosphere felt so still was enough to convince me that everything *is* moving.

We did eventually lose interest in watching them clamor around, so we turned our beams to the tree tops. Mostly we saw the subtle sparkle of freshly spun spider webs, but once, we found ourselves face to face with the eerie green reflection of nocturnal eyes. A sloth was climbing down from the top of a palm tree, and if he saw us, he certainly didn't seem to care, because he continued to move languidly down the thick green branches towards the sand. We shuddered as we imagined what else could possibly be hidden by the tops of these palms, and hurried back to the safety of our matte brown tiles.

The next morning, feeling inspired, we took the liberty of removing some tarps that hung across the space between our roof and the nearby trees. Jon found a twenty-five foot ladder on the property, dug its legs into the sand, and climbed up effortlessly, balancing on his toes to snip the taut ropes, sending tarps and leaves raining down around us. We raked, placed the tarps and all salvageable ropes in the bodega, and walked upstairs to admire our recently unveiled ocean view.

The house was definitely hotter without the shade provided by the tarps, but we thought the view was worth it.

We stood on the balcony and allowed the dramatic change in scenery from low to high tide distract us. We exchanged mischievous smiles and bolted down the stairs, shedding our layers and jumping into the curling waves that were now crashing onto the sand, treading above the rocky pools where the birds had fed only hours before. We dried off in the sun, its beams glinting off our sleepy smiles before we headed back to our hammocks to toss sticks in opposite directions for Marley and Luna to chase.

Jumping in the ocean and rinsing off in an outdoor shower had kept me clean enough for cleaning a beach house, but I thought it might be time to wash my hair. I unbraided and detangled the mess that was beginning to take on a new texture (thanks to the salt water), dug some shampoo out of my packed toiletries, and headed to the baño to test the indoor shower.

I peeled back the plastic shower curtain decorated with childish drawings of fish and seashells, and turned the nozzle. The water was cold, which I expected, but the pressure was low, so my hair didn't get much cleaner, and half way through the washing of my face, the hose detached from the shower head, spraying chaotically in all directions. I shut off the water and tried to reattach the nozzle, my slippery hands and soapy eyes the worst tools for the job, but eventually, it refastened, and I started the water again. The fourth or fifth time the hose fell off I swore loudly, which brought Jon tumbling into the baño. I explained to him what was happening, and he chival-rously held the hose in place for me, fighting the cling of the plastic curtain, while I finished bathing.

All in all, it was not bad for a camping shower. That night we lounged in the hammocks, watching the twilight sky turn it's fantastic shades of yellow and pink over the silver slate of ocean. We kept our feet up and away from the crabs who were emerging from the sand and watched our surroundings slowly disintegrate into dark shadows until the ocean was no longer visible, its presence just a rhythmic crash and a haunting, salty breeze.

We heard a familiar *"hola!"* and the circles of our flashlights illuminated Granjero, who was approaching from the beach, Tigra and Oso at his heels. Whatever he wanted to show us was immediately drowned out by the ferocious squeals of Tigra and Marley, who were suddenly conjoined, jaws to necks, limbs flailing, in a loud and sandy uproar. Tigra was winning, but luckily Luna rushed to Marley's rescue, forcing Tigra to retreat towards Granjero who chased her away with his trusty dog-weapon-stick. Granjero apologized profusely, his speech rapid and not limited to the elementary Español he usually reserves for us, and we could tell he was nervous.

We wished we could explain to him that no one but Marley was at fault, showing up in Costa Rica and thinking other dogs were on his turf. We eventually communicated to each other that everything was fine, and we found out he had come to tell us that he had plátanos at his farm. We told him we would come by tomorrow, and he waved before heading off, flashlight-less, in the direction of Tigra.

We sunk back into the hammocks, burned a treat in a pipa, and then a pile of leaves. The smoke distorted the shadows and fumigated the insects that had been attracted to our flashlights. We listened as the tide crept higher, both expecting to see a salty arm curl around our small fire at any moment.

Our hypnosis was suddenly broken by a rustling to Jon's left. Reflexively, our flashlights pierced the night shining in the direction of the noise. There was Dylan, eyes glowing green, diligently digging a rather large hole in the sand. He turned his back to us and squatted on the edge, ears twitching, the rest of his body rigidly still. After a few moments, he rose up, eliminated all evidence of his presence, and slunk off into the trees.

Plan de Vida

JON WANTED TO GO RUNNING. I hate running, but the fitness instructor in me knows I have to get my heart rate up. So, with relatively little grumbling, I put on a sports bra, shook my sneakers to check for scorpions, and spun my braid into a bun.

The tide was low, so with a perfect lane of beach as a track, Jon and the dogs galloped off in the direction of Rio Lajas, their strides long and their faces relaxed and happy. I took a deep inhale and flung myself forward. As my feet pounded into the squishy sand, I tried to focus on my breathing rather than the rattling of my skeleton. Looking up, I could see Marley tearing ahead, Luna frolicking happily behind him, and Jon sprinting effortlessly in their wake, each limb in his body working in a harmonious rhythm drawing him closer to his destination. I fell behind, legs heavy, choking on my own breath, wondering what to do with my arms.

I was proud of myself for taking only one break, and eventually, I caught up with the others at the river. Jon was glowing with his runner's high in the early morning sun, and he was tossing a stick to Marley, who was enthusiastically swimming after it. Luna was wading, cooling off in the lagoon. She looked like a strange parody of the Lochness monster, her torso buried but her smiling face and wagging tail emerging from the green water. I plopped onto a nearby log and braced myself on my twitching knees, trying to breathe deeply and mentally force the red flush from my face. After a few minutes, Jon bounced over, with a coy smile he asked, *"Ready to run back?"*

We returned to Casa Playa and after a rinse in the outdoor shower, the day began to pass in a strange fog. Despite the scorching sun, my mood and energy felt dark and damp. On days like today it was so unclear, what exactly am I doing with my Life? What is my Plan de Vida?

I want the time to answer my most burning philosophical questions, but feel exhausted in my attempt to do so. Then, I can't help but imagine my scenario from an outside perspective, and from there all I can see is myself lying on the beach. The guilt overwhelms me as I try to reconcile the many definitions that "work" has come to mean to me.

"What do you do for work?", asks Everyone. It is the common thread that brings us all together. Well, when I am teaching and writing, I am in the zone. I am doing exactly what I was meant to be doing: using my unique expertise and personality to further the work of great minds from the past. But, so far, I have made little to no money doing it. Does that answer your question?

Would it have been more relevant to say that I have worked part time since high school: flitting from tanning salon reception to retail to administrative assistance? My jobs don't tell anyone anything about me, but still, they remain my only source of money. Once I say that, I have to admit that I only have an education, and the time to pursue my passions, because I was born into luxury. I never *had* to work for money. I was taken care of by my parents and then my boyfriend/husband. Because I have been able to pursue the things that appeal to me, I have been able to attempt to figure out who I am, and I can wonder what I could do that will make me, my community, and my planet a better place. But so easily, in our world, I could have lived a lifetime without ever even asking myself what appeals to me.

So maybe I should just participate in the Economy rather than constantly damning it. Maybe I should just accept that I am lucky and be fine with it. Maybe I could save some energy and some sanity by simply getting a job. It probably wouldn't be exactly what I am meant to be doing, but wouldn't I be fulfilling some sort of moral obligation to do something that pays above the poverty line?

So what if I think I know my Plan de Vida? That isn't Real Life. Maybe if everyone had the right, the chance to find their plan de vida... but what makes me so special that I get to sit here in Costa Rica and contemplate the meaning of existence while other young women across the globe are struggling just to get by?

To make matters worse, the busy days at Casa Playa have zapped my energy and creativity, and my concentration is weak. It is so easy to want to be a writer and a teacher but showing up every day is challenging no matter what the task. Plus, the ability to disappear into my mind and create for hours on end has been taken over by the responsibility of a high maintenance house and a new dog, and I can't shake the feeling that I have been through this before...

I felt lost, and hypocritical, and worse, hypercritical. Then the guilt set in. Is work meant to be what is important to me personally, or what has been deemed important by my fellow human beings? I like to think it rests somewhere in the middle, because all good work is both personally and culturally relevant. Unfortunately for me, I have chosen preventative health and philosophy in an era that is largely ambivalent to those things...

So who is wrong? Me or the masses? Probably a little bit of both, so... What exactly am I doing with my Life? What is my Plan de Vida? I physically shook my skull, trying to escape the mist of self-doubt that had nestled into the crevices of my brain. I needed to get out of my head. I wanted to do something fun with Jon, maybe something where we could talk to someone other than The Dogs...

But there was no one to talk to here in Cabuya. Conversation was a frustrating battle with Granjero, who we longed to know better, but the relationship had somewhat plateaued due to the language barrier. We missed Cabuya Joe and Dolly, but more than anything we missed everyone back home...

Immediately, I remembered feeling disconnected back home, too. When we were able to go against the monetary grain in search of a more simple life, we felt isolated from the busy world around us. In Costa Rica, the isolation is even more intense. If we do run into a fellow human, even if we share common interests, there is usually a debilitating language barrier, and never is there the comfort and camaraderie of a lifelong acquaintance. We both want to dedicate this time to writing, to communicating on a mass scale, so we both strive to find a connection with people, our fellow earthlings, our theoretical audience, and yet we both have this foreboding feeling that the harder we try, the more we are losing our connection with our entire species.

Jon was immersed in his work and I knew better than to interrupt, so I wandered over to the neighboring cabina. I knew its inhabitant spoke English, and taught Yoga, so maybe, this could be a friend.

She sat, staring at her computer, a long braid hanging over her shoulder and a black dog curled up at her feet. I was struck by the slightly distorted mirror image and with a friendly smile and an awkward wave I asked her if she wanted to hang out. She returned the smile, inviting me to join her and we sat at her patio table, chatting for the better part of an hour. She was the girl we had met at La Panadería weeks ago, the very one who had given us Granjero's phone number. I thanked her profusely, but she just laughed it off with a wave and a "Pura Vida." She offered to take me to her class that night at Montezuma Yoga, and genuinely excited, I told her I would see her soon. I skipped back home to put on stretchy pants and grab my mat.

When I returned, she motioned for me to hop on the back of her motorcycle, and I timidly admitted that I had never been on one before. Honestly, they frightened me.

She said, *"Don't worry, I don't drive fast,"* and then warned me that one of the pegs was broken so I would have to be careful not to let my foot get scuffed by the rear wheel. Eek.

I summoned my courage and climbed on, mat on my lap, left foot aloft, fists clenched around the bars behind me that she had suggested I hold on to. Her final words of advice were to *"Move with the bike."* Right, Okay. Everything is Moving.

She revved the engine, and turned us onto the dusty road. I could feel every muscle in my body cramped with fear, and I begged myself to relax and enjoy the ride. As the tiny moto lurched up and down the rocky hills, I regretted not having a helmet, and wished I had spent the day being nicer to Jon.

Eventually, I did start having a good time. I could never again say that I hadn't been on a motorcycle, and truly, it was a wonderful way to see the countryside. When I focused on the scenery, I forgot my fear. To my left, rolling pastures and mountains lined the clear blue sky. To my right, patches of ocean, tumultuous in the high tide, shone through the breaks in the trees.

We approached Montezuma Centro but turned before its now familiar intersection, heading up a dusty trail that led to a large, circular, wooden hut, open to the air but covered with a roof. We dismounted, and she insisted that I had done well, and that I wasn't even the most nervous person she had taken on The Moto. For the second time that day, I was proud of myself for stepping outside of my comfort zone.

Yoga was amazing with the ocean as my drishti, and I was truly humbled by how much I missed taking class. Since we have been in Costa Rica, I have been practicing my Sun Salutations and doing my Pilates' Hundreds but the act of actually going somewhere and dedicating an hour to learning something new wields a strange power over me. I felt the boredom and the isolation wrung from my body as I twisted and folded, taking the time to bask in my strengths and acknowledge my weaknesses. I could feel my heart pulsing rhythmically inside my chest, conducting my breath and the flow of my blood. In that raw moment I reconnected with my purpose, and with everyone I have ever known: my family, my friends, my past teachers, my acquaintances, even my "enemies"...

I knew that each and every one of them has affected who I am today, and will affect my future, whether or not we hold the same interests in the same moment. These people, the ones who have merely passed through my life, the ones who will always be fundamentally en-grained in it, all of them were looking me straight in my third eye and telling me that distance is no match for memory. Fear is no match for love.

After class, we got to talking about teaching and we were so engrossed in our conversation that Neighbor for-got her boyfriend, Novio, and his daughter, Niña, were waiting for her outside. When they finally called out to her, she danced happily towards them, introduced us, and secured me a ride back to Cabuya in Red Van, a tank-like contraption filled with surfboards and childrens toys. I was grateful not to have to ride The Moto in the dark, so with a sigh of relief, I settled down into the sturdy seat and fastened my seatbelt.

When I got home, I found a note on the patio table: *"AT THE BEACH"* sprawled in a familiar scratch across a page ripped from a familiar journal. I grabbed my flashlight and headed towards the glow of a little campfire, ducking through the drooping palms, Marley and Luna orbiting around my ankles. We found Jon lying on his back, on a plank of wood, staring at the sky. A second plank was placed nearby, and I lowered myself onto it, gazing out at the peaceful scene. Everything was illuminated by the large, bright moon, the stars were shrouded in glowing clouds, and the ocean was gently purring its own lullaby as it lazily slipped off the rocks and drifted towards the horizon.

Today I had undergone a change as dramatic as the space between high and low tide. I had experienced the encompassing depths of self-doubt, and the radiant peace of self-love. Yoga had once again helped me feel inspired. It is so easy to get lost in my own thoughts, allowing physical tasks to become unconscious. I walk for miles, but never think about walking. Always my mind is occupied elsewhere: thinking about this book, or old friends, or what needs to be done at Casa Playa. During class today my mind could be occupied with nothing other than practicing the asanas, and just to be, a Mind-Body, doing something, anything at all, with 100% of my conscious energy, was pure and absolute bliss.

I don't remember going to bed, but I awoke to a dull ache in my legs that begged the question of why I had returned to running and yoga on the same day. With much effort I pushed myself out of bed and shook the stiffness from my joints, then trudged down the stairs more slowly than usual.

Breakfast at Casa Playa begins with the boiling of a few cups of water and the heaping of four teaspoons of café into an oblong filter that hangs from a hand painted wooden rack. The filter was once called an Elephant Condom by Cabuya Joe, and neither of us can go a morning without cringing at the vivid description.

While I waited for the water to heat up, I absentmindedly filled two bowls with a generous amount of strawberry cereal, then grabbed two clean spoons from the sink. Placing the spoons into the bowls, my sleepy focus immediately sharpened. The cereal was moving.

An army of ants was marching proudly through the oats and clusters and over the pink mounds of dried fruit. I gagged and began brushing everyone I could out of the bowl. Disgusted, I called for Jon, and he brilliantly filled the bowls with milk. We observed our own form of genocide as the ants began floating to the surface. Pura Vida. He skimmed the drowned ants from our grains. I poured hot water through the loaded Elephant Condom and into our kettle.

We ate the cereal, both joking that we should stop telling people we were vegetarianos now that we ate fish and ants, but then seriously, we decided to do another scouring of the kitchen. When we took everything out, we could identify the two areas where the ants seemed to be coming in: an open pipe near the ceiling, and the unraveling corners of a green screen that serves as both a dish drying area and a wall behind the kitchen sink.

Jon splashed the walls and the floor with bleach and began scrubbing away with a mop, while I climbed onto the sink and attacked the screen and the many corners of the wooden dish rack with a toothbrush. I evicted pregnant spiders from their hidey-holes and wondered if The Man, kicking the recently impoverished out of their hidey-holes, felt as much remorse as I did.

We filled in the vulnerable corners with small rocks and then sprinkled the rocks with black pepper, a natural ant remedy suggested by Google. After rinsing the walls, the pipe got peppered as well, and we waited, hoping the ants were successfully deterred. After ten minutes, none had resurfaced, so we congratulated ourselves on the cleaning, which had taken only half as long as last time.

Since we had run out of beans, it was a day to have something other than a casado for lunch, and Jon had purchased the ingredients for coconut curry shrimp. While he prepared the rice, I sat in my hammock, gazing out over the high tide, fully engrossed in my writer's block. What am I doing with my Life?

Well, I spent the morning contradicting myself by fighting Mother Nature's ants for living space, and eating sugary grains. Now I am staring at the sea, feeling the pressure of helping the collective human MindBody to heal. I can't shake the feeling that my Life's Work hinges on the ability of everyone on the planet to do their Life's Work, because only when we all have the freedom to pursue our arts and sciences, can the human MindBody balance itself.

If some of us don't have that chance, then my work is nothing more than narcissistic rambling. From the looks of it, that reality isn't coming anytime soon. Working seemed as futile as trying to keep a jungly beach house clean....

Obviously, I was happy to be distracted from my musings by Neighbor. She was wandering by with little Niña, her dog, Buddy, and a couple of squirt guns. They asked me if I wanted to play, and I did. Play is good for the MindBody, after all. We filled our weapons in the sea, chasing each other with jets of water and squeals of laughter. Marley, Luna, and Buddy joined in, running in circles around us, barking, flashing pink-tounged smiles.

It was then I realized that my so-called distraction wasn't a distraction at all. It was a slap in the face. An opportunity to see that every experience is a way of showing up and focusing on my craft. My work is not necessarily in the time I spend typing or teaching, but in the time I spend elucidating the connections that exist all around me. In trying so hard to define the meaning of Life, the meaning of Work, I had accidentally stopped those things from actually happening.

We invited Neighbor and Niña to join us for lunch, and they agreed. I apologized for our mismatched dishes, and jumped to explain that our only cup was a wine glass, and that Jon and I usually share it. To us these domestic details couldn't matter less, but somehow in the self-consciousness of company, they seemed like horrific pitfalls. Niña sternly informed me that I was not supposed to drink wine until after dark. I laughed and agreed, but the meal passed awkwardly while I worried about etiquette and realized 5-year olds don't care much for curry.

After lunch, it was time to go to the grocery store in Cabuya, which was farther from Casa Playa than any of our other residences, but we hadn't been "downtown" in awhile, so we were looking forward to the journey. As we came upon the road, we ran into Granjero, who was sweating, and spraying the dust with a hose. Luna and Tigra exchanged snarls while Granjero explained that he was taking care of the road by pouring molasses on it.

Apparently, after the last rains of the season, if you pour molasses on the road, the stamping of the cows and the horses will pack it down well, eliminating the dust. He explained that it is good for the road and for the people, but that it is very expensive, so he pays for it himself, to help his community. Impressed, we wished him luck and turned toward the store, our flip-flops sticking on the recently sweetened road.

About half way there, Luna got exhausted. She sat in the middle of the road, wagging her tail, looking in the direction of home. Despite her begging, we pushed onward, and soon she recognized a familiar puddle, ran to it and jumped in, cooling off by pacing in the murky, shoulder-deep, water.

Just when we thought she would stay right there, wading in the shade, waiting for us to return, she jumped vertically out of the pool and ran, without shaking, in our direction. Her belly swung, sending water flying frantically in every direction, her tiny legs pushing her drenched body forward in a comic sprint. We cheered her on and finally, the four of us made it to The Supermercado. The humans shopped, The Dogs sat patiently outside.

Luna received pats on the head from many patrons who recognized her, and she seemed glad that she had joined us on the last leg of the journey. We walked back, Luna jumping in the puddle again, and we were welcomed home by the saccharine scent of the new road. I couldn't help but think that Luna's adventure was similar to me riding the The Moto yesterday. We both overcame our instinct to experience something worthwhile. That ability has to exist in all of us, but we almost always need someone to talk us into it...

The next day, we woke up determined to spend the entire day in our hammocks, working. I had just started *Freakonomics*, and Jon had half-jokingly challenged himself to listen through our entire iTunes library, playing every album and discarding anything without artistic or nostalgic value. After some limones, we settled in and buried ourselves in our projects, Marley and Luna panting happily nearby in the sand.

Unfortunately for our work, the high tide brought in a particularly lively afternoon. The usually serene expanse of water and sky was completely occluded with a recent migration of pelicans. The birds, which are surprisingly large from this close distance, fill the sky and the sea. Some float in huddles, bobbing and squawking along with the waves, while others dive spectacularly into the swells, often in unison. Fisherman had noted the feeding frenzy as well, and four of them stood waist deep in the water, unique bobbing figures in a sea of birds, casting handheld lines below the sloshing sea. They would emerge from the water frequently, bare feet unaffected by the sharp stones, faces smiling and hands full, ready to deposit their bounty into coolers.

Having watched the fish feast all day was no doubt the reason for our pescatarian craving, so Jon went about preparing shrimp tacos at least an hour before our usual dinner time. We reminisced, as we always do on taco night, about the idea of opening a restaurant, a tiny place with good, simple, nutritious food that plays interesting music: a haven for intellectual thinkers and tortilla enthusiasts alike. Wait, what are we doing with our Lives?

Energized from our early taco feast, we decided to try stargazing again, hoping the night would be clear. We traipsed through the dark yard towards the silence of the low tide, flashlights aloft. When we emerged from the cover of the palm trees and onto the beach, we found the stars were not out. Regardless, we were met with a most poetic view of the universe.

The moon seemed larger than usual, slung low over the horizon, her hue a smoldering gold, dim enough to allow me to stare right at her, taking in the details, the shadowy shapes and textures. Sparse, silver-gray clouds encircled the glowing orb like puffs of recently exhaled smoke. I would be lying if I said I didn't have the urge to howl.

The Goddess

THE PRESENCE OF THE FULL moon was intoxicating the ocean. Her high tides were higher than usual and her lows tides were lower than usual.

This is probably common knowledge for anyone who lives anywhere coastal, but for a girl from the Midwest, this was a fascinating phenomenon. I even Googled it. Evidently the line formed by the Earth, Sun, and Moon during the new moon and full moon amplifies the tidal force, creating what is known as Spring Tide (Thanks Wikipedia). I highlighted the low and high tide times for the next few days on a moon calendar I found in the local magazine, planning to run out to the edge of the property and look out over the exaggerated scenery, soaking it all in to my sensory memory.

It was a good thing I marked the times, because that afternoon's high tide would have totally stolen our stargazing planks. We ran to retrieve them, shins bombarded by rushing water, ankles sinking into wet sand. Against all odds we moved them near the trunks of the palms, where we felt certain they couldn't be hit by the frisky waves.

After our evening casado, we walked amongst the crabs towards the edge of the trees, to experience the low tide. The atmosphere was so quiet in the absence of the sea, the sound of the distant waves imperceptible, muffled by the night wind. I stood on my plank, which was now positioned at the edge of a rocky cliff (the water had come so much closer than I had imagined possible), and gazed at the full moon, its light revealing calm pools in the distance.

When I grew weary of the glare, I dropped my eyes to the basin of sand below me. I had bathed in the sun there, chased The Dogs there, earlier today I had stood there and moved a plank. Now that chunk of Earth I had taken for granted was gone, eroded away in a matter of hours.

I felt as though I was looking at a double exposure: the new landscape ahead of me superimposed on the old landscape of my memory. Something about seeing the past and the present simultaneously made me wonder about the future. What would this shore look like tomorrow at high and low tide? What would it look like weeks from now? Months? Years? Centuries? Even if it seems to look the same, will it not also be totally different? How could one spot be so many things?

The next morning, we used the low, low tide as an opportunity to walk across the exposed ocean floor to Isla Cementerio: the beautiful tuft of trees floating on the horizon where local Ticos are laid to rest. After breakfast, we lathered up with sunscreen, put on our sneakers, grabbed a bottle of water and the camera, emerged from the shelter of the palm trees, slid down the new rocky cliff, and walked onto the white sand that reflected brightly in the morning sun. Ahead of us, the sand morphed seamlessly into black rock, and the spiky scene extended all the way to the horizon, Isla Cementerio looming in the distance.

As we transitioned from sand to rock, both of us felt like we had stepped into an apocalyptic movie. The space, sometimes teeming with rolling water and well-fed pelicans, was now a barren wasteland of sun-dried rocks, spotted with sulking vultures, lazily plucking at the bones of yesterday's catch. The sounds were different, and the air felt different, but we acclimated to the atmosphere as we headed southeast.

We passed fishing boats balanced precariously on the uneven earth in the absence of the water, their paint withering in the sun and salt, and we reminisced about our first day on these shores, when we left The Cabina to see this desolate and rocky field, remembering how deeply disappointed we were to have moved to a beach with no ocean. Having since seen many a high tide, we were once again humbled by the sheer magnificence of the dramatically shifting landscape. We were glad to be able to really appreciate the beauty of the low tide, instead of solemnly wondering where the water was. Pura Vida.

The walk to the island was long and hot, the rocks slippery and surrounded by puddles the sea had left behind. Peering down between my feet was the archeological expedition my inner adventure heroine always imagined. The jagged terrain was littered with chunks of dehydrated coral, shimmers of sunlight caught in swirling shells, and vertebrae of all sizes and evolutionary phases, their detail even more fascinating out of the context of the spines they had once composed.

I thought back to the night before, seeing the double exposure of the past and the present, and realized this idea was perfectly demonstrated by the existence of sand. What we call sand is simply billions of particles of decomposed matter. Sand is literally the future of all things that live and die in the ocean: rocks, shells, coral, vertebrae, all are decomposed by the turbulence of the sea into grains of sand. In the present moment, I could see evidence of all of these things, all at different stages on their common journey towards becoming sand. Billions of years of evolution was taking place right before my very eyes.

The scientific observation was fascinating, but what was even more impressive was the fact that it all seemed like some epic work of art: expanses of colorful beads separated into colonies by flat sheets of granite that periodically jut diagonally towards the sky. Each speck, gem, and boulder had its own history, no two exactly same, yet they created an image that was undoubtably homogenous. Grappling with existence was hard enough without having to consider its all encompassing beauty.

My brain felt as tired contemplating the terrain as my legs did traversing it, so I had to quiet it and concentrate on climbing, exiting what would be a deep lagoon in just a few hours.

We stood on the edge of the island, sweating, staring at a white arch whose outline we have seen everyday from the sands of Casa Playa: a proud man made creation, shining in the rays of the sun, dwarfed only by the superlative stature of its ancient neighboring palms. We snapped a couple of photos and then, we moved on.

Through the arch, a path led us through the trees. Hidden in the shade of their canopy, we found universal symbols signifying the loss of a loved one: white crosses, shiny plaques, wreaths of tropical flowers- some dead, some dying, some vibrantly alive. The place had such a different energy from any graveyard I had ever been to, but perhaps that is just a feeling that comes with being in a cemetery without anyone you actually know buried in it.

It was silent, and I was sure we were the only living humans on the island. Humbly, we took in the scenery and I couldn't help but wonder what it would have been like to say goodbye to my loved ones in this place, wrapped in the arms of Mother Nature, serenaded by her wind and waves.

I was instantly transported back to my 18 year old self, in a dorm at Hope College, knuckle in one ear, cell phone on the other, listening to my Mom who was babbling, urging me to pack a bag and head east, because it was time to say goodbye to MomMom...

The next thing I knew I was holding MomMom's withering hand, selfishly wanting to pour my heart out to her, hopeful for one last dose of her encouragement and advice, but her lips moved wordlessly in a conversation that I was not a part of, so I sat there in silence, hopeful I had said "I love you" enough times in the past to adequately express the depths of gratitude and affection I would always feel for her. She kept calling out for Jack, my PopPop, insisting that he was standing right in front of her, despite his death years before. I remember that she didn't seem like herself, but I also remember that she didn't seem afraid.

That night she died, and then she was gone, and I was sad, but not devastated. I couldn't be. She had a great life, and my life was better because she was in it. Even then I knew in some ways she could never be gone, because there is a part of me that would preserve her spirit, and pass it on to my own children.

I returned to the present, to Isla Cementerio. Looking around I saw Death, The Past, everywhere. It was in the tiny carcass of the fly forgotten within the crumpled and vacant spider web, whose remaining corners were stretched between a brown palm leaf and a decaying coconut shell, each half-buried in the sand, which to me now represented the decomposition of the previous millennia, which just happened to be cradling the remains of Cabuyan humans. Death wasn't the opposite of Life, it was Life. Pure Life. Pura Vida.

When we got home I sunk into the hammock and thought. The tide seemed to be bringing in memories that I was supposed to have left at Isla Cementerio, allowing space for nothing else.

As a science enthusiast, I realize why death is inevitable. Everything has to die, it is fundamental to biology. Apoptosis (programmed cell death), is necessary for organisms, because cells have to die in order to make enough space for other cells to exist, reproduce, and evolve. Matter cannot be created or destroyed, so there is no such thing as infinite growth or immortality.

Wouldn't that also mean there is no such thing as permanent death? Even if, as a species, we decide to blow ourselves up in some geopolitical environmental crisis, won't the molecular construct of our planetary ashes simply become the sands of some interstellar beach, caressing the toes of some Life the likes of which we could never even imagine?

I felt my third eye pulse deep in my skull: duh, you silly human- We are All One. There is no reason to fear death, as Granjero would say, *"es natural..."*

Earlier this week I had assumed that I was the same fundamental person throughout my life, but now I could clearly see that parts of me have experienced death and rebirth before, and other parts of me would experience those phenomena again. Probably someday soon.

Later that day, when we were sitting at the patio table, mugs in hand, deep in conversation, Niña announced herself and came skipping around the corner. She stopped in her tracks as soon as she saw us and blurted out, without even a hello, *"Why are you drinking coffee? Did you just wake up?"*

We explained that we had been up since this morning, but that we enjoy coffee so much we sometimes drink it twice a day. I couldn't help but smile, remembering back to our conversation about wine glasses, amazed by her knowledge of the time appropriateness of certain beverages. She asked if we were busy, and I found myself trying to explain to a 5-year-old that I wasn't busy per se, but my mind was racing, and I needed to sit, think, and write. She didn't seem to understand and said bluntly, *"Can you come play with me? I feel lonely out here all by myself."* Stunned, I agreed. I knew what it was like to feel lonely out here all by myself.

Cabuya was a lonely place, the census maybe nearing one hundred when filled to capacity with transient tourists. Here, meeting interesting people was inevitable, but establishing relationships was incredibly rare. Niña was certainly more honest about the solitary vibe here at the edge of civilization than anyone else I had met thus far. She was extending her tiny hand to me in friendship and I had to take it, because aren't I the one who is always talking about the importance of human connection? Did I really need to lose myself in my own thoughts for yet another afternoon? We walked towards the beach, and at some point she plopped down and resolutely went about digging a hole in the sand.

Digging holes in the sand is a well loved past time of Jon's, so he soon joined her, shoveling sand and rocks away for some unspoken purpose. I backed away, using the opportunity of their distraction to curl up nearby in the hammocks and write, watching the high tide pulse closer and closer to the shore.

My electronic device sat idle as instead I eavesdropped while Niña and Jon conspired, their conversation muffled by the sounds of the sea. I could make out two voices, one high and excited, the other low and calm, echoing one another's laughter, implementing some sort of master plan that included the words "fort" and "sand fairies". I was touched by Jon's natural ease with the child, and felt a wave of maternal longing watching the two of them crouch, knees to chest, hands busy in the dirt.

Rationally, I knew a f-animal-y was enough responsibility for two vagabond artists pondering existence, but still, I fell in love with my husband, the father of our future offspring, just a little bit more in that moment.

I allowed my thoughts to return again to MomMom. The woman that I had known was only one exposure of a dynamic journey through time, but I do know she dedicated most of her life to raising children. At a young age she married the love of her life and started having babies. From then until her death she spent all of her time entertaining and cleaning up after them, their friends, their neighbors, and eventually, their children and grandchildren.

I always saw that as something I wouldn't want for myself, something she was chained to as a back-in-the-old-days woman, but watching Jon and Niña made me remember that she had loved it, and that we had all loved her. She had created Life. She was a Goddess. Thinking about her made me wonder, what exactly does it mean to carry that extra X chromosome and a baby making facility in one's MindBody? What does it mean to be a woman?

I had always been told that women could be more than wives and mothers, so I always assumed those things couldn't possibly be enough for a happy life. Yet today I had been forced to contemplate the circle of Life, and being present with one another seemed so much more important than pursuing ever more competitive professional and financial goals.

I always associated Feminism with the phenomenon of women being liberated from the work of the home and demanding the opportunity to work outside of it, just like men. This was great. Hooray for working women! But, hadn't all of those women been doing super important work *inside* the home? Raising and educating children, producing and processing food, pediatric and geriatric nursing, housekeeping, etc. Who was there to take over the most intimate and formative aspects of our humanity when women went to "work"?

Novio retrieved Niña, Jon returned to his guitar, and I became distracted from my own tangents by a few frantic rushes to the baño. Soon I realized that the twanging in my pelvic region hadn't been maternal longing at all, it was a burgeoning UTI.

Guh, a urinary tract infection, an affliction I am all too familiar with. I knew as time went on the pain would become unbearable: I needed antibiotics, but I had no idea how to go to the doctor in Costa Rica. I returned to Casa Playa and started Googling things, finding resources that insisted there was a doctor in Cobano, but none that could help me find the location of said doctor. I tried to find natural remedies to see if there was any chance I could cure this thing here at Casa Playa, but my search only solidified my previous hypothesis: I needed antibiotics.

Interestingly, in my search I came across a connection between UTIs and the use of scented soaps. Apparently, scented soaps should never be used "down there" as they kill benevolent bacteria, contributing to the proliferation of the wrong kind of bacteria. I had used scented soaps "down there" my whole life, something I assumed I learned from MomMom, but regardless, as it turns out, I might have been giving myself all the UTIs I had acquired over the last decade or so.

How could I have lived to be 25 without ever knowing that? How did it never come up with a friend, considering all the times we have bitched about the discomfort of UTIs? How did it never come up with a doctor, after years of being treated for the same problem? Here I was trying to grapple with Life, Death, and Feminism, when despite having been a woman for years, one with some training in medicine, I had no idea that I might have been causing my own UTIs…

UTIs must be one of the most universal female predicaments, second only to the realities of menstruation. Yet somehow these topics, ubiquitous for women, remain shrouded in some taboo mystery, never to be mentioned, let alone pondered upon, especially aloud.

I closed my computer and headed to Neighbor's, she was a woman, hopefully she could help me figure out how to see a doctor. I explained my situation, and she sympathized, having struggled through the same in the past. I was right, UTIs are universal. They are also very awkward to talk about. She told me that I didn't need to worry about getting to the doctor, that I could just go to the farmacia in Cobano and get antibiotics… without a prescription. I was relieved, and then shocked. No prescription? I could just pick up the meds I knew I needed, no co-pay, no translating "burns when I pee", no need to figure out how many colones an out-of-pocket trip to the clínica would be?

I thanked and said goodbye to Neighbor, and walked back through the trees, hoping to get some rest. In the kitchen, I kissed Jon goodnight and downed an extra glass of water along with a Uristat I had packed in the first aid kit. Then I was off to the baño, where I cringed through the emptying of my bladder, before ascending the stairs of Casa Playa, bracing myself for a bad night's sleep, stopping only to scratch Dylan behind the ears.

In the middle of the night, I had to go back to the baño, and when I stepped outside, a chill went down my spine. I could *feel* the silence of the tide. I closed my eyes and inhaled the altered atmosphere, sympathizing with Mother Nature as a woman, acknowledging her constantly shifting moods, and wondering if the pollution in her waters felt anything like a UTI.

Then it was mañana and we were off to Cobano to locate some antibióticos...

Jon checked the bus times online before going to bed, but when we arrived at the bus stop (which was unfortunately in the opposite direction of Cobano), we waited and waited, eventually learning from a passerby that the bus left at 8:15A.M. & 10:15A.M., not 9:15A.M. like our source had insisted. Pura Vida. We started walking back and stuck out our thumbs in hopes that we wouldn't have to wait another hour to embark. Right at Casa Playa, just as were about to give up, a white SUV slammed on its brakes and waved us in. We told him we were off to Cobano, and he said he could take us about half way to Montezuma. That was better than nothing, so we hopped in.

Unfortunately, while we were boarding, Marley heard our voices, and was now speeding up the path, excited to jump into the car. We yelled and told him to go home, but he ran after us, jumping up at the windows, like he had the day we moved from La Hacienda.

The driver was greatly agitated by Marley's antics, insisting, rightly, that he was going to get killed if he kept it up. He honked and we all berated out the window, but it was to no avail. Finally, the driver slammed the brakes again, jumped out of the car with a rage filled *"God damn it!"*, and chased after Marley hurling curses and rocks at him, his unbuttoned tropical shirt billowing around him as he ran. Marley high-tailed it home, and the driver returned to his seat with a calm and sympathetic smile, explaining that was what it took to get a dog to listen. We nodded silently, hopeful the violence was over, glad Marley was no longer chasing the car.

It turned out that our driver was a dog lover. His daughter was a veterinarian, and he has been training and working with dogs for years. He informed us that dogs in Cabuya respond to having rocks thrown at them. He quickly added that the point wasn't to hit them, the threat was enough, and we were glad to try a new training tactic with the ever rebellious Marley. Through our conversation we found out that our driver had financed Luna's spay a few years back and had been the one to find homes for every one of her puppies, injecting them with the suggested vaccinations before scattering them across the peninsula.

I knew what he had done was normal and humane, but in my current state of mind, I couldn't help but see it all from Luna's perspective. Her puppies stolen, her womb left barren, unable to participate in the miracle of Life. Or maybe she was glad to be able to live out her days responsible for no one but herself. I have certainly been glad to have that privilege, and believe that every woman should have the right to choose whether or not she becomes a mother. Why wouldn't that apply to canines as well?

But why was I so hung up on Luna? I had done the same thing to Clover…removing her ovaries before she was even old enough to try and figure out what they were for. Did I help her or hurt her? How am I ever supposed to know? And also, why was I so hung up on being a woman? Had I not castrated Dylan and Marley as well? Is the question of what it means to be a man not worth contemplation, even if the experience isn't mine?

Our driver pulled into his driveway on the outskirts of Cabuya and told us he would be driving the rest of the way to Montezuma in about ten minutes if we still needed a ride. We thanked him and introduced ourselves; his name was Chris.

We walked for a bit, both reflexively checking over our shoulders, expecting at any moment to see Marley emerging from the trees, still chasing after us. Marley never came, but soon the rattling frame of an army green jeep advanced noisily up the road, and pulled over at the sight of our outstretched thumbs. He explained that the car had only one functioning seat, so if we wanted a ride, one of us would have to sit on the floor of the seatless backseat. Jon didn't seem to mind, hopped in, and held on, while I took the front seat.

Our new friend was from Czechoslovakia, was going to Cobano, had lived in Canada, and was a cook. Also, his name was Chris. We talked a little, but mostly we passed the windy ride lost in the scenery.

Every drive through the countryside is a reminder that the landscape is alive. The soil, the trees, the animals, each piece its own MindBody existing within a greater MindBody. The insane detail that can be found within this swatch of green and beige and blue expresses so beautifully the constant state of flux that propels our existences. It simply derails one's consciousness from the perpetual reel of human anxieties. The feeling of camaraderie with the very air around you lets you know a peace that needs no other validation, because it is the truth of who we are.

I looked to the ocean, and thought, sure, to be an alive human, an alive woman, a complex network of energy and matter, was a miraculous thing. Even more miraculous was the ability to understand my existence as part of some larger network, some Body that was not physics as humans would explain it, but rather a realm of understanding where I was some benevolent bacteria poised at the entrance of Mother Nature's sacral chakra, wondering why I kept getting doused with scented soap.

And then we turned away from the water into the hills of pastured farmland, and to look around was to see Mother Nature relaxing amongst the hills. The cows and humans her children, climbing across her gaily, seeming to disrupt her, but truly, her rest deeper, just knowing they are there.

Finally, we scaled up a tree-lined slope that deposited the shaky car right into the heart of Cobano, and then I couldn't see Mother Nature anymore, all I could see was The Man. We bid Chris farewell, turned, and entered the farmacia. We walked up to the counter and were greeted by a smiling, young woman who was wearing a stiff, deep blue medical jacket with a Viagra logo on it.

"Hable Inglés?", I asked hopefully. *"No"*, she said apologetically. Well, here goes nothing. I explained my predicament in broken, rudimentary Español, and received a sympathetic wince and a nod in return, because evidently UTIs feel the same in every language.

She asked me something in Español to which I responded (also in Español), *"Can you repeat that more slowly, por favor?"* She did, and I still didn't understand, but by the third time I was able to confirm that I wasn't alérgico to any antibióticos.

She went to the back of the farmacia and returned with a tiny packet of pills. I looked at them, recognized the word Nitrofurantin, and thanked my past experiences for the instant relief of knowing that I was going home with a trusted cure. She instructed me, *"Uno por la mañana, Uno por la noche para cinco días."* I understood and thanked her profusely, adding a *"con comida?"* and receiving a smile and a *"si"* in response. That hadn't gone badly at all. Pura Vida!

We decided to grab a few things at the grocery store and wandered the aisles of the Mega Super, laughing about how weird of a coincidence it was that both of our rides had been named Chris. We didn't trust the bus times Jon had gotten online, and we assumed it would be easier to hitchhike than to figure out the bus schedule, so we started towards the Road to Montezuma, thumbs aloft. We were offered a ride before we even left the Mega Super's parking lot.

This car would have been considered nice and clean by suburban standards, so I was extra aware of the sand and sweat covering my legs as I settled my agitated pelvis onto the textured, posture adjusting, inflatable ball that rested on the passenger's seat. Our middle-aged, long-haired, well-tanned, driver was headed back to his cabina, just outside of Montezuma, where he and his wife were vacationing away from their children for the first time.

When we found out that his kids were our age, I felt another wave of existential awakening, as though I could see the spectrum of my adulthood before me and know that I was very much at the beginning of it. We also found out that he knew Novio and little Niña. Of course. The Nicoya Peninsula was both a small town and an infinite universe.

The driver pulled over at his cabina and we got out of the vehicle. We thanked him and Jon introduced himself, sticking out his strong hand for a friendly shake. The driver smiled warmly, grasped Jon's hand, and looked up at us through friendly blue eyes: *"Chris"* was the only word he said.

We walked away in a stunned silence, could that actually happen?! Three hitchhikes, with three different Chrises? It couldn't be. Maybe it was hitchhiker code to protect ones identity and a local inside joke to use the name Chris. Either way we were spooked, and gingerly held out our thumbs, wondering how many Chrises could possibly live on the peninsula.

The next car to stop was a completely full pick-up truck that motioned for us to hop in the back. We did, the wind whipping our hair as we watched the world around us zoom away, as though we were riding back-wards on a dusty, scenic roller coaster.

When we neared Montezuma Centro, Jon banged on the side of the truck. It pulled over and he jumped out in one smooth motion, held a hand aloft to help me, and with the other hand waved goodbye to our chauffeurs, joking that at least one of them could have been named Chris.

I was hungry and wanted to take my antibióticos, so when we found a restaurant that advertised french toast and bagels, we happily sat down and ordered. Unfortu-nately, the bagel-making girl had moved back to New York a few days ago, but I was able to order my toast (with bananas and cinnamon), and Jon settled for an egg, tomato, and avocado sandwich.

We added bagels to the list of things we wanted to eat in our future, other items included: Thai food and deep dish pizza. We found out that it was only 11:00A.M., and I reasoned that despite the adventure, the procurement of antibiotics really was more convenient than the US mod-el. We picked up a few more things from the super and, backpack full, headed towards the bus station. The bus to Cabuya wasn't for another hour, so we decided to set out on foot again, thumbs aloft.

Before long, a car pulled over, and we hopped in, happily recognizing our friend who had given us a ride home from our last excursion to Cobano, the thirteen dog, eight cat lady. We talked about everything that had happened since our last meeting: we moved to the farm and the beach, she had gotten much better at driving stick and adopted two more dogs.

The ride passed quickly, and soon we found ourselves back at the driveway that led to Casa Playa. Marley tore up the path as we gathered our bags and said our good-byes, the coincidence striking me mid-sentence...I hadn't even thought of her name until the words *"Thanks Chris-sy!"* came out of my mouth.

Is it all some cosmic joke? Is Mother Nature as funny as she is wise and beautiful? My mind remained consumed with this thought throughout the night and it percolated in my dreams when my body eventually fell asleep.

The return of high tide woke me up, and I knew it was around 7:00A.M. thanks to my study of the tide calendars. My limbs were too heavy to lift off the bed, so I lay in a drowsy stupor, listening to the chatter of the squirrels in the treetops.

I heard Jon get up and head downstairs, but I remained, comfortable and comatose, my eyelids stubbornly shutting out the daylight. Some time later, my dreamy state was interrupted by a shrill giggle from Niña, followed by a soft chuckle from Jon, and I found that I was smiling. Relieved to have regained muscular control of my body, I pushed myself out of bed, stretched, and walked down the stairs to find Jon and Niña in the kitchen.

He was on the laptop Google-ing "good iPad game young child" while she was confusedly flipping the device, trying to play *Monopoly*. My appearance immediately distracted her from the task and she jumped from her chair and grabbed my hand, hoping I wanted to play. I suggested a movie instead and, thankfully, she agreed. I set up the laptop on the patio table and began Disney's *Beauty and the Beast*, while Jon prepared café and cut up watermelons, removing the seeds from Niña's portion.

Novio came around the corner, apologizing for the early hour, explaining that he had told her not to come over, she just hadn't listened. We assured him it was fine and insisted that it had been our plan to watch Disney movies all morning anyway. We offered him some café and he and Jon struck up a conversation, discussing spiders, surfing, and local gossip. Niña narrated the entire plot to me as we watched, weaving in some imaginative developments along the way.

It had been years since I had seen this flick, and it had always been one of my favorites, so I was glad she chose it. Unfortunately in my current state of mind I couldn't help but be overwhelmed with the Feminist perspective of the Disney Princess. Here was Belle, likely the most well read of the Princesses, but still most appreciated for her doe-like brown eyes and ability to make men fall in love with her.

Above all, she desired adventure, but at the end of the day she settled for a guy with a nasty temper whose only redeeming quality was his superlative wealth. Even the supporting cast didn't seem to care that she was a unique and magnificent being, they were just excited that she was young and female (cue *"it's a GIRL"* in Lumiere's exaggerated french accent).

Sure, the point of the movie was that she could see past Beast's horrid appearance and get to know the man underneath, but lets pretend for a moment the roles were reversed. What if she had been a kind soul trapped in a less than attractive body? Would she have still been the princess? Or at the end of the day, is being beautiful the most important part of being a woman?

When Beast reclaimed his humanity, Niña turned to me with excited brown eyes and said, *"I am so happy. Are you happy?"* Moved again by the honesty and wisdom of this child, I wanted to answer with the same openness...

Was I "happy"? Well, I think society is destroying itself in some high-stakes, cartoon-like, *Monopoly* game, and I am bewildered about why, and what to do about it. There are crabs in my shower and ants in my kitchen, and I have to walk or hitchhike anywhere I want to go. I am unsure about the future, unfocused in my passions, I miss my friends and family, and I have a urinary tract infection.

On the screen, Belle and her prince embraced in the magic of rewarded empathy, their true love evaporating all darkness from the scene, leaving smiling, celebrating humans singing and dancing in its wake. Despite all of the terrible things that can be, Life is a wonderful miracle. I giggled, and said, very honestly, *"Yes, I am so happy."*

When Niña and Novio left for their beach house, Jon hitchhiked to Montezuma in an attempt to find guitar strings, leaving me alone at Casa Playa for several hours, a rare opportunity. I opened my journal...

When Jon returned I heard him greet the dogs and approach the hammocks, feet sifting through the sand. I looked up from my screen and was met with an adorable, lost expression. His hair was rumpled and dusty, his face and signature gray tee-shirt streaked as well. His golden brown eyes were glazed. Their surrounding sclera a shocking shade of pink.

"I'm so stoned", he admitted.

"How?!" I laughed,

"I dunno", he responded, *"just let me be stoned for a second."*

He plopped into the other hammock and I continued to type away until he was finally ready to tell me his story.

He hadn't been able to find guitar strings at a store, but he had hitchhiked with a couple, who happened to be staying in The Cabina, who happened to play guitar, and who happened to have an extra set of strings. He exchanged information with them and did some grocery shopping in Montezuma before he started for home, thumb aloft. He managed to hop in the back of a red pickup truck piloted by two surfers, accounting for his wind blown hair.

Inside the truck, each surfer was smoking his own joint, and one politely turned around to pass his through the tiny back window. Jon obliged with a *"muchas gracias"*, hit it once, and handed it back. Apparently, they had been able to find better weed than we had, because Jon was still wandering around in a smiley haze, hours later.

I wondered: was there any less coincidence in Jon hitching with musicians and a couple of generous pot heads than there was when we rode with all the Chrises? Is life always full of these coincidences? Is it just that no one has time to write them all down?

War and Peace

MARLEY HAS BEEN SPORTING RED scratches around his neck and chin for awhile now. We assumed they were from a fight with Tigra, but as the days pass fight free and the scratches remain, we have lost confidence in our diagnosis.

We turned to trusty Google, trying to locate images that reminded us of Marley's affliction, but we were unsuccessful and grew weary of the gruesome images one finds with the Internet search "dog skin lesions". One day Jon struck up a conversation with a French woman, Voisine, who lived a few beach houses down, and was willing to pull back Marley's fur and take a look. She wasn't a vet, but she had some antibiotic cream that we could use on the open scratches, and told us that in her unprofessional opinion, it looked like Marley had fleas.

Fleas. We hadn't even thought of that. All of our animals are on preventative flea/tick medication, they have been for years, we thought they were immune, but now as we look closely, the scratches lining Marley's neck do appear self-inflicted. We put the antibiotic cream on the worst of the scrapes and called a vet to make an appointment. We sat back down in front of the computer, motivated by a more specific search, and found out what fleas looked like and what symptoms of an infestation might be.

Grabbing a flashlight, we rolled Marley onto his back and looked at his belly. The scratches were surrounded by patches of irritated skin, covered in a light black crust which we now recognized as flea dirt. As we studied the patches, a tiny vampire crawled into our line of vision and I grabbed it between my fingernails. It jumped from my grasp immediately, and we looked at each other with pursed lips. Marley definitely had at least one flea.

Google informed us that garlic is a great remedy, fleas hate the taste, but Google also informed us that garlic is horrifically poisonous to dogs. Hmm. We crushed a clove and ran it over Marley's fur, hoping the smell would be as offensive as the taste, and found that it certainly was to human nostrils. The vet never returned our phone call, so we called another one (the only other option in the local magazine) and crossed our fingers. We looked at each other and reassessed the situation, if Marley had fleas, Luna definitely had fleas, and what about The Cats?

Luna's diagnosis was easiest, simply pulling back the fur at her tail revealed a flurry of activity, fleas crawling over one another in every direction, explaining her strange habit of suddenly jumping 360° and biting at the air as if she was trying to catch a bug that had just leapt onto her tail. We groaned and each grabbed a cat. We found only one lone flea on Dylan's belly and theorized that it could have jumped from Luna on to us, and from us onto him. Clover of course, was pristine.

The second vet called us back, and gave us a free phone consultation. He told us about the Animal Co-op in Cobano where we could buy flea powder, explained how to sterilize the house with it, and insisted that we should not use it on the cats. He wanted us to continue using the antibiotic cream on any of Marley's open cuts, and gave us a natural remedy as well. If we could find it, he told us there is a tree called Madera Negra, whose leaves can be made into a flea-repulsing, skin soothing tea used to bathe the dogs. Even rubbing their fur with the foliage should help, and it was safe to use on The Cats. He told us to increase our Frontline application from four weeks to three weeks and explained that if the situation got worse, he would come and pay us a house visit. We were glad to have a plan of action, but flea powder would require another trip to Cobano, and there was no way that was happening until tomorrow.

We rubbed another garlic clove over Marley, did the same for Luna and took to the sand for a twilight stroll, hoping to distract the canines from their scratching fest.

The low tide had left tiny pools between the rocks, and they were surrounded by Ticos, shadowed by the dying light, plucking tasty marine life from the fractures in the rocks. It reminded me of the birds I watched weeks ago, and it astounded me to see how much we had learned and could still learn from the world around us.

The serene setting simply wasn't enough to squelch our anxious moods, and up until we kissed goodnight our conversation kept returning to our poor, itchy ani-

mals. Jon woke up early to hitchhike to Cobano and I settled into the hammock to write, tossing stones at Marley
and Luna to stop them from scratching. Some time later
Jon returned, but unfortunately, he had not been success-
ful. He had a hard time hitching a ride and had therefore
walked many exhausting kilometers in the Costa Rican
sun. When he did eventually arrive in Cobano, he found
the flea powders expensive, and labeled in Español, and
decided he couldn't buy anything with out more information. He had bought some fresh onion loaves though
and quickly prepared a delicious lunch: tomato and avocado sandwiches. At least we wouldn't have to ponder
the flea situation on an empty stomach.

We read somewhere online that it is possible to drown
fleas, but the technique requires the dog to be submerged
neck deep in water for at least ten minutes. It seemed like
a valid option, so we digested a bit before heading into
the sea, calling for Marley to come and join us.

He swam bravely into the surf, his little face bobbing
over the waves until he reached us. Jon supported him
under his belly, but his paws continued to kick instinctu-
ally. We tread in the water, holding and calming our hy-
drophobic dog who refused to let us submerge his shoulders and neck, forcing me to ladle handfuls of water
around his face to drown any fleas that had perched
there. After what we assumed was ten minutes, we headed back in, not particularly hopeful that this flea killing
scheme had worked.

We dried off in the sun as Marley shook and
scratched. Luna wandered over and started digging into
her ears with an exuberance that made Marley's frantic

itches seem lazy. We frowned as we discussed what to do about Luna, a wild dog, no collar, no master, no monthly flea treatments. But Luna also likes to curl up next to Marley when he sleeps, and from everything we've read, treating Marley without treating Luna was an exercise in futility. Just then we noticed movement in the treetops.

A louder than usual howl suggested that the friendly monkeys were around. We sat still, silently observing, and they eventually showed themselves. One at a time they came into view, black bodies, white manes and faces, long arms swinging from the branches with acrobatic ease. Their playful jumps were aided by their tails which could grab and hold the branches with phenomenal dexterity. One brave monkey shimmied down a post near a neighboring dining table. He looked around questioningly before leaping, swiping a few plantains, and scaling back up the post and into the tree tops with a victorious yelp to his friends.

We stood up and followed as the monkeys scurried towards Casa Playa, and we found them convened above the breakfast nook, enjoying their bounty. Their hands were so familiarly human, peeling and feeding, and their chewing faces too, glowing with the good fortune of a tasty snack. Marley let out a growl at one who hung on a low branch, but the monkey simply returned the sentiment, accenting his snarl by hurling a stick in Marley's direction. Tail between his legs, Marley slunk off to resume his scratching while the primate pack lounged on the boughs, tails hanging in curled contentment, bellies round and full. Pura Vida.

Late in the afternoon, Granjero came by and we tried to explain the flea situation. After minutes of looking bewildered, I ran into the kitchen and typed "fleas" into Google Translate. *"Pulgas!"* I shouted, turning around just as an expression of understanding came over Granjero's face. He raised his pointer finger to the sky and motioned for us to wait, dashing into the bodega and quickly returning with a white plastic bottle with no label. He pointed at Marley and then at the bottle, and we nodded, wide-eyed, wondering what he was about to pour on our dog.

Jon held a confused Marley, I poured the contents of the bottle along his spine, and Granjero rubbed the mystery liquid through his thick black fur, rustling the fleas from their hideouts. When Marley was finished, Granjero motioned for Luna, and we gratefully grabbed her, repeating the process again over her larger surface area. When Luna was finished, he bathed Buddy as well, determined to eliminate the pulgas from his properties. As he turned to leave I remembered the natural remedy and asked him about the Madera Negra tea. He seemed excited I had heard of it and with a *"Come! I show you"*, he walked me to a tree at the edge of his property. He grabbed a handful of leaves and slid them off their branch, showing us how to wring them out in order to get the best odor. We thanked him and took the leaves, rubbing them over Dylan and Clover who had emerged from their afternoon napping places, ready for their nightly crab hunt.

We awoke very early on Saturday and took the dogs for a sunrise stroll. Their hearts weren't in it though, as their itching had increased since the application of the mystery liquid the night before. Even Marley couldn't run very far without plopping on to one hip and scratching vigorously at his head, neck, and shoulders with his flailing back paw. We felt so bad for them, and wished we could explain that they would feel better if they would just. stop. scratching. We decided there was only one thing that could help them at this point, so we got them stoned.

Jon inhaled a large gulp and exhaled directly into Marley's face, while I did the same to Luna. Buddy was our control subject, since we felt it was unethical to get someone else's dog high. Within minutes, those under the influence were sleeping peacefully, paws still, and expressions peaceful. Buddy persisted in the scratching of his floppy ears a few minutes longer, and his paws continued to twitch even after he had slumped into the sand, following his compatriots into dreamland.

It was still very early in the morning, and we were now very stoned, so of course, Mom called. Skype's video camera instantly gave away our current state and she shook her head at our debauchery. We talked for awhile, mostly about fleas, until she had to hang up to get to yoga class. I threw in a load of linens that had come in contact with the animals, and instead of spending the rest of the morning writing, we decided to cut all the long pants we had brought with us into shorts.

That afternoon, we checked the animals again to see how the pulga situation was panning out. We were disappointed to find Luna still thoroughly infested, Marley still marginally infested, and Dylan with three fleas now instead of one. Clover, of course, was still pristine. We decided it was time for another tactic, so we headed to the edge of the property and grabbed as many Madera Negra leaves as we could carry. Back in the kitchen, we boiled them as the vet had instructed, and after steeping and cooling, we gave Marley a bath in the tea. It smelled delicious, and Jon wondered aloud if *we* could bathe in the tea as well. We rubbed our wet hands over our legs and arms, basking in the beautiful perfume, then scattered the remaining soggy leaves around the sand near the patio, hoping to discourage any pulgas from pouncing off the pups and populating the perimeter.

Jon headed back to the tree to gather enough leaves to make a bath for Luna, and I went to take the now flea-free animal bedding off the clothes lines. I pulled a sheet, shook it out, and accidentally deposited an entire army of fire ants onto my flip flops.

I howled as they bit me, slapping them away and hopping from foot to foot as I tried to escape without dropping the clean sheets in the sand. It was too late, and as I returned to the matte brown tiles of the patio, the welts had already started to appear. Exhausted, and now as itchy as the animals, I suffered through Luna's bath and Jon's tacos, before we settled into our uncomfortable plastic chairs for a movie marathon. We started and prematurely ended one bad movie after the next, finally giving up and heading to bed early. I sported my most colorful pair of socks in an attempt not to scratch my swollen feet.

The next morning, I sunk my afflicted appendages in an oatmeal bath that I had packed in the first aid kit.

Within the cold, murky water, my feet continued to crawl with the sensation of millions of tiny ants, the desire to scratch the largest of the welts distracting me from all other activities. I looked sympathetically to the dogs, who also itched to the point of distraction, and I tried to lead by example by not giving in, not deliciously digging my nails into the irritated flesh.

I blogged: editing and posting a passage about moving from The Cabina to La Hacienda. The event felt like a lifetime ago considering the overwhelming week it had been since hitchhiking to Cobano for antibióticos. As I wrote, I would take my feet out of the bath and let them dry, plunging them back into the grainy depths of the bucket whenever the itching would resume. When I finished the blog I felt as though I had worked enough for the day, but when I looked at the clock I realized that it wasn't even close to lunch time yet. Jon mentioned that he had bookmarked a long documentary, and I theorized that if I took notes it was technically research, which as a writer should be considered work…

The documentary was called *Thrive*, and had I not been confined to my oatmeal bath, I probably would have turned it off prematurely, as it delved into alien conspiracy theories with very little foreplay. It wasn't great art (cheesy graphics) or great science (super biased), but I am glad we stuck with it, because in the end, it inspired us both by paraphrasing ideas that we have been struggling with, and introducing us to some new ideas that were intriguing and relevant to our work. After the documentary, I needed a change of location, so I pulled my feet from the water one last time and dried them on a towel before slipping the spotted, soggy skin into my flip flops and heading to the hammocks. As I left, Jon crossed his feet on the patio table and began absently strumming his guitar. I was proud of us for leaving behind the drudgery of our sick day to escape into the endless possibilities of our imaginations.

I thought about the documentary, which I suppose could be considered a sort of summary of some of the most famous conspiracy theories: The Rockefellers and Co. (i.e. "The Illuminati", or the 1%), are enslaving the rest of us, through their invention of an economy that depends on resource scarcity to give Them complete control. They suffocate all media with their Propaganda Machine so they can poison our food supply, sterilize us through vaccinations, cover up communication from alien species, instigate perpetual war, and surreptitiously control the world's governments... I know this sounds crazy... because I think I might actually be crazy, and still, all this sounds crazy to me...

However, I can't help but see the parallels of this diabolical master plan and my theory that monetary profit is to blame for many of the problems we face today. I want to participate in society without the assumption that the powers that be are out to get me, but shouldn't my null hypothesis assume it equally as likely that they are? Modern society is based on the idea of perpetual growth, but don't we know by now that perpetual growth is impossible on a finite planet? How does one navigate the fine line between conspiracy and skepticism? Either way, whether the truth is a diabolical master plan or a random act of evolution, isn't the need for a solution still valid?

The narrator advocated for a philosophical shift to nonviolation, basically, a human understanding that Thou shalt not violate and Thou shalt not be violated. The concept is idealistic for sure, but I think it is agreeable to all, even Bears and Packers fans. Anyway, the nonviolation idea illustrates that mutual respect could be the tool with which we build a better future; one without war, yet with the freedom to feel safe enough to follow our instincts. If business, health, agriculture, etc., were to adopt the principle of nonviolation, our world would be unrecognizable. It made sense to me, and fit in with my new worldview of needing to live as one with nature.

The narrator explained our current time as the largest social movement in history, a time of mass awakening, a consciousness shift that is allowing people to imagine a world of abundance and prosperity for all species. It might seem like a fringe movement, but only because it is taking place on a global, not a local, scale. It is a shift that continues over time. It was the philosophy of Jesus, Martin Luther King Jr., and Ghandi, of John Lennon, and John F. Kennedy, and...
Wait, why do all these non-violent activists keep dying such violent deaths?

The narrator went on to suggest that if war is the weapon of choice for Them, and if They are as powerful as They seem, then We cannot possibly hope to win in a war. However, with the "weapon" of nonviolation, we could withdraw our support at the base of the pyramid, and end The Game by forfeit.

At the end of the documentary, there was a vignette about a man "waging peace" between the Crips and the

Bloods. He basically attributed gang violence to decades of unresolved conflict, and made it his life's work to mediate that conflict. When he convinced gang leaders to meet and put aside their differences, the enemies embraced. Later, they both admitted that they had expected to be stabbed in the back by their rival. So is that what it takes to be nonviolent? To stop fearing death? To look at every moment as though it could be your last and be grateful for the time that was, not greedy for the time that can never be? To reach out for an embrace, even if it means getting stabbed in the back?

A familiar whistle from Jon announced that it was dinner time, and over our casado we discussed the cultural contrast of our sick day. We had been able to get more work done being sick, vs. the typical "sick day" in The States where one waits until one's sickness is so contagious that one is forced to call their boss and grovel for time-off before spending a miserable few days on the couch, doing nothing.

I remember pushing through sickness during finals week at NU, it seemed like clockwork the way my sinuses or stomach would flare up in response to the extra studying. I remember counting down the hours until I could collapse on my bed and let the illness run its course. I knew the stress, the pushing it, only made the sickness worse, had I just relaxed when my nose started running, maybe I could have avoided spending my spring/summer/winter breaks with bronchitis. But professors don't think like that, unless one looks like death warmed over, one isn't really sick enough to take time away from one's responsibilities.

So, we spend a good week in denial. *"Oh its just aller-gies…"* we say, as we hop ourselves up on DayQuil and cough all over each other's Scantron sheets. What other option do we have?

Fail Out? Get fired? Lose Money? Not get paid? Those aren't options when every penny counts. So we cart our insidious microbiota around our community while simul-taneously running ourselves into the ground. We think the war is with the invading microbes, but maybe they are simply trying to give us a sign, proving to us in the only way they know how that our lifestyles are taking a toll on our MindBodies.

Sorry guys, but we aren't listening. We insist that our rampaging work ethic is survival of the fittest, and we put our stuffy noses to the grindstone.

No normal boss would have let me take the morning off to soak my itchy feet in an oatmeal bath and watch conspiracy theory documentaries. Regardless, by the end of the day, I had still chosen to do my work. I had put in more than eight hours, without getting paid, and the kicker- it was a Sunday.

Is there enough internal motivation present in the human race to pursue "work" that is relevant? Does our society need to be forced into progress? Or would progress simply happen if we had the time to cultivate our heath and our talents? Not that we can't have jobs, but must those jobs limit all other areas of our lives? Should some people work eighty hours per week, while others struggle to find employment? And isn't technolo-gy coming for all the jobs anyway? What should we do then? We talked in circles about work and jobs and The

Man until we were almost too delirious to make it up the stairs. I reapplied my colorful socks and went to sleep, feet prickling, head spinning.

In the middle of the night, both of us awoke at the same instant, wondering aloud, *"What was that?!"* A suspicious noise had entered our unconscious, sleepy brains, and after a moment, our fears were confirmed. We heard something, something *large*, moving near Jon's side of the bed. My fingers wrapped around the handle of my flashlight, thumb instantly igniting the beam and pointing in the dark towards the noise.

There, in the spotlight, tongue and tail wagging, was Luna. She had busted through the screen on the door and was eagerly awaiting an invitation into our bed. When we were finally able to compose our laughter, we shooed her away and closed the heavy wooden door, blocking the now open screen from any more intruders.

Our first thought in the morning was that we missed the ocean breeze, so we fixed the screen with a few thumbtacks. Our second thought was that we had to start setting more boundaries for Luna. She had fleas, and was now bringing them upstairs to The Cats, and as of last night, into our bedroom. The mystery liquid has dampened their presence, and the Madera Negra baths seem to soothe the itching (even if they do unfortunately turn her green for an hour or so), but her infestation is still a danger to our f-animal-y. It was now time to aggressively pursue tactics to keep her downstairs.

We found a small table that effectively blocked the stair landing, preventing Luna from continuing up the second set of stairs. We were sure The Cats would be able to crawl over or under it, but we were worried that our tenacious Marley would try to overcome the barrier, running up or down the stairs in the middle of the pitch black night, and seriously hurt himself. We went upstairs and called him up, wanting to see how he would react to the barrier. He climbed over easily, as if he hadn't even noticed its presence and on the way down he leapt past it carelessly. So far so good, hopefully it wouldn't be so easy for Luna. We both practiced climbing over it a few times and finally decided that it was safe enough.

Around twilight, Granjero showed up waving and smiling from the property line, asking permission to come inside and spray for pulgas. As he walked toward the bodega, and disappeared inside, we cheered, excited for this next mission in the War on Fleas. He emerged with a machine that reminded me of something a mad scientist would have handy: a multicolored hunk of levers and hoses, any labels or instructions for use either non-existent or long since rusted over. He hoisted the heavy apparatus on to his shoulders like a backpack, and snapped a medical mask over his nose and mouth. He attached the bottle of mystery pulga poison to one hose, and wielded another, pointing it towards the ground. He hooked an elbow around a contraption on his left side and began pumping his arm enthusiastically, until the mystery liquid coughed out of the hose and onto the sand near the patio.

Whatever he was spraying had a strange and suffocating odor. We holed up in the kitchen, comforted by the faintly lingering smell of fried fish, and burned a stick of incense while we watched his progress. He walked the perimeter of Casa Playa pumping vigorously, his bouncy gait poorly suppressed by the small, shuffling steps he took to ensure that every inch of the sand was sprayed thoroughly. He looked like a comical ghostbuster and I couldn't help but imagine the horns and cymbals of a one-man band, and wonder if there were any other uses for this obscure machine. He smiled while he worked and after a few minutes, he waved goodbye, shuffling over to Neighbor's, pumping and spraying as he went.

The next morning was considered a victory in the War on Fleas, between the Madera Negra tea and Granjero's mystery treatments, the itching had subsided. During inspections, even Luna was clean. We decided not to go to Cobano for flea powder unless the situation escalated again. My feet were also feeling much better, so when Neighbor came by, wondering if I wanted to walk with her to Rio Lajas, I gladly obliged. The dogs followed us happily, but Marley turned around not far from home, unable to deal with the separation from Jon.

Two little boys talked with us in Español as they splashed and wrestled in the water, and my confidence soared as I followed and participated in most of the conversation. When they left, we stood up and walked along the rocks. I slipped, cursing as I felt a small stone pierce my big toe. Aggravated by yet another foot injury, I immediately wanted to head home to the first aid kit. We did, our progress slow, my gait awkward as I tried to keep the sand away from my bleeding hallux.

Close to home, we were stopped by a group of Ticos gathered around a tiny fishing boat. They spoke to us and I understood not a word so I just stood wide-eyed as

Neighbor laughed and joked with them. To think, only moments ago I had two functioning feet and thought I could speak Español.

As we walked away she translated for me: They were going lobster fishing and invited us to join them. Neighbor had politely declined (phew), but told them where to find us whenever they were ready to part with their catches. We finished our walk excited, it looked as though tonight would be lobster night.

I cleaned and covered my foot while chatting with Jon, who was cutting up fruit from Granjero's farm. After our snack, I composted the remains to Crab City while Jon sat at the kitchen table, the laptop open, headphones on, right fingers expertly maneuvering the mouse across a screen of recording levels, left fingers wrapped around the neck of a guitar that rested, seemingly forgotten, across his knees.

I grabbed the iPad and headed to the hammocks, looking out at the beautiful and ever changing sea-nery and thinking about the balance between War and Peace.

How is our War on Fleas different from the War on ____? We saw a threat to our way of Life and attempted to obliterate the offending party. We stood our ground at the perimeter of our property, wielding soggy tea leaves and mystery liquids, caring not for the fact that The Fleas probably have a purpose in our ecosystem of which we are unaware. How do I protect myself and my f-animal-y from diseases spread by fleas without demeaning and destroying an entire culture? Does this prove nonviolation impossible? Is there a way to coexist? Or, does peace with the pulgas mean plague for the perros? Maybe in a balanced state War is a fight for Peace, and Peace requires ethical and logical War.

Marley came flying by, prompting Luna to gallop after him, and I looked up from my work when they started barking in unison. I stood to see a friendly Tico who was pointing to a large pot that he held over his head while shouting *"Tengo Langostas!"* — it was the lobster guy! I whistled for Jon, who had luckily taken off his headphones, and we approached the lobster guy together, ogling his treasure: five lobsters, alive and shuffling over one another. I was so busy taking in the creatures, the ornate armor of their exoskeletons, their other worldly antennae extending long past their container to timidly scope out the atmosphere, that I barely noticed the man talking rapidly in Español and Jon staring pointedly at me for translation.

I tore my eyes from the crustaceans and tried to listen, the conversation difficult. Finally I understood: Cook until orange in garlic and mantequilla (which was an Español word that I didn't know, but was told was "like oil" and that I intended to look up in the dictionary) and the lobsters were 4mil a kilo. I told him we wanted two, but he told me we should buy three, so I accepted, and he charged us the 4mil. Jon ran back into Casa Playa for colones and a langosta container, while I attempted to stop the dogs from leaping onto the lobster guy and catching some seafood for themselves.

When Jon returned, the lobster guy peeled three langostas from their compadres and placed them neatly into a blue plastic mixing bowl where their curious sensory appendages immediately began caressing Jon's muscular wrists. We thanked him and he bounced away, leaving the two of us looking helplessly at our still moving dinner.

I never had to kill the food I intended to eat. What an interesting take on dinner in the midst of contemplating War and Peace. Jon and I have talked about living off the land before, and we both agree that killing a fish to eat would be easier than killing a mammal to eat, but still, we have never actually done it. I guess *Dexter* put it best, *"Tonight's the Night...."*

We had no idea what to do with our new animals, and then it dawned on me to go and get Neighbor. Not only did she speak Español, and know how to cook langostas, but she definitely wanted to buy some from that guy. I sprinted over shouting *"hola?!"* and told her, *"the lobster guy was here, well he left, but he was here, and we bought three, and they are alive, and we don't know what to do..."*

She laughed at my anxiety and told me just to throw them in the fridge while she headed to the beach to pick up a few more. When I returned to the porch, Jon was staring into the bowl and I had a suspicion that he was playing with the alien looking things we were about to slaughter. I told him about the fridge and he cleared the bottom shelf, placing the bowl inside, and staring at it, hands on his hips, frowning. The inquisitive antennae reached out of the bowl and towards the warm air swirling around his knees. Shuddering, he closed the door.

Neighbor returned quickly with four langostas and told us that Novio would come to Casa Playa around 5P.M. to teach us how to cook them. She also relayed the message from the lobster guy that mantequilla is butter, that she had some she would bring, and that she would make a salad. We asked if there was anything else we could pick up, and she suggested sweet potatoes, a delicious and cheap way to feed many people. Woo hoo! A dinner party!

While Jon headed out on foot towards The Super in Montezuma, I cleaned up the place, collecting anything that could be considered flatware. Jon returned more quickly than I expected. He ran into Novio and Niña at The Super, and hitched a ride back with them and Buddy in Red Van.

Neighbor had to meet with a client, so I took on the responsibility of playing with Niña while Jon solemnly followed Novio into the kitchen, about to kill his first lobster. I was (somewhat ironically) trying to teach my little amiga how to play "go fish", but she didn't quite seem to understand the concept, preferring to hoard her cards rather than give up her pairs. However, she squealed with delight every time she got to say the words "go fish", so we both remained entertained, although the games never concluded with a clear winner.

At some point Jon exited the kitchen, paler than usual, the bowl once containing the squirming crustaceans now piled high with a mixture of their shells and sweet potato skins. He dumped the remains on Crab City and when I asked how it went he only shrugged, meeting my eyes with a look that said "but...".

I gave him a sympathetic smile as he headed back into the kitchen and then my attention shifted to the three dogs eagerly sniffing around the compost pile. I shook my head as Marley emerged as the alpha- the first to run off toward the beach, lobster antennae protruding from his jaw. Evidently he had no qualms with lobster murder.

I was distracted by Neighbor's *"hola"* as she came around the corner, and in the time it took for me to turn my head, Niña had screeched, ran, and entangled herself around Neighbor's lower half, the adult continuing to walk forward as though none of this had happened. I laughed as I collected the cards, then suggested that we set the table. Niña swiftly changed trajectories again, bouncing into the kitchen to collect the plates and inform the boys. The two men were gathered around steaming pans tossing liberal amounts of garlic and mantequilla into them, and the scent was making everyone's mouth water. Soon, the five of us sat down and dug in, my fork piercing the meat that was muscle not so long ago. It was delicious, no doubt, just like the ribs had been at Cabuya Joe's, but I couldn't shake the feeling that the cost was too high, especially when my palette seemed even more drawn to the gentle sweetness of the potatoes, and the crispy crunch of the colorful salad.

We sat back, full, and enjoying a good conversation. We found out that a few nights back, Marley had spent the night in Red Van. He snuck in under the cover of darkness and wasn't discovered until Novio left for work the following morning. We were still laughing when Niña bluntly admitted, *"I want to go now, I'm tired."*

Novio whisked her up and carried her through the trees to their beach house while Neighbor stuck around to help us with the dishes. When she left, I asked Jon if it was worth it, and he gave me an uneasy look.

Los Vecinos

AT 7:00A.M. THE TREES WERE shaken with an ear-splitting,
almost too ironic, blast of Guns and Roses', *Welcome to the
Jungle*. We tried not to judge, but we missed the sound of
the waves. After a few songs, we figured we should at
least use the amplified adrenaline as motivation to clean
the house, so we rewashed all the rugs and fabric that
might have come in contact with Marley and The Fleas.

That afternoon, Neighbor came by inquiring about
the music and explaining that she had a lot of free time
on her hands over the next few days because Niña was
across the gulf in Puntarenas with extended familia. She
suggested we accompany her to Karaoke Night that
evening, an event hosted every Friday by Novio, at his
B&B in Montezuma. We accepted. Then she wondered if I
was free now to do some yoga. I was.

We walked through the sand, passed the hammocks,
and once we reached the sea we headed north until we
found a nice rock-free stretch to vinyasa. From this distance the music was not all consuming, and I found that
the tunes as a background for the waves was downright

pleasant. My chaturanga wobbled as my toes and fingers squished in the sand, the waves sometimes stealing the ground right out from beneath me. Eventually, I got the hang of it, and it was fun to dance at the edge of the earth.

To say I love to dance is an understatement. I suppose it began one summer, when Bella and I, toothless and tan, decided to try out for cheerleading. We made the cut, and my parents were thrilled that I had a hobby that didn't require me to sit silently in the house, soaking up black marks on pieces of paper (I spent much of my childhood time reading and playing the piano).

A few summers later, I expressed the desire to become a ballerina. I was in my first week of Sports Camp, adolescently trying to get through the summer without playing any sports, when Mom in her clunky gray car pulled up a few hours early, waving for me to get in. She had located a ballet studio, purchased a leotard and tights, and was here to take me to class if I wanted to go, but we were late, so if I did, we should hurry.

After the class, we immediately registered for the Summer Intensive Ballet Camp. It started the week prior, so I was already behind, but I was elated to have found a ballet school AND a way out of sports camp...

It was hands down the toughest summer of my youth. I woke up early every morning to lay in a series of stretches, willing myself to stretch further, determined to catch up to the other girls. After a full eight-hour day, I went home to soak my aching feet in ice and place heating pads on my overstretched 11-year-old muscles. After dinner, I practiced piano, then grabbed a book, polishing off a few chapters while stretching on the floor.

I learned so much about discipline and pain, about beauty and failure, about friendship and rivalry, and about how to correctly point my toes. By autumn, I was attending regular ballet classes, then Ballet Camp every summer after that, with the expectation that I would someday be a professional ballerina.

72 hours before I was to leave for college on a scholarship to study dance performance and kinesiology, I broke my ankle during a performance. With the spotlight on me, the choreography called for a series of piqué turns, each one diving directly into a penché, and on my fourth I slid, my ankle bending awkwardly with an audible *"crunch"*. I stood up, immediately knew that I was hurt, and took a bow. I hopped off the stage prematurely, my foot already swelling out of the delicate satin of my pointe shoe. So much for my childhood dreams... I was jerked into the present moment by Paul McCartney yelling at me over the distant speakers: *"You may be a woman, but you ain't no dancer"*.

The memory of my loss stung anew, but quickly, I reminded myself that all of it, even the painful stuff, made me who I am today. When I decided to return to Casa Playa, Neighbor remained to take Buddy for a ten minute flea dunk in the sea.

Back home, Jon was nowhere to be found. I wandered around, peeking into all the rooms, even the bodega, and started to worry. As I meandered towards the laundry to switch the linens, I heard his familiar whistle and turned to see him, hidden in the trees, lying on his back atop the picnic table that had deposited me onto the ground on our first day here. His left hand pillowed his head, and the fingers of his right were curled around a glass of icy rum that rested on his shirtless belly. His eyes were glazed and he pointed to the sky, as if The Doors blasting from the neighboring speakers were explanation enough for his early imbibing. They were.

To say Jon loves music is an understatement. His dad and older brother were in local bands when he was growing up, thus spawning a love for listening to, playing, and writing music. When I met Jon, when he drew the ring on my finger with a Sharpie, he was in a local band. That band turned into a band that he fronted, which led him to join a more popular regional band, who eventually disbanded. A couple of part-time jobs and incomplete college semesters later, Jon got a gig on tour with an even bigger regional band, working as a guitar tech and videographer. Only a few months on the road, he met and became the bassist for a soon-to-be-famous-internationally band. From there, the group toured the world.

They were on all the magazine covers, and all of the late night TV shows. Jon co-wrote an album with them, and performed and released a live record as well. Then, after five years of rising tensions between members and outside influences, the band abruptly split. Jon and his writing partner were confused, but had a handful of songs, so they formed another band. Unfortunately, conflicts from the past carried into the new project, and it ended before it really even started. Jon was devastated, but left with an education in the music business, a refined songwriting craft, and enough money to pay off our debts and float us while we searched for the next chapter, whatever that may be…

When The Doors album ended, a more abrasive set began, and Jon hopped off the picnic table, announcing that a good set of speakers was another luxury that he truly missed.

I rinsed the sand from my skin as the concert continued, the guitar solos never ending, the shrill falsettos presenting the annoyed birds with stiff competition, and the cranked bass literally vibrating through the sand.

It was so funny to have a Rock 'n' Roll soundtrack to life at Casa Playa. It made the contradictions in my own life feel more normal. I found myself humming along as I untwisted my braid and chose a cute dress to wear to Karaoke Night. We jumped in Red Van with Neighbor, Marley and Buddy in the back, and headed down the dusty path.

We stopped in Montezuma Centro, picked up two pizzas, then headed up The Hill to the B&B. When we arrived, only Novio was there, looking lonely in the absence of Niña, and tangled in a messy array of speaker cords. Jon crouched beside him to offer his professional services. They opened two beers, started fiddling with the wires, and in no time, the system was up and running. Afterwards, they each stood with a mic in hand, manipulating their voices as they tried to outdo one another with ever more ridiculous sounding *"check"*s.

Neighbor and I stood guard at the doors, training Marley to stay outside. Eventually, the boys grew bored of checking the mics so we all migrated over to the pizza boxes. Once the pizza was gone, it was 6:30P.M., so even though it was only the four of us, Karaoke Night had officially begun.

Neighbor cracked open a "Cuba Libre" (rum and coke in a can) and was the first to grab the mic, admitting to her small audience that all she sings is country. I cringed internally at the mention of my least favorite musical genre, but smiled encouragingly with the bottom half of my face as the words illuminated themselves on the screen.

I am sad to admit that singing is most certainly not my strong suit. I inherited a loud croak from MomMom, and I am usually edged away from at parties whilst singing *Happy Birthday*. I have never performed karaoke in my life, but still enjoy getting drunk enough to watch others do it, and since Jon is good enough for the both of us, we always have a great time.

Neighbor finished belting out in her pretty soprano a song about how frustrating love is when you are cheating on your spouse, and then Novio sang *What I Got* by Sublime, before handing the mic to Jon who chose Roy Orbison's *You Got It*. He lifted his eyebrows as he imitated Roy's dramatic vibrato and periodically he would turn with a sweeping motion and extend his arm to me, emphasizing the most romantic of the lyrics. I bit my lip as I fell in love with him all over again.

During Neighbor's second country song, a tenant of the B&B showed up with a bottle of tequila, and a couple of Tico-Gringos. I was relieved there was enough of a crowd now for my non-participation in the karaoke to go unnoticed. While we were introducing ourselves, a huge spider wriggled over the threshold of the porch where

Marley and Buddy lay. Everyone turned, noticing its presence, and Novio identified it as a baby tarantula. Jon squatted down nearby and stroked it's fuzzy back, coaxing it to crawl onto his arm. The spider was slow and clumsy, reminding me of the Dylan that I used to know, seemingly unaware that it was given graceful appendages.

Distracted by the spider, we failed to notice the ever growing party. When Jon set our new arachnid friend down on a ledge outside, we were surprised to find ourselves facing a crowded room. An array of people were wandering about and taking turns on the mic, some were patrons of the B&B (like the tequila lady) others were karaoke regulars (like the Tico-Gringo's), and a few were transient wanderers, unsure of how they arrived in Montezuma, let alone at Karaoke Night.

I sat at a table on a patio amidst the jungle, successfully stopping Marley from running inside the establishment by scratching his ears with my feet. I chatted with a teacher, a builder, and a masseuse, all of whom stopped talking to listen to the Bob Dylan impersonation that was happening inside. There was Jon, drawling through *Just Like a Woman*.

After his performance, Jon cornered a guy who walked in with a package of guitar strings (he still hadn't been able to purchase any). Unfortunately, they were a gift for Novio's brother, Bro-vio, and had come all the way from The States. We talked to a man who had met Michael Jackson, the story bringing drunken tears to his eyes, and we also met someone else from Chicago. Jon took the mic again, this time taking on Johnny Cash's

Ring of Fire. Someone on the patio lit a fat joint and the entire party shifted to form a large circle as we passed and puffed. Everyone laughed when Jon dropped the mic to join the circle, leaving the vocal-less song playing in the background.

I looked around and wondered: Who were these people? I met teachers, and natural health practitioners, people working in organic food and solar energy. They were people who preferred smoking pot to drinking, people who were multilingual, well-traveled, and all on Facebook. I felt a great companionship with everyone around me. Although I was, admittedly, slightly over-served.

The best connection we made was with a couple, traveling the US in an RV. They had crossed the border in Texas as part of the journey, and somehow wound up all the way down here. Back at The Townhouse, before coming to Costa Rica, we had seriously contemplated a similar lifestyle, and to be honest, we still hadn't ruled it out. It would be a fun way to tour…

We impaled them with questions, asking everything from what they ate to where their favorite places were. We gave them advice about their first trip to New Orleans and pouted when we learned they would pass through Chicago while we were still in Costa Rica. We sat engrossed in our conversation until the karaoke had ceased and Novio was shooing us outside.

We woke up early and hungover, groggily agreeing to get pancakes at the hotel near La Hacienda. We tied Marley up outside and told Luna and Buddy to *"va a la casa!"*, before walking in and taking a seat in two comfortable leather chairs. We ordered the pancakes with honey and sugar, and while we waited for their arrival we watched colorful birds hop between the treetops and the ceiling eaves, attempting to snag some pancakes of their own. Suddenly, Marley came zooming through the eating area, bee-lining for the beach, having obviously wriggled free of his harness. A squinting and uncoordinated version of Jon grumpily got up and chased after him.

When we returned to Casa Playa, Neighbor was heading to the organic market in Montezuma and offered to give us a ride, which we readily accepted, excited to pick up some good lettuce and not have to watch it wilt on the walk home.

In Montezuma Centro, the usually secluded park had taken on its Saturday morning bustle: a circle of vendors set up in a large common area, some selling freshly prepared food, others cute, handmade dresses, others obscure, yet intriguing works of art.

When the vegetable truck arrived, the volunteers set out wicker baskets filled to the brim with colorful, seasonal fruits and vegetables. They asked the milling crowd to refrain from shopping until the truck was completely unloaded. The crowd listened and gathered, the excitement palpable. I couldn't help but compare the energy to the culture of lining up outside a music venue, everyone perky in hopes of hearing the hot, new band.

Suddenly, two, tall, 20-somethings, dressed in elvish attire, began a magic show in front of the unloading truck. They spun clear balls across their limbs, cracked whips, and expertly tossed batons to one another to the polite applause of the adults and the amazed shrieking of the children. At the end of the performance the she-elf shouted:

"*Ladies and gentleman, please look around you: this is your community. Whether it be just today, this week, or forever, we have all come together, here in this place, to share in and support our food system. Let us thank the sun and the rain for these beautiful treasures and the farmers who toiled to harvest them for us. It is food that brings us together, and it is organic farmers who are saving our food.*"

The male elf translated this message en Español and then invited the crowd to start shopping.

The market was chaos again. Arms flinging in all directions, reaching into baskets with no marked prices, fingers curling around the choicest of items. We were too slow to get any cucumbers, so I grabbed some edamame instead, and stood my ground in the rapidly growing line while Jon continued to shop, joining me to dump more produce in my heavily burdened arms before disappearing again into the bustling crowd.

Our friend Konstnär checked us out, explaining that the edamame was very expensive and that's why the price tag was so high. We got it anyway, now that we were both craving the salty snack. We reconvened with Neighbor back at Red Van, making a multiple-point-turn on the narrow road and lumbering back in the direction of home.

The rest of the weekend passed in a blur. We cleaned, wrote, read, gave the dogs another bath in Madera Negra tea, and gave everyone (excluding Luna) their tri-weekly spot-on flea treatment. On Monday, we washed all blankets and rugs again, swept, then mopped the floors, determined to sterilize everything that might have come in contact with the pesky pulgas.

That evening, we decided to go out again, this time to Organico's Open Mic night. We mentioned to Neighbor that we were going, and she offered to give us a ride, jumping on another adult social opportunity in the absence of Niña. After dinner, Red Van rumbled off again in the direction of Montezuma Centro, its interior buzzing with the discussion of the dessert options at Organico.

They had dark chocolate gelato, so Jon and I split that and settled in. The tiny place was packed, the tables completely full, latecomers like ourselves loitering in the walkways. We stood near a ledge, messily strewn with books, and home to a laminated sign announcing a book exchange. I surreptitiously glanced through the titles, but found nothing worth parting with anything in my current collection for, so I turned my focus to the crowd.

Everyone was focused on a small stage adorned with microphones and creatively mismatched lighting schemes. They were all smiling and grooving along with a crooner who was slapping his acoustic guitar whilst belting out a song that was evidently funny (it was not in English, so I couldn't be sure). The effect was charming and Jon and I were impressed, both with the musician and the attentive audience.

The night continued this way, the range of music astonishingly varied. Singers belted in Español, English, and more, the communal acoustic guitar playing everything from classical, to folk, to rock. Some people brought their own instruments, breaking up the night with ukulele solos, electronic beats, and even a riveting ten minutes of a didgeridoo.

Open Mic ended at 9:00P.M., and we couldn't wait to come back next week. We were ecstatic to have found a place for live music, and Jon was already thinking about what songs he was going to play. Back at Casa Playa, we heard Neighbor calling for Buddy, so we called for Luna, assuming they were together.

The next morning when I crossed the tree-line with my mat, Neighbor was already astride The Moto. She informed me that Buddy had run away last night. He had followed us all the way into Montezuma, trekked up The Hill to the B&B, and sat there in the dark, waiting for Neighbor, until Novio had found him there this morning.

Our class at Montezuma Yoga was fun, the instructor helping me in to my first ever headstand, and we left, yoga-buzzed and hungry, agreeing to grab lunch in town before heading home. We went to her favorite place, Sano Banano, and I ordered a veggie sandwich. We people watched, and she filled me in on local gossip.

Half-way through lunch, Neighbor received a phone call. Despite hearing only one side of the conversation I could tell that the news was exciting. When she hung up she explained that her boss, Jefe, had an unused aerial silk, and had agreed to give it to her. When met with a blank expression from me, she explained that aerial silks was a hobby she had picked up over that last few months... a circus-esque practice that looks a lot like yoga, but is performed at dizzying heights, suspended in the air, limbs wrapped in long, silky, flexible fabrics. I told her I wanted to try it and she squealed with delight.

A few days later, when Jefe arrived in Cabuya with the extra silk, Jon helped him to fully extend a 25ft ladder and balance it precariously between the sand and the thick trunk of a nearby tree. The three of us watched with bated breath as Jefe climbed carefully up the narrow rungs, the tangerine hued silk tucked under one arm and draping dramatically behind him. At the top, he secured the silk around a rung and bravely flung himself onto the tree branch, pulling and tugging with all of his strength to make sure that the branch would hold our weight.

Finally, sure it was satisfactory, he maneuvered back onto the ladder and fastened the silk around the branch with a simple yet sturdy knot. Silk hung, the fear we hadn't even noticed evaporated from his body language.

Then, we were presented with problema número dos: a crooked, pointy branch stood poised like a sharpened spear, a few feet below where the silk hung, ready to impale the first silkist to dare attempt a dance. The boys returned the ladder to a less dizzying height and Jefe climbed again to the top, slipped a hand saw into the notch between trajectory and trunk, and pierced through the dry bark.

The progress was slow and he and Jon alternated often while Neighbor and I watched from below, cheering redundant encouragements. When Novio came around the corner, wondering what was going on, the saw was resting momentarily, wedged into the tree so that only its glinting edges were visible. He smugly explained that we were attempting to saw through Madera Negra, one of the hardest woods in Costa Rica. Jon and I glanced up, squinting into the distance, above the silk, way above our

roof, and into the leaves, which were instantly recognizable.

Neighbor and I sighed with relief that the branch
would most definitely hold our weight, but Jon and Jefe
rolled their eyes as they finally understood why this tiny
tributary had been so tough to tear down. They were
both more than happy to recruit a third set of testos-
terone enhanced biceps, and encouraged Novio up the
ladder.

It was Jon who struck the final blow, calling out an
overly dramatic *"Timmmbeerrr!"* as the disconnected log
plummeted to the sand. As he scaled down the ladder,
Novio handed him a cold cerveza and they clinked their
bottles, taking a well-deserved seat at the patio table. Jefe
left just as Neighbor was showing me how to wrap my
foot in order to step into the silk.

We both cheered when after many torturous tries, I
hovered inches above the ground, hands cramping and
brow sweating profusely. She insisted that I take a break
and stretch my hands while she took the silks into hers.
She ascended easily, her body moving with the silks instead of weighing them down, and she proceeded to flip
and spin them around her, while I watched from below,
jaw agape. Once in awhile she would strike a pose and
hang there smiling, asking how it looked. The perfection-
ist in me blurted out, *"point your toes"*, when what I
meant to say was *"beautiful"*.

We continued to alternate and I eventually got the
knack of pushing my feet into the silks to help my puny
arms lift my heavy skeleton. By my last attempt I stood
panting, about five feet off the ground, shaking with the

effort of holding on. She showed me a few cool down stretches and I was hooked. The silks were so impressive, and such a challenge for my personal weaknesses, I was determined to keep practicing.

Soon, the monkeys came by to see what all the commotion in their treetops was about, so we respectfully braided up the silk and retired for the evening. We discussed the wonder of the monkeys and Novio explained that if he were a monkey he would want to be a Central American monkey because *"only the "new world primates" can use their tails like a fifth hand"*. I smiled, because he *was* a New World Primate, his monkey ancestors just developed kick ass thumbs instead of kick ass tails.

I spent the rest of the night and most of the next day obsessed with the silks, climbing as many times as my limbs would allow me, already imagining my tricks into choreography that went along with whatever Jon happened to be strumming at the time.

The Red Tide

MY PERIOD WAS LATE. It had been fifty days since my last period, twenty-eight is normal. I wasn't *particularly* worried, things haven't been regular lately, still, childbearing was on my mind. Maybe because Bella was due in a few weeks...

Did I want to have a baby? For most of my life that answer was a resounding *"no"*. All of the advice is: College, Job, Date, Travel, Delay Children for as. long. as. you. can. Yet, there had been a shift for me lately. I found myself thinking about children more often.

It was a Friday when Niña came back, her absence not truly felt until she was standing there, shoulders thrown back, eyes intent and open, asking me to hang out. She had a hula hoop, and challenged me to a contest, and although I have never been able to hula hoop, I shrugged, stepped into the striped circle, twisted, and flung it around my ribs. It orbited once or twice then wobbled, and with each rotation the hoop slowed and awkwardly slid down my spastic hips and legs. Niña laughed aloud,

I joined her, then she grabbed the hoop explaining, *"You do it like this."*

She spun the hoop around her, and it floated magically about her waist, neck, and arms while she effortlessly walked around. She finished with a flourish, handed me the hoop again, and I tried, with slightly more success. After a few more giggles and pointers, I held the hoop aloft for about thirty seconds…a lifetime achievement!

Jon emerged from the kitchen, snatched the hoop from my hands and hula'd with technique almost as good as Niña's. We were still playing when Granjero came by, wanting to spray for pulgas. Jon offered to help him, and to escape the fumes, I took Niña for a walk to Rio Lajas.

On the way, we saw a dead shark and Niña bombarded me with questions. Some I knew the answers to, most I didn't, many I never would have even thought to ask. For example she wondered if it was a baby shark or just a small shark. I realized that my midwestern denial had just assumed it was a small shark. Obviously nothing big enough to have pushed that out of its vagina could possibly be lurking in these waters…Wait, do sharks even give birth? I asked Niña, she didn't know either. After the river, when we returned to Casa Playa we Googled it. The answer is that some species of shark do give birth, and some don't.

She was hungry and wanted to go home, so she skipped towards the trees. She halted only for a moment, pointing to the hula hoop, discarded on a nearby stump, *"I will leave it here so you can practice."*

I settled into the hammock and thought about my morning and how much I had learned from Niña. As an adult, it is so easy to forget to look at the world with fresh eyes, to try new things, to ask more interesting questions. Children can remind us to do those things. I wanted to see the looks of awe and joy that I saw on Niña's face on the face of my own child. I wanted to be a parent. But was I really ready for all that responsibility? In most ways I was still a child myself.

Last summer, I stopped taking The Pill, not because I wanted to have a baby, but because I stumbled upon an article that suggested vegan diets are particularly dangerous for women taking it. Apparently, it leaves us deficient in some nutrients, including but not limited to, B-vitamins. This wasn't even Vegan Conspiracy Theory stuff, this was academically published information. What?

I started taking The Pill at the age of 13. Not because I was sexually active, but because a doctor attributed my bipolar mood swings to PMS and my anemia to a heavy flow during my period. He figured birth control should, well, "control" both of those things. So before I could even drive, every morning, as soon as I woke up, I took The Pill. Everything did even out, just as the doctor had predicted. Years passed without my questioning its use, and eventually I wanted to use it for other purposes.

From there on out, it was tucked in every suitcase and in a drawer at every apartment and house I ever lived in. I went annually for physical exams, and even changed doctors as I changed geographical locations. No one ever mentioned B-vitamins to me.

I remember the rage that boiled up from a depth inside me. I had always thought birth control had given me the right to make decisions for my body. How did I not know this information after taking it for so long? For over a year I had been ridding my self of all processed foods and negative vibes, conscious of everything I put in and got out of my body. Yet every day, without question, I swallowed a white or blue pill that, apparently, had a whole list of side effects.

Immediately, I told Jon I wanted to stop taking The Pill, delving into my rationale and reasoning, never stopping to take a breath. He listened patiently and when I finished he exhaled slowly, *"We still get to have sex, right?"*

Of course. But birth control would now be his responsibility. He seemed up for the challenge, but I was nervous. I had been on The Pill since puberty. I had no idea what to expect from my cycle or my mood without it...

That all happened a few months before we arrived in Costa Rica, and so far the worst has been that my periods are super irregular. Unable to put my period on the calendar when I open a new pack of pills, I actually have to listen for the rhythms of my body, and so far, it sounds like an untuned and disjointed calliope.

I never really thought about it before. Every month my body prepares to have a baby. Then when I don't get pregnant, it strikes the set, and starts preparing for the next one. Whether or not "I" want to have a baby, biologically, my body is going through the motions. Every month.

How was I not more aware of this part of myself? How could I bring a child into this world when I was just now starting to concept my own role in the proliferation of our species? I was distracted by the sounds of construction, and flicked my eyes to the clock in the corner of the iPad. I had been staring at a screen for way too long. I wandered back to Casa Playa in search of food.

The next morning, we hitched a ride with Neighbor to the market, and as we drove I noticed a rotten smell. When I mentioned it, she explained that it was just the Red Tide: a seasonal accumulation of plankton. For a few weeks, the organisms occur in such massive quantities that the sea appears stained. Neighbor continued, explaining that some fish die after ingesting the creatures, hence the rotten smell. She admitted that the sea creatures weren't particularly harmful to humans, but she still recommended to avoid swimming in it, and not to eat any shellfish for a few weeks because they absorb the plankton in high enough quantities to definitely cause gastrointestinal distress in humans. I thanked her for the local knowledge, and she threw a distracted *"Pura Vida"* over her shoulder as she checked her blindspots and turned into town.

After we got our veggies, Neighbor offered to drive us home again, but explained that she had to stop by the B&B because Red Van needed gas. Hanging with Neighbor sounded easier than hitchhiking home, so we agreed.

When we arrived we found out that the B&B was also out of gas, so a trip to Cobano was in order. We could go collectively, or send Bro-vio on the mission and wait here at the B&B. Really, all we wanted was to go home, but now that meant hitchhiking down the hill *and* to Cabuya, so really our only option was to go or not to go to

Cobano. Deciding we would rather not, we collapsed onto a couch that we had previously occupied at Karaoke Night.

We sat engulfed in a huffy silence, hungry and bored. Frequently, we were interrupted by Niña who was trying to convince us to play hide-and-seek. Jon refused, but I finally consented, hiding and searching in turn. When we ran out of good hiding spots, Niña started adding complicated rules to the game, and I grew exhausted, eventually wielding some sort of "grown-up" veto and convincing her to instead check out the board games.

We plowed through a few rounds of *Candy Land*, then *Dominos*, then we both suffered through the tantrum when the *Dominos* had to be cleaned up. Afterwards we settled on a "quiet" version of freeze dance, where we rapped our nails on the floor to manipulate one another's movement.

I looked over to Jon, eyes calmly focused on a book he had found, he was absently twisting his beard between the tips of his fingers. I felt a pang of jealousy. I wanted to be reading, thinking, learning. I had wanted to go to the market and work today. Instead, I am running out of energy, and wishing I was playing with my own nieces. Did I want to have a baby? A baby would grow into a child who would need nurturing and discipline. I was still living the dream of being a writer who lives in the jungle. If I am not ready to wrap my creativity up in board games, doesn't that mean I am not ready?

Niña noticed my sour mood and seemed determined to pull my triggers. At some point, my patience ran out, and I told her I didn't want to play anymore. I returned to the couch and slouched on it, covering my eyes with my elbow. We waited and waited, my hunger negatively impacting my mood. I sat up, attempting to read over Jon's shoulder, hoping my scowl would be interpreted as concentration.

It was early evening before Red Van returned, and as Neighbor drove us home she complained that because of the late hour she would have to turn right back around to teach her yoga class that night. I felt guilty that the day had been stressful for everyone and we rode in silence, looking out over the dull waves, our collective breath shallow in the presence of the odorous Red Tide.

The next few days felt like Winter. We were confined to the indoors because of the literally stinky weather (the stench of dead fish was oppressive, and the waters were murky, ruining a perfectly good view). I wrote from the patio table and tried to let my creativity flow despite missing the monotonous swing of the hammock.

I read up on Red Tides, and learned that they are getting worse, each year the migration starting earlier, lasting longer, and causing more damage. February was an alarmingly early onset. I guess phytoplankton are also pursuing perpetual growth at the expense of the environment around them, and we humans are helping them do that by acidifying the oceans.

Just as my brain was wrapping around the connections, I was interrupted by a whine from Marley, who had come running up to Casa Playa, with a gruesome cut on his leg. The cut was clean, but deep, the blood flowing freely onto the sand and patio tiles. I felt panicky and irresponsible. Did I want to have a baby? How would I feel if I were covered in his blood?

I whistled for Jon and we were able to staunch the current. Upon inspection the cut appeared to be the consequence of a run in with a barbed wire fence rather than another animal, and that was a relief. Still, the prospect of keeping the open wound disinfected here at Casa Playa was daunting. We needed a plan...

Our best brainstorm was to rent an ATV in Montezuma that we could take to Cobano. There, we could visit the Animal Co-op to buy first aid materials and more flea powder, which we recently found out was the mystery liquid Granjero was using to treat the property. We could take advantage of our transportation to run other errands. For example, el banco. We needed to pay Granjero a lump sum, and get cash for our upcoming trip to Nicaragua, but we were hassled by ATM limits and fees in Montezuma. We could also stop at the Mega Super to stock up on rice and liquor, and maybe even pick up a pregnancy test at the farmacia. Then, back at Casa Playa, once Marley was treated and bandaged, we could lock him in the recently cleaned kitchen to get some rest. We could take the ATV on an adventure across the peninsula, to finally spend some quality time in Mal Pais. Win-Win-Win.

The next morning, I awoke early and sat on the bed in the closet room, staring at my suitcase, my pre-coffee frown more defined than usual. What was I even supposed to wear on this ATV ride? Keeping comfortable and cool in the equatorial sun while being equipped for a trip to the store, the beach, and a dinner date wasn't exactly an easy task, especially since every once and a while an ominously gray cloud would grumble, twist, and hiss a threat to rain.

It *would* rain on adventure day I thought to myself, but then I shook the depression from between my ears. The clouds always threaten and it never rains, and if it does, so what? Pura Vida. We needed to treat Marley's cut, we need to get rid of The Fleas, so I needed to get up, get dressed, and get over it. I put on my bikini, covered it with a stretchy pair of yoga shorts, then threw a bright yellow cover up over the black ensemble. I knotted my hair on top of my head, clipping and pinning it in place, hoping it would retain its shape with as little tangling as possible. I lathered up with sunscreen and bug spray, then threw a cardigan in the backpack, just in case it did rain.

Breakfasted, we walked towards Montezuma, periodically turning around to look for potential hitchhiking vehicles. We laughed when we saw Luna, who had snuck under the gate, and was scurrying to catch up to us. The three of us strolled, lost in our thoughts, until a pick-up bounced down the road and we hopped in the flat bed. I crouched across from Jon, wedged between the tailgate and a baby stroller, and watched as the world slipped away. Luna sprinted behind us loyally, but was left in the dust as the truck swerved through the trees.

At the ATV kiosk in Montezuma Centro, it was $60 to rent the ATV for six hours, which would give us until 7:00P.M.. We asked if there was any way could have the vehicle until 8:00P.M. and the attendant not only agreed, but gave it to us for $55, since he had seen us around town before. He asked for a credit card and a passport, but no driver's license.

He gave us keys and helmets, and explained that we could fill up with gas in either Cobano or Santa Teresa, or return it with an empty tank and pay an extra $10. With that, he gave Jon a very brief tutorial about how to drive the thing. I stared at the warning label that read "NEVER RIDE AS A PASSENGER", accompanied by a drawing of a stick figure flying off the moving vehicle and landing on its bulbous head. Hmm.

The attendant handed us a couple of nets for our grocery trip then walked briskly back to his kiosk with a smile and a wave. We put on our helmets and climbed aboard the ATV. I donned the backpack, taking its usual place by latching myself tightly onto Jon's torso. He squeezed the handle bars and we lurched forward, in the direction of Cobano.

The Road to Cobano begins with a rare slice of concrete that lies in a dizzying spiral around a steep hill. Our progress up this slope was slow and choppy, the quad jumping and leaning as Jon practiced shifting gears while navigating the climbing loops, a challenging beginners attempt. Once over the peak, the terrain was much calmer, but the concrete was gone, replaced with the dusty (sometimes recently molassesed) road we have grown so accustomed to. The quad seemed more at home rattling over the bumpy gravel, and Jon's driving improved too, the gear shifts becoming more transparent with each attempt.

Once in Cobano we went to el banco, and detoured into a butcher shop so we could bring a treat home to Marley, who was cooped-up and miserable. Jon ordered four bones and at the sound of the saw, I turned on my heel and walked out, averting my eyes from the displays of red flesh behind the glass counters. Bones cut and stored safely in the backpack, we started for the Animal Co-op, detouring once again, this time into a delicious smelling bakery.

Afterwards, I sat on the quad with the pet stuff and fiddled with the fit of my helmet, while Jon ran into the Mega Super. He soon returned, filled the backpack with a bottle of wine, a bottle of tequila, and two six-packs of beer, then secured a big bag of rice on top of the big bag of cat food on the front of the quad. We climbed back on our vehicle, and I had to sit astride the big bag of dog food attached to the rear and cling to Jon, who revved the engine and headed for home.

The second drive was significantly more fun than the first, although speeding down the concrete, coiling hill carrying so much extra weight was pretty frightening. When we parked near our gate we unloaded our heavy groceries and popped open a beer, celebrating a success-ful trip to Cobano. As soon as I opened the drink I real-ized I had forgotten to buy a pregnancy test. Pura Vida.

We cleaned Marley's wound again, applied the cream, and were about to give him one of the bones when we heard Granjero's familiar *"Hola!"* from the vicinity of the ATV. He wanted to treat the house for pulgas and we proudly produced our recently purchased package of pulga powder. He was genuinely grateful for the poison and used his giddy mood to make a joke about how I looked like a banana. Then he headed to the bodega with a frantic wave.

We gave Marley his bone and locked him in the kitchen. We also gave a bone to Luna, who flopped happily in the sand and went to town. Jon put the quad in reverse, inching out the way we had come in, and I closed the gate before hopping back on.

This time we turned left, zoomed deeper into Cabuya, passed La Hacienda, The Only Bar, The Café, The Cabina, and straight up the hill that we had once traversed on foot. The quad took on the challenge with little effort and we sped through the pendular jungle hills, appreciating the height of the trees and the dips of the valleys, exhilarated by the speed and the scenery.

Soon, the clinking of our helmets had become a toast to all of the beauty around us. Occasionally, other quads would pass us, their occupants helmet-less, donning sunglasses and face masks to squelch the dust. We waved, flashed smiles, and thought aloud about how we must look like silly tourists, and then about how much we didn't care. Why not be on the safe side? I imagined us as two adorable little astronauts exploring planet Earth. We pointed out the obstacles along our journey that had forced us to question turning back on our previous attempt, and when we finally pulled into civilization, and turned away from the Fish Market, we shook our helmets, unable to believe we had hiked that crazy road.

We continued towards Mal Pais Centro, making a quick u-turn when we passed a sign for the Papaya Lounge, a bar/restaurant we wanted to check out for the time my parents come to visit. We parked near some other ATVs, hooked our helmets over our elbows, and started up some stairs.

When we reached the landing, we turned 90° to see another long, arduous flight, ascending through the foliage. This second flight was followed by a third, and a fourth, each new set trickily occluded from view by sharp turns and leafy appendages. We eventually lost count, but continued up, panting, calves burning. I was so glad we had done this before bringing my middle-aged parents along.

It was worth the climb. At the top we stood amongst the trees at the edge of a cliff, looking down on the valley below. It was a patchwork of greenery and hidden homes billowing into a flat expanse of infinite blue ocean. The waves curled high compared to the ones on the gulf, and I laughed as I saw myself, a midwesterner that had thought I'd moved to the ocean, only to realize months later it was only an estuary.

The restaurant was posh, all surfaces shiny and decorated, tables set around an ornate bar that was backed by a giant painting. We strolled over to an outdoor lounge of sorts, where cushioned wicker couches huddled around tiny tabletops. We chose one and sat down, ordering an expensive blackberry daiquiri, a reasonably priced beer, and a very cheap appetizer. This would be our first sunset over the *real* ocean, and we both kind of wished to see it here, sitting so high above the sea, but we still had so much exploring we wanted to do before the sun went down...

We decided to come back here with my parents for the exact purpose of watching the sunset, knowing they could be pried up the stairs by the promise of delicious daiquiris. We tumbled, me a little tipsily, down the mountain of stairs and hopped back on to our little cruiser. Jon was great at driving now, and revved the engine, spinning smoothly out of our parking spot, and back onto the main road.

We motored through Mal Pais and into Santa Teresa; the strip taking on a funkier vibe as we continued north. Unlike the seemingly untouched road between Montezuma and Cabuya, this dusty path was lined with a fully functioning city, and therefore occluded with a respective traffic. The road was wide and full of people, young surfers, parents, and entrepreneurs, all walking, dogs at their ankles, mouths wrapped in scarves of all fashions to protect their lungs from the haze of dust that hung in the air.

When we noticed the sky growing paler, we searched for a place to watch the sunset. A driveway opened up and Jon spun in, parking the quad near a tree. We dismounted and looked out at the twilight, jaws hanging: we were standing on a sandy beach, completely secluded but for the two of us. The sea's silver waves were purring and curling dramatically in the dusk, no evidence at all of the Red Tide in her waters. The entire scene was framed by enormous rock formations: solid stones, baking in the heat, jagged silhouettes against a pink and yellow sky. From one granite tower grew a lonely tree that jutted out parallel to the ocean, reaching bravely for the sinking, orange sun.

The sun itself glowed a neon shade of amber and seemed to be conducting the atmosphere into frenzied colorful motion. The sea and the sky were determined to outdo one another, showing off to prove who could reflect the sun's light more boldly. A few clouds, patches of streaky vapor, shadowed the brilliant shades into deeper, more somber hues and we watched as the sphere sank lower, hovering over the horizon, shimmering with its own radiance. I laughed. I laughed until I cried at Mother Nature's ability to repeatedly blow my mind.

Just when I thought I had seen enough to understand her beauty, and known enough to understand her power, she ups the ante with an effortless wink, reminding me that anything is possible and that Everything is Moving.

I wondered if she felt ready to be our Mother, or if our race had blindsided her, then eclipsed the Life she had worked billions of years to build. As her spoiled children, do we even notice our role in her situation?

I inhaled the glorious moment and sat my hiccuping, teary-eyed self on a tree skeleton next to Jon, who was snapping photos of the sky's metamorphosis. Together we watched the great ball of fire as we hula-hooped around it on our continuous journey through the cosmos.

In an instant, the last pixel of sunlight vanished from the horizon, and the sky softened in the afterglow until everything around us had faded into shadow. It was too cloudy to see any stars, so we donned our space helmets and settled back onto our quad, hungry, wondering what time it was. Jon flipped on the headlight and started the quad in reverse, reentering the bustling street, this time heading south.

Speeding through the sleepy city, arms wrapped tight around the love of my life, chin resting on his strong shoulder, our surroundings only vaguely illuminated by the glow of the headlight, was impossibly romantic. I felt free yet fundamentally attached, safe yet closer than ever to danger, calm yet screaming with delight. *"You're looking for the Thai place, right?"* Jon yelled over the roar of the engine. I gulped, not wanting to admit my distraction but unable to lie, *"I don't think we passed it!"*, I shouted, but it sounded like a question even to my ears.

Luckily, I was right, we hadn't passed it. Soon I pointed to a sign carved with a fat, happy Buddha, proud to have succeeded in my navigation task. Jon parked the quad, again we hooked our helmets over our elbows, and entered a cool zen garden, all stones and dark wood, spotlights unveiling colorful depictions of many-limbed animal gods. We sat at the bar, found out it was 6:45P.M., and ordered Pad Thai, Fried Rice, and a Papaya Salad. We also got a bebida de frutas for an appetizer, the frosty drink soothing our dusty lips and throats. The food was amazing and we ate savagely, amazed at the voracious appetite we had worked up riding around on a quad appreciating Mother Nature all day. Full and sleepy, we paid as soon as we finished, and climbed aboard the ATV for the final time.

We filled the gas tank in Cobano and pulled into the kiosk in Montezuma at 8:03P.M. We turned in our key, helmets, and grocery nets, and thanked the attendant for the fun adventure. We walked away into the night, legs wobbling, evidently unaccustomed to working after a full day of not being our main mode of transportation.

We stood under a streetlight, swaying sleepily, waiting for a car to pass. Finally a van pulled over and waved us in, chauffeuring us home in a sleepy silence.

A few days later, I finally got my period. Part of me was relieved, but part of me was disappointed. Did I want to have a baby?

I thought back on the intense feelings that had surrounded the previous week: the dredged up anger about the birth control pill, the frustration of being stuck at the B&B, the anxiety I felt when Marley cut his leg, my inability to get dressed in the morning, even the tears of joy I had shed at the beach in Santa Teresa… all that emotional upheaval, was it even real?

I felt defeated knowing I had been PMSing. Yes, normally I *can* cope more gracefully, but when my estrogen and progesterone have just dropped out, and the cleaning crew of my microbiome is faced with the daunting task of clearing out fifty-seven days worth of nesting material, I suppose I may be feeling a bit sensitive…

On Valentine's Day, The Neighbors wanted to go out and wondered if we didn't mind babysitting. We didn't, and when the sun went down we crossed the trees separating the properties, to find Niña already in her pajamas curled up in a hammock. Jon joked with her while I took in all the vital information for putting her to sleep. We played for awhile, wished upon a star, and brushed our teeth. Niña introduced us to the colorful toothpaste-loving crab, Elvin, that lives in her bathroom sink, and we laughed and spat as he danced happily along the porcelain.

I tucked her in, closed a mosquito net around her, perched on the edge of her bed, and plowed through *A Kitten Named Mittens* twice before she fell asleep. Once her breathing was slow and deep, I was able to sneak out and down the stairs, smiling a wordless affirmation to Jon before we both settled into our books.

It was totally silent but for the sound of the insects, the flipping of our pages, and the ticking of a loud chartreuse clock that hung above Neighbor's patio table. By 9:00P.M. the clock had lulled us both and we felt deliriously tired, heads lolling on our shoulders, laughing at one another's increasingly unfunny jokes. In an attempt to stay awake, we stood and stretched, but our muscles were too tired, so we hugged instead, supporting one another's body weight in a sleepy slow dance. Jon whistled *Dance of the Sugarplum Fairy* (which he would refer to as *The Tetris Song*) and the two of us giggled and swayed until we heard the familiar roar of The Moto. We returned to Casa Playa, trudged straight upstairs and passed out, luckily having already brushed our teeth.

Isn't that what everyone says parenting is like? Sheer exhaustion? But they say its worth it, don't they? Creating a younger version of yourself to take your place in solving the next generations' challenges of being alive?

Did I want to have a baby? I think so. Or maybe, I am simply ovulating.

Nicaragua

IT WAS OUR EIGHTY-SOMETHINGISH DAY in Costa Rica, so in 48 hours, we were required to leave for Nicaragua.

In order to enter Costa Rica on a tourist visa, one must prove that one will be leaving the country again. Our return ticket to Chicago was enough proof to let us into the country, but still, our visa expires after 90 days. To renew the visa, we must leave, and re-enter the country. These border hops are common for expatriates who have relocated here, most using the deadline as an excuse to travel around Central America, or return to their homelands to see their families.

The easiest trip was Nicaragua. It was the closest border and the currency there was notoriously inflated, making travel seriously cheap. The Internet suggested we stay in either surfer haven San Juan del Sur, or historical, colonial Granada. We eventually decided on Granada, missing the vibes of The City. We made a reservation at a hostel downtown that offered $20 massages and an organic restaurant, excited for a romantic get away from the f-animal-y (Granjero and Neighbor had agreed to look after everyone while we were away).

We would travel to Nicaragua by bus. There was an 11:00A.M. Transnica bus which would take us from Barrancas, Costa Rica to Granada, Nicaragua. However, Barrancas was a twenty minute drive from Puntarenas, the ferry port on the other side of the Gulf de Nicoya. Neighbor told us that we could purchase a bus ticket in Cobano that would include the ferry ride to Puntaranas, so all we had to do was catch a 7:00A.M. bus in Cobano...

We woke up ten minutes before our 5:00A.M. alarm and started walking in the dark towards Montezuma where we would catch a bus that left for Cobano at 6:30A.M. Luna followed as we hiked through the misty grayness over familiar stones, and my mind raced: What did I forget to pack? What was the cordoba to colones to dólares conversion rate again?

I like the idea of being nomadic, but traveling is so stressful to me. The "what ifs?" blow my anxiety out of proportion. I *wanted* to go to Nicaragua, but every moment that ticked by where a vehicle didn't pass made my heart pump a little faster. I focused on my breathing. We wound up walking all the way to Montezuma Centro, along the ocean against a most spectacular sunrise, arriving at exactly 6:29A.M. We boarded the bus that immediately pulled away, bouncing through the intersection, and up the spiral, concrete hill.

Once in Cobano, we found our loading dock and waited. We stood alongside working Ticos and Tico-Gringos, and an assortment of travelers, some alone, some in clusters of similar ages, similar languages, or similar ancestors. Onboard, the bus was full, but we squeezed into a little alcove that was reserved for wheelchairs, and propped ourselves against the wall, shoving our heavy bags between our feet. People continued piling on, standing in the aisles, a solid block of bodies from window to window slowly filling up the non-air conditioned vehicle.

The ride was a little over an hour, but felt much longer. Our tired legs wobbled while we attempted to stay upright on the old bus that was lurching up gravelly mountains and around hairpin turns. As my body acclimated, I found I was glad to be squished up against the window instead of standing in the crowded aisles. The view was worth the agony in my quads. The reminder of how far we were from modern civilization was humbling. The countryside was somehow more vibrant than ever. We passed Tambor, and pointed to the tiny airplanes that my parents would soon be arriving on. Finally, we arrived in Paquera.

The bus driver stood up and gave lengthy instructions in Español, I concentrated fully but when he finished the only thing I truly understood was that we were in Paquera. We blindly followed the masses dismounting the bus and collected our yellow tickets for the ferry. We passed an eatery that smelled delicious, but we were reluctant to detour, preferring to remain close to our fellow bus passengers. We followed them straight onto the ferry.

The deck offered rails and benches with beautiful views of The Gulf, and we stood, looking out for a few moments before checking out the interior of the boat. We found a nearby door and entered a large, air conditioned room, reminiscent of an airport boarding lounge: rows of cushioned seats surrounding a glimmering pastry case, the walls lined with televisions, all playing the news.

Currently, all sets showed the stoic face of a female politician who was giving a speech in Español. I couldn't tell from her expression if she was relaying good or bad news, but no one in the room seemed to be paying much attention, so I figured, either way, it was unimportant news. I was amazed at the contrast and the similarity, words I would never actually hear, yet had somehow heard a million times.

After awhile, we exited the room and walked up another flight of stairs to the sun deck: a stadium of plastic chairs filled with people in hats, eating snacks, and chattering in the sun. I was absurdly reminded of a baseball game, and then realized I might be searching for the comforts of home up against so much transitory chaos.

We found a few empty seats, which appeared to be in the shade, and rested our legs while gazing at the town of Paquera, a dock surrounded by a mass of jungly trees, a few brightly colored corners of buildings poking sporadically out of the wilderness. At 9:30A.M., on the dot, the intercom exploded into life and I listened intently to the Español announcement, picking out random words and trying to piece them all together. Thankfully, the message was repeated in English, and I learned there were two rules aboard the ferry: wear a shirt, and don't feed the birds. With that, the ferry chugged forward, the aviators hovering nearby, gliding on our currents, winking at the tourists, daring them to break that second rule.

Not long after, I was officially hungry and wanted to check the pastry case before digging into the cereal reserves we had brought from Casa Playa. We coaxed our legs into taking the journey down the stairs and back into the air conditioning. The vegetariano options were limited but we walked away with two cafés, a piña danish, and a huge slab of cornbread.

We sat at a little table near the snack bar and enjoyed our snack, turning our attention to the TVs which now presented a cooking show en Español. A beautiful woman in a fashionable apron smiled as she poured prepared ingredients into a baking pan, taking the time to position her hand so the label and her manicure showed.

We used our disconnected iPhone as a notebook, writing down our travel costs thus far and reiterating our travel itinerary: Arrive in Puntarenas. Taxi to Barrancas. Transnica to Granada. Taxi to our hostel. We noted the time and stowed the iPhone safely in the backpack, returning to the sun deck to watch Puntarenas approach.

As soon as the ferry stopped, we walked towards the exit, and immediately noticed that seasoned ferry takers had long ago lined up at the gates. They were poised to avoid the crowded decks that were now draining by two single file lines down narrow staircases that led to a chaotic harbor full of taxis and vendors screaming offers in the blistering sun.

The slow descent was excruciating seeing as we were already slightly behind schedule. The chaos of the port was disorienting, but we eventually found a cab and told the driver our destination. When I peeked at the clock, I gasped. We only had twenty minutes to make our bus to

Nicaragua. I asked the driver how long it would take us to get to Barrancas. *"Fifteen minutes"*, he said, *"más o menos."*

Eighteen minutes later, he pulled up to a corner on an urban street where a group of people loitered, evidently waiting for a bus. We paid him and looked around, hoping for a station where we could redeem the tickets we had reserved online. Noticing our lost expressions, a man in a uniform waved us over and asked for our passports. We handed them to him, he checked our name off a printed list, then gave us some immigration forms. My Español was able to get us through the transaction, and I even found out that the bus stops relatively soon for a lunch break. My tummy, having since burned through our sugary breakfast, cheered.

Transnica pulled up and we boarded the sparsely populated shuttle. We walked to the back, grabbed two secluded seats and sighed, we made it. We settled in, pushing our bags under our chairs. I grabbed my book while Jon unraveled his headphones.

The ride, which included lunch and a border crossing, took the rest of the day. When we finally arrived at the hostel I was relieved the receptionist spoke English, my sore brain exhausted after a long day of travel translation.

He handed us a key for a locker, and showed us to the dorm where we had reserved a bed for the night (our private room was not available until the following evening). The dorm was clean and bright and had a queen bed waiting for us, so we relaxed completely and shoved our stuff inside our locker, asking the owner where we could get food. He suggested the hostel's restaurant.

We returned to the lobby, passed the entrance to the dorms, and entered the atrium: a café/lounge/garden in the middle of the hostel, under a large opening in the roof that was currently exposing the night sky. We sat, waiting for our dinner, and saw a guy who was wearing a Chicago Cubs teeshirt. We struck up conversation with him, finding out that he was from Jamaica, but grew up listening to the baseball on the radio. Our chat was overheard by a middle aged acupuncturist who also grew up in Chicago, but now lives in California, and has been scuba diving for a week here in Nicaragua.

Our dinner was cheap, as promised, but it was also delicious, contrary to what we had heard in Costa Rica about Nicaraguan food. Afterwards, we both took a well-deserved shower before hopping into bed with our books, excited to fall asleep. We officially felt old, curled up in the hostel dorm, dozing off, while everyone around us was getting dolled up to hit the town. We fell asleep, but not deeply, our nostrils stuffed with various colognes, ears full of unfamiliar city sounds on the other side of the wall. We awoke early and awkwardly, unable to snuggle in our morning tradition surrounded by so many other sleepers. We got up and changed quietly, tiptoeing out of the room and onto the streets of Granada, familiarizing ourselves with the surroundings. We hunted for a cup of café in the sleepy streets, but most businesses were still closed, and the vendors at the street market were just starting to pile goods onto their kiosks.

We picked up a bag of freshly chopped fruit for ten cordobas ($0.04), then headed to La Caldaza: the cobblestone street lined with bars, restaurants, and shops that was considered "downtown" Granada. Everything was closed, but advertised happy hours that we planned to attend later.

We found a cup of café and a croissant, and sat outside, enjoying our breakfast. It was so strange to be in The City. The bustle of activity, and the scent of the overworked sewage system, lay in such stark contrast to our last few months in Cabuya, a town where the locals are outnumbered by the tourists, and the tourists are outnumbered by the dogs. There were a few stray dogs here too, skinnier and rougher, hunting for their breakfasts in littered curbs.

Back at the hostel, I inquired about a massage since my low back was screaming after a full day on bouncing buses. When the time came for my appointment, I was informed that the lady who usually does the massage was not available, but that the "*blind masseuse*" was on his way. Blind? Yep, he can't see. Okay. Interesting.

Moments later in the atrium, a hotel employee showed me to a curtain and we both went inside. There, a large man waited for us, sunglasses on, facing our general direction. The employee and the masseuse spoke only Español but I gathered that I was to take off my clothes and lay down. The employee left, and as I disrobed a few feet from the man, I had a gut wrenching feeling that he wasn't blind, that it was just a sales tactic, and that right now he was watching me undress.

I shook it off, I wanted a massage right? If he was lying, that was his problem, not mine. I climbed on the bed, face down, nervous for the first time in my life about a massage.

I didn't have the Español to explain the chronic tension in my right hip, or that as a fitness professional I prefer a more aggressive technique to an aromatic lotion application. So, I simply inhaled deeply, exhaled slowly, and waited.

Over the next hour, I came to the somewhat hysterical conclusion that the best massage I will ever have was from a blind man in a hostel in Nicaragua. The idea that his hands had acquired an extra sense to make up for his lack of sight had to be true, because he was able to feel the chronic tension in my right hip, and worked on it, twice as long as he worked on the left, until it gave in to his persuasion. He spent time on my calves, a place I would never have asked for, but obviously desperately needed, and he used techniques, like the rapid karate chop thing, that I have hated in the past, but understood finally.

I felt relaxed, but also inspired by his knowledge of anatomy. He counted vertebrae to find muscles' insertion points, using a light touch to find the anatomical landmark before delving expertly into the belly of the muscle. I realized he could see a leg, whether or not he could see my leg. I let my mind wander, wondering what this man thought of me. He probably guessed I was from the States by my accent, and an athlete by the feel of my build, but he didn't know the color of my skin, my hair, my eyes. He didn't know if my jewelry was expensive, or if I sported any tattoos. I wished for a moment that I couldn't see people, and rather had to use other senses to learn about them, how would that change my interactions? How would it change the way others felt about me?

When he finished, I slid off the table, my bones unsupported by the soup that was now my musculature. I tried to tell him that he had a gift, but I might have told him that he had a ruler. Either way, he smiled and thanked me as I placed a generous tip, a bill of an amount he couldn't tell, into the palm of his hand.

Relaxed and hungry, Jon and I hit the streets again, heading back to La Caldaza.

Granada was much busier now, the cobblestones packed with horse drawn carriages winding through vendors and shoppers, the outdoor tables full of people eating, drinking, and laughing. Our noses were immediately drawn to a Mexican restaurant, but we continued down the strip to compare options.

Along the way, we passed a free art gallery and cheered, loving anything creative and free. We walked through an exhibit of beautiful sketches, their titles in Español and their interpretation therefore unlimited. We both admitted that we did miss the kind of culture that one only finds in The City. We wondered if our hearts felt more drawn to the seclusion or to the bustle. The tiny gallery of sketches opened up into a large outdoor atrium (obviously a cornerstone of architecture here in Granada), rows of trees surrounded by tiny rooms, reminiscent of an outdoor mall, each "store" housing a different artist's paintings.

We wandered through, floored by the talent, and feeling solidarity with the other artists of the world. Our favorite was a giant rendition of John Lennon's face, suspended above an ocean sunset, a closer look at his scraggly beard showed palm trees growing from his chin and towards the sun and water. We returned to the Mexican place for happy hour, and ordered a cerveza and a margarita, totally comfortable in our knowledge of Español when reading a menu.

Full, we went to a super to buy some rum, realizing that we had started drinking early and were now forced to keep up if we didn't want an early evening migraine. Plus, Flor de Caña was made here in Nicaragua and was cheaper than in Costa Rica, so we could stock up on a few bottles for my parent's visit. When we returned our private room was ready, so we grabbed our bags from our locker and moved in. We poured a glass of rum and flipped on the TV in the corner of the room, watching the second half of *Harry Potter and The Chamber of Secrets*, overdubbed in Español.

Deciding to be social again, we returned to the atrium to make some friends. Jon recognized a tall man from Canada who he had met in line at the super and they started chatting. Our friend from Jamaica introduced us to a lady he had recently met, who was traveling from Israel. The five of us eventually decided we were all hungry, so we hit the streets as a group, looking for something delicious. When we finally headed home, we were drunk and shocked to find it was 11:00P.M. We stumbled into our private room and snoozed.

We woke up on Sunday and had breakfast at the hostel before attempting to buy a Transnica ticket that would bring us back to Costa Rica. We called a few times, but had no luck, so we finally decided just to show up at the station in Granada in the morning, hopeful they would have a seat for us. After that, we went to explore the hostel and ran into Israel. As we chatted, we found common ground in our love for Yoga, and she wondered if I would teach her a quick Pilates class. I readily agreed, so we found a private corner in the atrium, and got to work.

When we finished, we got wrapped up in a very emotional conversation in which she talked about her current recovery from an eating disorder. I was shocked that she was telling me all this, I was a stranger after all, but maybe it was easier that way, to say something to someone who doesn't really know you. So for the first time in my life, I verbally admitted to my eating disorder…

I was always thin, so I never worried too much, until about the age of twelve when ballet really fueled my obsession with weight. I spent my days with bony girls who would cut their M&Ms in half and teachers who explained that I was thin, just not dancer thin. Everyone's advice was to start drinking a lot of water before I ate, so that hopefully, I wouldn't eat as much. I took these tips to heart and always tried very hard to get skinnier.

However, as a product of my culture, many of my meals were fast food, or whatever could be found in convenient stores. My studio was situated next to a Little Caesars, and once a week at Ballet Camp, the ballerinas would all split a pizza, cutting the nasty, greasy slices into quarters so that we wouldn't get fat.

As I got older, I gave up ever trying to be as thin as the girls around me. I actually liked my body, and if anything I wanted my boobs to be bigger instead of anything else getting smaller. I stopped obsessing as much and adapted to The Western Diet without so much stress and self-hate.

Then I went to college, and stopped dancing. My appetite seemed to think that I was still burning thousands of calories a day, but the truth was I was sitting around a lot, reading. I would hit the dining hall and get what I considered a healthy meal: vegetable stir-fry soaked in oil, with a sugary iced-tea, and a cookie. Not so bad right? It wasn't a bacon cheeseburger with fries and a Coke, which was also an option at the dining hall. I picked up going to the gym as well as walking the long way to all my classes. I started substituting meals with Nutrigrain bars and Jamba Juices. Still, I didn't look like the images of beauty all around me...

Then, Jon joined the band. Now I didn't just have to feel confident walking around on campus, but I was actually going to MTV's VMAs, and had to look good next to Paris Hilton. Are you kidding me? I amped up the workouts and started a tradition of "juice fasts" that my sorority sisters teased me mercilessly for. Basically, I would refuse to eat anything but smoothies for days to slim down before visits to Jon's tour.

Then it got worse. I would be hungry and frustrated and my desire for food would reach the point of distraction, so I would binge on everything I could find in my apartment, reveling in the tastes and textures, and then rush to the bathroom, put two fingers down my throat, and remove the calories from my body before they had time to stick to my tummy. The first few times it was disgusting and emotional, but then it became normal. Part of my meal time routine. Unfortunately, I didn't get any skinnier.

Luckily, when I started Pilates, I was able to exercise my body without exhausting it, feeling sexy and confident even if I wasn't as skinny as I wanted to be. I started to feel good about my body again, even though I still wanted bigger boobs. I stopped bingeing and purging in the literal sense, but still continued to take down sweets and deep dish pizzas with ferocity only to burn them off later with two hours on the Reformer.

It was my outrage towards processed foods that actually cured my eating disorder. Wondering what my food was and where it came from, I gained a new respect for eating, and kicked my addiction to the embellished food stuffs that had haunted me for years.

The minute I decided to become healthy, I was instantaneously more beautiful in my own body then I had ever been before. Rather than an enemy to eliminate, my body became a friend to support. I hoped MindBody awareness would offer a similar path of healing for Israel, a beautiful woman sitting across from me, wiping tears on her sweater, trying to escape a prison of unattainable expectations.

Israel and Jamaica had to leave, the hostel was full for the night, so they were off to another one. As we hugged I thought about how far Israel and I had to travel to be here together, supporting each other through our abstracted mirror images. When they were gone, I missed them, even though I barely knew them.

We ate at the hostel again, this time with Canada, the tall guy, who explained that if we didn't catch our bus and were stuck in Nicaragua tomorrow, we should check out his friend's hostel in San Juan del Sur. We nodded enthusiastically, but hoped to be home, then we retreated to our private room to watch *The Bodyguard* in Español. It was much more difficult to follow than *Harry Potter* had been, since neither of us had seen it before.

First thing in the morning, we found out that we couldn't catch a Transnica bus to Costa Rica that day, so we took Canada's suggestion and hopped on a bus to San Juan del Sur instead. When we arrived, we ate lunch and hung out at the beach before walking up a hill to find the hostel. There, we sunk into the hammocks on the deck, taking in the beautiful view of the town and the bay tucked between its limbs. After awhile, we met a German world traveller who hates American airports and loves to drink beer in the afternoon. We soon found our conversation teetering on whether gravity exists, or if it is simply a figment of the limited human imagination. Then, he impressed us with a vision of the world that proved we are all sound waves, and he and Jon sat huddled, brains close together, working on the theory until they were interrupted by German's travel companions, one another German, the other from Idaho.

They were three men, ambiguous in their middle age, who had been lifelong friends and had decided to meet, after about ten years of absence, here in Nicaragua. They teased German #1 for entrapping us with his crazy con-

versation, but we assured them that we loved crazy con-
versations, so they settled into the hammocks to join us.
The beers went down along with the sun and we had
many breakthroughs. They challenged our theories, forcing us to sharpen them, and I felt glad for the stimula-
tion. Eventually German #2 got hungry enough to convince the five of us to spill down the hill and onto the
dark streets of San Juan del Sur.

They wanted to go to a place they kept calling *"Free
Toña"*, a barbecue joint where each meal comes with a
free beer (Toña is a beer brewed and bottled in Nicaragua). As sort-of-vegetarianos we didn't want to get
barbecue, even with the promise of free beer, so we
waved goodbye and headed for a hole in the wall taco
shop we had seen earlier in the day. A crowd of people
stood outside, eating delicious smelling creations from
styrofoam plates. I ordered two fish tacos and Jon got a
veggie burrito, and we waited and watched as the cook
prepared them. We squeezed chipotle and picante sauce
over our tortillas, and after the first yummy bite, I immediately ordered two more. The dinner was delicious and
we topped it off with a scoop of ice cream, enjoying what
would hopefully be our last date night in Nicaragua.

When we got back to the hostel, our friends were still
at Free Toña, but a few other surfer dudes, all wavy hair
and sleeveless shirts, were gathered in the common area,
talking about traveling, and drinking not-free Toñas. We
sat silently in the hammocks listening to their laughter,
intertwined with the city sounds, intertwined with the
sounds of the insects, until we drug ourselves to bed. We

had a long day of traveling that started very early in the morning.

The dogs were relentless through the night, screaming over one another, keeping us awake, reminding us of our first night at Casa Playa. When our alarm went off at 5:00A.M., the buzzing sounded like a soft and soothing lullaby compared to the squawking of the roosters.

We shook the sleep out of our heads and grabbed our bags, heading into the crisp predawn air, and into the center of town. We hopped in a taxi to the Transnica bus stop, and were able to purchase two tickets. When we boarded, the comfy seats were packed, and we walked the entirety of the aisle, squeezing our bags close to our chests, but still bumping into sleepy looking Nicas, as we took the very last seats on the bus. We crossed the border, rode the ferry, and eventually found ourselves in Paquera, boarding a bus to Cobano.

Waiting for the bus to Montezuma, Jon ran into someone he recognized from Open Mic and when their conversation turned to guitar strings, the comrade pulled a set out of his backpack, selling them to Jon right then and there. We disembarked in Montezuma and I ordered two casados while Jon went to The Super. As soon as the food was ready, Jon came back, forearms bulging under the weight of four heavy bags. We started for home, our over-packed bodies struggling to hold out our thumbs.

Three Ticos in a pickup truck stopped and waved for us to hop in, they weren't going all the way to Cabuya but could get us most of the way there. We jumped in, smiling into the wind, anxious to see Marley. The truck pulled over, still far from home, and the English-speaking driver explained that they were stopping here to look for a tree. Jon asked, Madera Negra? And the guy nodded, frowning at his good guess. *"We have one in our yard if you take us home"*, Jon suggested, and the Ticos glanced at each other suspiciously, wondering if these two gringos could possibly know what they were talking about. They shrugged and took us the rest of the way to Casa Playa.

It was dark in the shade of the palms. We were chaotically greeted by all the dogs and Niña, and simultaneously reprimanded by Neighbor for bringing strange Ticos onto our property. After they cut a few branches from the tree at the edge of the property they rolled up a fat joint of sticky green weed. As we coveted the beautiful flower (a stark contrast to the brown brick we have been smoking), the English speaker admitted he had grown it himself. Jon got his number in case we ever needed more greenery, and the guy agreed, introducing himself as Jonathan. The two boys bonded over their common nomenclature, and we inhaled the smoke and the smell of the sea, glad, at last, to be home.

La Familia

IT IS NOW MARCH 4TH, Mom's birthday, and ten years to the day since Jon drew the sharpie ring on my finger.

Last year, March 4th was the night before our wedding. Mom was throwing a birthday party for herself at the hotel bar, and it was epic, of course, especially considering that her East Coast family and her local crew were both able to attend the bash. It did end considerably early though. Around 11:00P.M. she boasted, *"the only thing more important than birthday parties is mother-of-the-bride beauty sleep"*, and left her own celebration. This year, Jon and I are staring at each other over a casado and two mugs of Flor de Caña. Mom and Dad are going to be here. At Casa Playa. In ten days.

If you have read this far, you have hopefully noticed the transformational journey that brought me to this particular place. To articulate how I've been feeling, what I've been thinking, to my parents, the people who knew the "old" me best, is, I don't know, daunting and confusing.

For example, one of my parent's favorite things to do is to go out and eat at nice restaurants. They like to meet friends for cocktails and appetizers at kitschy spots. As far as I am aware, they have never cooked a meal on a Friday night. They do cook on other nights, though. Dad delves into gourmet preparations for their at-home meals, and Mom has a four-course holiday dinner down to a science.

Jon and I eat a very simply, usually vegetarian, and we rarely go out to eat. If we do, it is usually to the cheapest place that offers the simplest, vegetarian options. We etched into our budget a week of touring the eateries that will most please our elders, excited to bridge this gap between our cultures. We also budgeted a week of taking taxis, since I doubted my parents wanted to walk twenty minutes to The Café, or hitchhike to Montezuma, or brave an ATV ride only to be faced with the stairs leading to the Papaya Lounge.

Another one of my ancestors favorite activities is watching TV. At Casa Playa, we have no TV, and more importantly, no couch. Once and awhile, we watch documentaries, or a favorite drama we have downloaded onto the laptop, but even then, we sit on uncomfortable plastic chairs that tempt us to move after an hour or so. We only have two of those chairs.

I hope the withdrawal from their favorite activities paired with the exhaustion of Life in the jungle doesn't put a damper on their vacation. Either way, they had already purchased their tickets, and Casa Playa was what it was, so we finished our rum, cleaned the kitchen, and went to bed.

The morning of March 5th dawned muggy and we woke up early, celebrating our one-year wedding anniversary.

Last year, the morning of March 5th had dawned snowy, and we slept late. We kept things simple: short engagement, no church, threw the whole thing in a hotel near the airport, no formal bridal party, pasta bar instead of fancy dinner, Jon made the playlist instead of hiring a DJ, etc. All I wanted was to be around family, and the friends that have become my family, wear an awesome dress, and solidify an already legendary commitment to the cutest boy I had ever met.

We wrote our own vows. One of Mom's judge buddies married us, he said a few things about for better and worse, and even held my bouquet as I placed a thing around Jon's finger and he placed a thing around mine. We were officially "The Walkers", and we kissed, surrounded by thundering applause.

We greeted and snapped photos with everyone, ate a delicious meal, and danced the night away. We danced alone, with our parents, with The Walker Brothers and The Sister Chicks, with cousins, Sorority Sisters, Significant Brothers, Bella, old bandmates, fellow Pilates instructors. I danced with an uncle of Jon's that I had never met before, and with two wedding crashers who had shown up at the sound of The Clash. One look at my dress started them apologizing profusely, but I was glad my wedding was fun enough to crash, so I just laughed and boogied alongside them before being whisked and spun across the floor by my new husband. Before I could believe it, the lights were turned on and the music stopped. Midnight had come and gone.

I walked to the lobby glad to see the party was still in full swing. A hotel cash bar had opened in the place of our open one and the bartender poured Jon a triple-shot of whisky on the house, which we took as a sign that our guests had tipped him well. We thanked him and looked around in awe at the sheer amount of people who were standing here in the lobby, showing no signs of leaving anytime soon. Eventually, the bar closed and a sorry-looking hotel employee informed us that we couldn't linger, so I invited everyone back up to our room, forgetting that it was our wedding night, which is traditionally set aside for more intimate purposes.

It was 5:00A.M. when everyone left. I was still in my dress, Jon in his tux. I told him that I had to pee but would need help with my dress and as the words left my mouth I realized I had not gone to the bathroom since I put my dress on almost twelve hours ago. He drunkenly fumbled with the corset tie, cursing at every hidden snap. He gave up many times along the way, before the satin ribbon finally flung from its clutches, and he collapsed backwards onto the bed. I dashed to the washroom, then chugged a few glasses of water. When I returned, Jon was safely under the covers, laughing. I joined him, and he put his iPhone on speaker so I could hear a drunken congratulatory message from a friend who had not been invited to the wedding. The voicemail contained more love than hate and was so funny that we both were reduced to sobbing hiccups, drunk and delirious, as the sun rose on

March 6th. We composed ourselves and kissed, excited to wake up for our first day as The Walkers...

An epic wedding would mean a disastrous morning after, and that is exactly what we had. We both lay, nauseous, nibbling saltine crackers, unable to move and having to request a late check out. We somehow drove home in a snowy slush and collapsed onto Bed Island, maybe tomorrow would be a better day to start our lives as The Walkers.

This year, as the sun rose on March 6th, I swung in a hammock, in an early morning reverie, contemplating just how much has changed in 365 days. I didn't even recognize the couple that got married on that night. The girl with the french manicure and the boy with a boutonnière. They certainly weren't the same couple destined to spend the day wringing fleas out of their sheets and hacking up coconuts with machetes. From the point of view of my hammock, it was so obvious that even our simple wedding could have been so much simpler. It wasn't that I don't look back on it with the fondest of memories, it's just that I didn't need half of the shit that I thought was necessary. I could have worn a simpler dress. I didn't need all the flowers. My cousins took better pictures than my photographer, etc.

Despite my efforts to make it not so, my wedding was still an unconscious product of my culture. It made me think of other paths I have walked unconsciously, riding the waves of the masses around me.

The sounds of construction were so distracting that I wound up back at Casa Playa where Jon and I cloistered ourselves around the kitchen table, elbows clinking as we tried to work, unable to think about anything clearly. We emerged at twilight, when the noise finally died down, and were shocked at what we saw.

Total deforestation of the property to our left. At least fifty trees no longer stood. We gaped at the casa that we hadn't known was there. Around it, the stumps stood proudly. They seemed as stunned by the sudden new scenery as we were, and appeared to be quaking with the effort of showing their blunt, flat wounds to the paling atmosphere. We walked numbly out towards the ocean, past stacks of horizontal trees, vibrant green leaves already wilting without their water supply.

Disgust rose from my stomach and into my throat. Something about this scene was inherently wrong. Those trees took years to reach that height. Machines took only hours to slaughter them, leaving the Earth exposed, suddenly naked without the shade of its oxygen factories and water filtration systems. Silently, Jon solemnly untied the end of one hammock swinging it to face another direction, adverting our attention from the gaping wound to our immediate left.

In what felt like a response to my frustration and fear, the moon appeared. A lonely shadow forming in the pink sky, it's shape full, it's location low, closer than usual to this grieving place on the planet. It continued to sharpen into focus, like an all seeing eye taking in the scene and burning it into the memory of the cosmos. It seemed to whisper, *"This is family too, Mother Nature and The Man. They will always struggle for power, and be divided between chaos and control, but you need them, so it is up to you to navigate the in-between."*

As their children, can we really continue to watch, afraid, as Nature, in all her exquisite beauty, takes the beating? As she lies, unable to raise her arms, unable to close her legs, instead forced to endure, eyes open, screaming curses and insults that too few will hear? Or will we stand up for her? Protect her from harm? Force The Man to romance her for the use of her precious resources?

A Tico in baggy jeans and a dirty baseball cap emptied the corpses from the yard, dumping heavy bushels of green branches onto the sand in front of us, where the tide would soon come to swallow them whole.

The calm of the low tide seemed to spit in revulsion, as begrudgingly, the ocean accepted her duty. The distant rumbling of her waves admitted that she had the power to absorb the trees, of course she did. It also issued a threatening hiss, a warning that she wasn't going to be around to clean up after us forever. A second wave of warning, a menacing echo of the first, a reminder that if she is not around to clean up, we will have already been long gone.

I forced my lids open as I watched, an aware attendant at my first tree funeral. I think I prayed, begging whatever good is in this world to fight for our planet. I stayed this way until the scene was sketched in gray shadows and I saw the Tico man ignite a long torch, pointing it purposefully at every corner of the pile.

The trunks and leaves, still wet with Life went up in copper flame and thick, heavy smoke. The smoke curled and rose, dragging my eyes above the fire, over the sea, and straight up to the bright, white moon. A shocking full circle, a whisper no more, a beacon now standing bravely in triumphant salute to the raw cuts in the trunks of the trees, whose skeletons were burning in the sand.

The lone Tico was joined by a few others, who hauled the huge logs atop the smoldering pile. I felt no anger towards these men, who had deforested a tiny plot of land for a good day's pay, like any hard working citizen would have done. In fact, I think I recognized something in their hunched gait, something that suggested that they too knew the tragedy in what had occurred here. They were just a few men, whose hands were guided by The Man.

There is no one to be angry with. There is no Us or Them. There is only we, a family of Earthlings, connected to each other, spiraling around one another, moving forward into the future.

Yes, Everything is Moving. The control we are looking for is never here to stay, it is always just some moment in a never ending spiral, suspended in a dream. Nothing is perfect, and the anger doesn't help. The suppression of the feminine won't be cured by the suppression of the masculine. We must discover our feminine energy, and integrate it alongside our masculine energy. Not out of hate, but out of true love for whatever it is we humans actually are.

Perhaps The Goddess has been subdued for so long that we can't remember her wisdom, but we can't be angry because of that. Instead, we must listen, try to hear her in everything around us, and try to embody her advice. We sat, watching flame turn wilting leaf to floating ash, until it was time for dinner.

My parents will be here in six days, and we are trying
to clean up the place. I keep having the strangest deja vu,
remembering having to clean up as a child in preparation
for MomMom's visits, only to have her to walk in the
door and start cleaning every spot that we missed. I
thought of how she might react to the amount of sand
and bugs in the kitchen, and concluded that it would
have made her faint, for sure.

She would have never believed we had been cleaning
Casa Playa consistently since our arrival. We have. It's
just that it is impossible to combat the mess on the beach.
The elements are intrusive and its easier to get used to it
than it is to try and control it. Granted, I have had a few
months to get used to it. My parents will only have a
week.

For example, the bugs. There are roaches (the largest
of which can fly) that live in the bodega, and bats that re-
side in the roof. Giant orb-weaving spiders leave clouds
of tunneled web strewn across the landscape that drip
with fallen leaves and intricately woven coffins. A no-
table one reaches close to our centrifugal dryer, its cre-
ator's body hangs in a stark, menacing silhouette against
the early morning sun. The arachnids are uninterested in
and totally harmless to humans, their webs are literally
amazing feats of Nature that exhibit tensile strength similar to that of steel, and there is plenty of evidence that
they help to keep the place bug-free-er. None the less,
their presence will most likely be appalling to suburban-
ites.

It is simply part of Life in the jungle to shake all fabric for dormant critters, and prudent to shine a light on all outdoor walkways after dark to avoid scorpions, centipedes, and crabs. Routinely, animals and humans need to be inspected for ticks and fleas, despite the coat of bug spray that must be worn 24/7 to ward off the mosquitos that carry the dengue fever (commonly described as *"the worst flu I've ever had"*).

I have come to see the bugs like I see the cold weather: environmental conditions that breed plague and malaise, ebbing and flowing with the seasons, creating patterns of aggravation and reprieve. The similarity between them is often overlooked because many humans don't migrate between dramatically different climates for extended stays. The cold kills the bugs, and where you find thriving bugs, you don't find cold winters, so as humans, we deal with the condition we are used to, and fear the one that we are not.

I think any Tico would be as petrified walking through a windy Chicago snowstorm as I am walking through an atmosphere that buzzes with a numerous and winged subculture.

My parents will be here in three days. They keep asking me what to pack. I am worried that their thoroughly Midwestern wardrobes just won't suit jungle life. They appreciate clothes for their aesthetic appeal and believe that perfect fit and understated style are fundamentals to any article.

Around Cabuya and Montezuma, style is of little importance, and even if it were, it is impossible to attain.

When we do come in contact with humans other than ourselves, everyone is in some stage of undress, the common elements a swimsuit, and non-waterproof clothes that are wrinkled, ripped, stained, or dirty. Fit is gone with the first wear. Sweat distorts and stretches the fabric before it is washed, hand wrung, and thrown over a clothesline to dry. The laundry must be done first thing in the morning, allowing it time to dry completely before nightfall when the creepy crawlies are tempted to move in. Clean garments hang outside, all day, in the dust, so my best packing advice is not to bring anything white if you would like to keep it that way. The important aspects of clothing here are that it keeps one cool, dries quickly, and provides some form of protection for your skin from the sun and the bugs.

We rearranged around the property after finding some extra furniture in the bodega, and threw the extra set of sheets in the washing machine. As I wrung and hung them, I wondered if my parents would rather sleep on the musty or the squeaky mattress. I posed the question to Jon and we eventually decided just to choose for them. Why present them with a question that is unanswerable, like *"would you rather vomit or have diarrhea?"* We gave them the squeaky one.

We were interrupted by Granjero. He had come to fix the toilet and hook up our "suicide shower". This is local vernacular that explains the process of obtaining a hot shower here in Cabuya, where there are few water heaters. It entails crossing the electrical wires in such a way as to create enough heat in the shower-head to warm up the water. Seeing as this is not a totally safe way to use electricity, it gets a shocking nickname, although apparently, no one has ever died using one.

We don't mind the cold showers anymore, but here is Granjero, whistling while rearranging his wiring, so my parents can enjoy warm H_2O. As soon as he is finished he turns his attention to the toilet, which has been backing up a lot recently.

Speaking of backing up, I need to rewind for a second here and explain plumbing in the jungle…

Back at The Cabina, a tiny laminate sign was posted at eye level (when sitting on the toilet), that read in both Español and English: "Please DO NOT flush toilet paper! Place it in the trash. Costa Rican septic systems are not built to handle non-natural waste." Not flushing toilet paper is a hard habit to break. Luckily, Jon and I had practice, since this "no flushing" rule also exists on tour buses. Signs like this exist in businesses and residences everywhere, and to throw one's TP in the trash is something that feels normal in no time at all.

The upside to having water that is not filtered through a system overloaded with the breakdown of non-organic products, is that it requires fewer chemicals to treat it. Cleaner, cheaper, win-win. Blue Zone Agua. (Granted, Blue Zone Agua is not due solely to the lack of flushed toilet paper. The TP thing is just one example of many that demonstrates Costa Rica prioritizes the protection of its natural resources).

The downside to these natural systems is that sometimes, the plumbing sucks. We first learned this at La Hacienda, where if we did a load of laundry and showered within the same hour, the water wouldn't turn on the next. Here at Casa Playa, the H_2O problem manifests as a poorly flushing toilet. Often, the water level is low, gurgling in the base of the bowl, and the handle needs to be held encouragingly for a few moments to inspire a powerful flush.

Obviously, this problem is only exacerbated by a number two, and of course our diet consists mainly of beans, rice, and bananas, the ingredients for a particularly efficient bowel movement. The two of us couldn't poop in succession, one disposal tiring the flimsy rush of water in the pipes. The sheer stress of trying to reschedule our colons was almost enough to drive us both mad. Once, Jon approached me looking particularly traumatized. When I asked what happened, he just silently shook his head, his expression caught between a sob and a hysterical bout of laughter. Eventually, he spat out, *"I just had to scoop my own poo out of the toilet and bury it in the sand...like The Cats..."*

I laughed until I cried, but Jon seemed genuinely unnerved, so I subdued myself and tried to comfort him. When his disgust was finally overwhelmed by the humor in the situation he repeated his statement again, this time interrupted by hiccups of laughter. I composed myself slightly to gasp, *"Where?!"*, but he swore, between gulps of air, that he would never tell me.

You could say my parents are slightly pampered in the bathroom arena. Dad brags about his splurges on expensive toilet paper, insisting that it is a product that is always worth the money. Mom keeps their bathroom at home like a spa, recently bleached walls and floors, adorned with colorful, creatively scented soaps, each perfectly poised for an occupant to enjoy a relaxing bubble bath. She is a self-proclaimed "product-junkie", her drawers filled with potions that soften, scrub, sculpt, shine, silk-ify, and scent the human body.

How am I supposed to explain to my parents that they will definitely have to sweep crabs out of their shower, and that they may have to bury their own feces? Oh, and by the way, the bathroom has no sink. We wash our hands beneath the spider web by the laundry, and we brush our teeth in the kitchen...

While I had been distracted by my cleaning and my musing, Granjero had not only emerged from the baño, but had also dug a massive hole in the sand below our clotheslines, uncovering a pipe that had been infiltrated by a tree root: the source of our shitty plumbing.

He opened the pipe, cut the root, and released the stench of who knows how many days worth of clogged excrement. I gagged at the smell, noting the sheets I had washed for my parents were hanging dustily above the hole that Granjero was now vigorously refilling. I guess I would be washing the sheets again tomorrow. Pura Vida.

On Wednesday, my parents arrived. We took a cab to meet them in Tambor, where their tiny passenger plane landed on a golf course. There were many hugs and much excitement and when we returned to Casa Playa, Jon made us each a delicious casado and we visited into the night.

When we woke up, I braided Mom's hair into something that could survive the humidity and bug-spray, then we headed to Montezuma to rent ATVs. We stopped for lunch at Bar Restaurant Montezuma, the spot above the beach, and afterwards, we learned that the ATV's were all booked for the day. Pura Vida. Mom suggested tequila at Chico's instead, and after a few we went home so Mom could take a hammock nap while Jon and Dad tried to conceptualize a theatrical jungle musical.

On Friday, Niña joined us for breakfast and she helped me braid Mom's hair while Dad looked up NFL stats on his iPad. We successfully rented the ATVs and drove to Santa Teresa by way of Cobano, jumping in the ocean before heading to Papaya Lounge for dinner. They complained about the stairs, but agreed the food and view of the sunset was worth it. We dropped them off in Cabuya before taking the ATVs back to Montezuma. Nervous in the jungle in the dark, my driving was slow, choppy, and hilarious to Jon.

The next day, we made it in time for the Organic Market in Montezuma and stocked up on produce. Uncharacteristically, we acted like Tourists, snacking on freshly made crepes served on banana leaves, sipping water from a straw stuck in a coconut, haggling with vendors about the prices of their souvenirs. Back at Casa Playa, we snuck in a quick hammock nap, then headed back to Montezuma and out on the town for St. Patrick's Day.

We started at Cocolores with a round of papaya daiquiris and noticed that the waves of the ebbing tide were glowing. It looked like electricity was crackling through the water and we *"oohed"* and *"ahhed"* as we perused the menu. Before we ordered, the Neighbors showed up, pulled up a few chairs, and joined us. They explained that the glowing waves were just another symptom of the Red Tide.

After dinner, we went to Chico's bar, but the daiquiris paled in comparison so we bought some expensive Guinness at The Super and took a cab home. We ended the night at the table on the patio listening to Mom drunkenly and nostalgically belt out old Irish folk songs.

On Sunday, we had pancakes at the hotel, and then lounged around Casa Playa until Monday, when we returned to Montezuma. We walked north along the beach to the Ylang Ylang resort for happy hour drinks and awesome vegan food, then we stumbled into Open Mic where Jon played a few of his new songs. Tuesday Granjero made us lunch before we went to La Cascada de Montezuma, a waterfall, that was not too far a hike from town. As we trekked up the river, I could see that La Zona Azule had rubbed off on my parents. Dad now somehow reminded me of *Indiana Jones*, and Mom was tan and make-up less, rocking the natural waves in her hair.

When we reached the pool we slid in and the water was cold but intensely refreshing. The view of the 30ft waterfall from its base was humbling, and some brave souls, including Jon, were scaling the rocks and jumping in from astonishing heights. When we grew tired of treading we dried off and hiked back to the dusty road for dinner at Playa de Los Artistas, the fanciest restaurant in the area. It had nice bathrooms, cushioned chairs, hot waitresses, and a gourmet menu. For a moment, I almost thought we were back in the 'burbs.

Wednesday was our last full day together, so we decided to do the most touristy thing of all and take a boat trip to Tortuga Island. We woke up extra early to get to Montezuma, but still almost missed the boat while we were drinking our café. On board, we took a ride through the gulf, headed north along the shore, and watched the blur of dramatic cliffs and tiny cities that exploded once and awhile out of the dense jungle.

We stopped twice to snorkel, and I coaxed Mom into the water, despite her insistence that she didn't want to know what was swimming around under there. I think she enjoyed herself, once she got used to the sensation of breathing through her tube, but she also got back on the boat as soon as we spotted a giant eel.

When we reached Tortuga Island, the crew made us lunch and we enjoyed a private island beach party. Small boats from around the gulf had brought their passengers here to hang out for the day, but they would all leave the island before dark, allowing after hours to be dominated by the wildlife.

We had brought a little joint and snuck away from our folks to enjoy it, only to get caught by our ship's captain. We were able to buy our innocence by gifting him the end of our stash.

We returned to the beach and waded into the perfectly clear ocean, any presence of the Red Tide gone from these shores. We looked back to the land to see my parents passed out on two lounge chairs, having obviously enjoyed their vacation, despite all the drama that jungle life contains.

On Thursday, we accented breakfast with a couple of fruity rum drinks, then they packed up their belongings. Before long, they were off in a taxi to Tambor, on their journey back to The States.

Immediately, we showered and had sex, glad to enjoy the Cabuyan privacy we had grown so accustomed to. Awhile later, we learned that my parents were stuck in San José and would therefore probably be spending the night in Houston. My mood shifted. I felt bad their travel had been stressful. I also felt hungry, now in the habit of eating large, rich meals every night. Mostly, I felt bored, now that we had coupled, we were lonely in the absence of my parents, and more than a little homesick.

Luckily, we were distracted from our depression by Neighbor who introduced us to her new kitten. Very, very new. The thing was only a couple of weeks old, its body resembling more fetus than cat. His name was Juniper, and as soon as he met us, he started running away to our house often, to avoid the overly aggressive snuggles of Niña. Juniper was a fluffy white with patches of gray tabby and therefore he assumed that Dylan was his father. I think Dylan liked the attention, even if he pretended to be annoyed. I watched as the f-animal-y expanded once again, to accept this tiny little critter that was part of our lives now, even though he wasn't "ours".

One morning over café, Jon absentmindedly scratched the kitten's spine and brought up leaving Costa Rica early. He wanted to return to The States, to get a head start on our next move. I pointed out that he only talks about this when I am PMSing, and the conversation ended there. Instead, we poured a bowl of cereal and sat down to watch *Bill Maher.*

During the episode, Musico called to confirm plans he and Jon had recently made to jam at his cabina (Musico hosts Organico's Open Mic Night). His English is rudimentary, his Español better than mine, but usually, he speaks in Italian with twinkling eyes and descriptive hand gestures. I eavesdropped on their phone conversation as Jon chuckled through it, repeating the Español words he knew, and filling in the rest of the details with slow, vague English expressions. His fingers were crossed, hoping everything was translating correctly. I discerned that he would be heading there at 2:00P.M. and that I was invited as well, to hang out with Musica while the boys did their thing.

I was grateful to have been invited and reluctant to turn down the invitation, but I hesitated. I had been planning to use Jon's jamming time to hunker down and get some writing done. I voiced my concern and we decided that it was still early. I could work now, and after lunch, and still accompany Jon to Musico's.

When we got there the boys fiddled with wires and the girls conversed, a familiar ritual in an unfamiliar setting. The language barrier dissipated once the boys held instruments, and afterwards we toured their beautiful property: a home, with a garden, on the river. It was a paradise.

On our way back to Casa Playa, we talked about our family and our friends, old and new. We talked about the social connections we can create when we share memories with the old, ideals with the new, and love with everyone. We came to the conclusion that family is something one is born with, but also something one has to make.

Época Verde

DURING AN AFTERNOON BREAK OF café, papaya, and a documentary about permaculture, Granjero came by with some mangos.

We loved eating mangos that had already been prepared for us, but so far we have avoided them in their raw form, finding them to be a sticky mess. Granjero laughed at us when we asked him how to eat it, but then patiently explained how to peel it before hacking a juicy, orange slice off for me, then one for Jon, then one for himself. As soon as we finished, we split another, and after that, I took another one and ate it all by myself. Quickly, mango became my favorite food, and a few days later we headed back to the farm to get more.

We entered La Hacienda through the gate and immediately noticed the once lush lawn was now an expanse of snapping twigs. As soon as he spotted us, Granjero used one arm to grab a large, empty box, and the other to wave us over with a *"Come, I show you!"*. Crossing the barbed wire into the pastures where we had watched the cows and horses graze months ago, we followed

Granjero single file down a narrow path, until we arrived at a mango tree. Each of its limbs were drooping under the weight of its colorful fruit, and I figured there were probably enough mangos on this one tree to feed everyone in Cabuya, Tico & Tourist alike. These trees were everywhere…

Granjero brandished a large stick and explained that he was going to hit the mangos out of the tree and that Jon was going to catch them. Granjero did his part all right, but the mangos would fly so haphazardly that Jon couldn't seem to snatch a single one. I set to picking them up off the ground and placing them neatly into the backpack, but my rhythm was disrupted as Granjero ran away from the tree, swatting around his head, yelling *"avispas! (wasps!)"*.

He assured us he had another tree with more mangos and fewer avispas, so we followed him deeper into the pasture. The vaca caca became more prevalent as we went, and soon the narrow path was a bit of a hopscotch game. Granjero pointed ahead to another mango tree, this one growing directly to the right of a large herd of cows.

We approached and the vacas watched us carefully. I waved and tried to communicate with my eyes that I thought they were adorable, hoping that they could somehow sense that I hadn't eaten beef for awhile. When Granjero started waving his stick at the branches, many of the cows turned and wandered off, but a few remained, chewing and staring, shifting their weight on their massive hooves.

Granjero swung and Jon darted beneath the tree attempting to catch the fruit that fell in all directions. I organized what he handed me, admiring the colors, reds, oranges, yellows, greens and purples, each fruit shaded uniquely. I learned that the yellow ones were the most sweet, the green ones the least ripe and the shades in between an indicator of when they would be ready to eat. Granjero had found a perfectly ripe one and handed it to me. *"Eat right now"*, he smiled. I wiped it off on my shorts as he would have done, and dug in. As I munched I watched Granjero wave the stick, and Jon, arms overflowing with mangos, chase him around the base of the tree, reaching dramatically for the falling fruit, and missing every time.

I thought back to our afternoon documentary. It seemed that Cabuya naturally resembled the idea of Permaculture, the use of human ingenuity to ethically harness and enhance the symbiosis of Earth's systems. I wondered what the implications could be if we actively designed our entire global system for efficiency and harmony instead of for profit. Then I wondered what the implications would be if we don't...

Just then, a loud *"Moooooooooooo"* made me jump straight in the air. The cows had smelled my mango and moved closer to investigate. I had never before been so close to a cow, and as much as I wanted to reach out and stroke the side of its skull, I was unsure about how the cow would feel about that, so, we just blinked at each other, curiously.

Jon finally got the pattern of trajectory and was able to catch a few mangos before we had completely filled a plastic bag, the backpack, and Granjero's once empty box. We headed back to La Hacienda, sat in the shade, and set down our heavy loads, taking the opportunity to thank Granjero graciously for everything. He seemed genuinely glad to share, proud to show off his beautiful land.

He gave us a bunch of bananas, and then a bunch of plátanos, and then he climbed up a ladder to his roof and opened a screen at the top, producing a handful of sun-dried plátanos. He gave us a few to snack on while he explained the process. We listened intently.

Afterwards we started back to Casa Playa, Jon having to carry both the backpack and the plastic bag, which was too heavy with mangos for my delicate biceps. We discussed our wonderful luck in meeting Granjero, then wondered aloud what to do with the fifty-plus mangos on Jon's person.

After devouring a few more mangos, I grabbed a copy of *The Grapes of Wrath* that I had found in the bodega, and I headed for the hammocks. I had read it before, and hated it, but in hindsight that might have been because I read it as a high school summer reading assignment, while on a 16-hour road trip with my parents. I felt ready to give it a another try. Only a few pages in, I couldn't believe how well the evils of modern society were illustrated in the novel...which was written in 1939. We have known the problem, but we haven't been doing enough to solve it.

Permaculture seems like part of a holistic solution. Transitioning to a permanent culture means thinking as a whole and redesigning human landscapes, institutions, and technologies to integrate, evolve with, and magnify the Earth's resources. Imagine a world in which all of us have sustainable access to water, energy, shelter, food, medicine, technology, education, travel, time…

We were about to sit down to dinner, brains buzzing with the possibility of it all, when we heard the rolling grumble of thunder. We looked at each other and shrugged, we had heard thunder before, but it never actually brought any rain. The rumblings continued and as we finished, the lights flickered. Jon rolled a joint, we put our feet up on the patio table, and settled in to watch the storm.

Too many weeks of beautiful days became boring, and we were genuinely glad for the change of scenery. Lightning flashed over the ocean and we listened to the staccato of rain drops that never hit the sand, collecting instead in the canopy of leaves overhead. We went to bed, breathing in the fresh scent of rain in the dust.

I awoke in the middle of the night to howling wind and saw Jon, already out of bed, flashlight aloft, peering out into the stormy night. We exchanged looks of doom as rain pounded the roof overhead and the house creaked around us. The act of waking up meant we both had to pee, so I grabbed my flashlight and stuck close to him as he slid open the screen door and we shuffled out into the tempest.

The wood floor of our second story was drenched, and the towels and swimsuits that had been left hanging above the banisters were now whipping menacingly inwards. We headed down the slippery stairs and stopped at the landing to see the aerial silk spinning like a flaming tornado in the chaos. Jon bravely reached out and grabbed it, tying it to the banister of the stairs while shouting over the wind for me to continue to the baño without him. I hurried down the stairs and tried to slip into my flip flops, only the realize they contained puddles. I chose to forgo the footwear and pressed on, my braid whipping around my face and brown leaves swirling around my ankles.

I entered the baño, flipped on the light, and closed the door against the intrusive wind. I had to hold the door with my foot to keep it closed, and I peered at the crabs hiding in eaves while I peed. I emerged and Jon dove in while I bolted back up the stairs to shelter.

Once safely back in the bedroom we closed the windows that have been open since we moved in. Much to our dismay, we found the window directly in the wind's current had a broken lock, so the heavy wooden plank swung precariously on rusty hinges with every gust. Jon found something to use as a wedge to keep it closed, and happy to be sheltered, I crawled back under the covers while Jon went once more into the night to rescue our towels.

Instantly, the power went out. I was shrouded in encompassing darkness without the light of the moon through the windows, and instinctively my hands searched the bedside table for the flashlight. I grabbed it and ran to rescue Jon, who was fine. He returned to the bedroom with our towels and with a candle, shoving the long votive into an old wine bottle. Jon decided to go watch the storm from the animal room, and I followed, unwilling to be left alone.

There, we found Dylan, Clover, Marley, and Luna, all curled up in separate corners, avoiding the downpour. We took a dry spot for ourselves and watched as sheets of water fell from the sky, bypassing the palms now, and saturating the sand. Clover hunted a bug that was attempting to find shelter while Marley and Luna shook and whimpered. I was with the canines: wet, cold, tired. Noting my discomfort, Jon suggested we try to sleep again.

Locked up in the dark box listening to the ferocious wind made sleep impossible. We recounted all the crazy storms we have read about, and in light of the truth of climate change, we wondered aloud if we may be amidst the apocalypse. Were we tomorrow's tsunami headline? Having grown up in tornado country, we both felt naive on the second story, so we decided that our safest bet was to spend the night in the kitchen. We stuffed our pillows under our shirts, and I grabbed a dress that had been discarded on the floor and used it to cover our blankets. We held our flashlights aloft, nodded to each other in the dark, then raced out the door, down the stairs, and on to the matte brown tiles. We struggled with the key, huddling around the door, protecting our dry linens as the rain wet our backs. The door finally gave and we spilled inside, slamming it behind us.

We wiped our wet feet and bodies while we searched the room for crabs. Finding none, we laid our blankets down in the middle of the floor and settled on top of them. The floor was hard against our skeletons, and the inky blackness of the night was constantly reminding me of every creepy crawly I had ever swept out of this room. I dozed, but never completely, and as the storm let up, Jon suggested we return upstairs. I groggily agreed and followed him, my feet clumsily hitting every puddle on the way up to our room. We arranged the blankets again, and fell heavily to sleep.

When we awoke, the room was damp and stuffy, and peering out a window we saw that the morning was gloomy and gray. We headed downstairs to see the damage and were unsurprised to find everything soaking wet and filthy. We made café and Googled the weather report, thunderstorms all week. Pura Vida.

As we were finishing our breakfast and wondering how to do and dry our laundry, we heard a familiar *"hola"* and saw Granjero standing near our staircase. He pointed to the rafters where tarps had once been hanging. *"Este"*, he pointed, *"no agua"*, he swung his pointed finger to our puddly staircase. *"Si"*, we agreed. He smiled and offered to help us hang them back up again. *"La época verde (green season)"* he shrugged. We nodded, thanked him, and returned to our damp kitchen. We were sad that our view would be impeded, but we were glad that tonight might be a little drier than last.

While Granjero and Jon went to work rehanging the tarps, I swept the soggy sand from the baño and the patio. Granjero unceremoniously untied the aerial silk, barely allowing it to billow into the sand before pulling a tarp taught across the space it had once filled. I gathered the fabric into my arms and laid it gently onto the patio table. I let go of my grief, resolutely marching upstairs to sweep, the tarps rising around me.

Once everything was clean, my glum mood improved and I was able to appreciate the lowered temperature and the sweet smell of the breeze. We ate some lunch, and a few more mangos, and used the rest of the rainy afternoon to mull over our future.

Our Costa Rican adventure was coming to an end, and we weren't exactly sure what to do next. Our latest plan was to return to The City, immerse ourselves in the culture, and continue our work. However, we were getting antsy about the high rent. Would we get distracted from our plan de vida by financial responsibilities? What other choice did we have? Buy a little cabin in The Country? It wouldn't be as cheap or as beautiful as Cabuya, and it wouldn't have the culture that we missed. Buy a foreclosed house in The Suburbs? The best of both words, a little culture, a little nature...or the unsustainable monoculture that we had come here to escape? We could buy an RV, tour on our own terms, see The States, avoid the unfavorable seasons. All the options seemed good, and bad, and each had a distinct rhythm. It seemed impossible to choose the right course.

We spent the whole weekend this way, stuck inside, each day philosophizing, finally concluding that we would stick with the plan, and go to The City of Chicago.

About a week later, the sun peered through the clouds, so we packed the backpack in hopes for a jungle adventure. As we walked to the market, Neighbor offered to throw me on the back of The Moto, and I accepted, wishing Jon luck as we shifted gears and sped forward. Over the roar of the engine and the crackle of pebbles on tire, we chatted about how sad we were that we weren't going to be neighbors anymore. We had learned a lot from each other, it was nice to live in our tiny commune with our extended f-animal-ies. We were definitely going to miss each other. She dropped me off at the bottom of The Hill, then ascended as I waved goodbye, walking in the direction of Montezuma Centro.

Just as I was entering the intersection, an SUV slowed beside me and Lessor shouted out the window, *"I have your man!"* A rear window rolled down, and I saw the backseat was full of smiling, but unfamiliar faces. Eventually, I noticed Jon waving from the trunk, so I opened the hatch to let him out. As we walked towards the park hand in hand, Jon explained that Lessor might be able to get us a cheap ATV for the day, and that she was having a party tonight.

After catching up with Konstnär and making our purchases, we visited with some of the other friends we have made in Montezuma. We reminisced about our first time here, how we stood awkwardly, knowing nothing of the people and the customs around us. Now we visited genuinely with friends and exchanged happy nods with familiar faces. This sense of community surrounding organic food was so powerful in this tiny jungle village, and I truly hoped we would find something similar back in Chicago.

I sat with all the groceries while Jon talked business with Lessor's ATV guy. He negotiated well, securing the ATV overnight for only ten extra dólares We cheered, we would not have to keep our eye on the clock tonight! As Jon listened to a quick tutorial about this particular quad, I wound up in a conversation with someone we had met at Karaoke Night, a fellow Chicagoan. We talked about traveling home and he wished us luck, explaining there was an incredible waterfall, La Cascada de Florida, that we should check out if we had an ATV for the day. That sounded perfect, so I asked him for directions.

He explained that we were to take Pura Vida Road, which is unmarked (obviously) but somewhere near a nature lodge and a bakery. If we missed the road it was okay, because we could just go all the way into Cobano and get on Pura Vida Road by turning right after the banco (we knew where that was!). From there we would drive about 5km (ATV sales guy interjected that it was actually 7.5km), until we saw a lavish gate with nothing behind it. Soon after, there would be a corral on our left, and a small house on our right. We nodded (although I winced slightly, hoping Jon knew what a corral was, because I certainly didn't). We were to go to the house and pay 2mil. Once paid, we would be shown to a gate. After passing through two more gates we would reach a large tree. There, we would find La Cascada de Florida. We nodded again.

Jon reversed the ATV and I climbed on behind him, groceries hooked around my elbows, the backpack heavier than usual, loaded with organic veggies. We were to meet the guy who rented us the quad at a tourism kiosk just outside of town where we would grab our helmets. Jon revved the engine and we sped out of Montezuma Centro, past the bus stop, and to the kiosk. We were greeted by a Tica who gave us two helmets, and we concluded that the ATV would need to be dropped off here by 9:00A.M. With that, we sped towards Cabuya, wind and sun in our faces, the journey quick and painless thanks to our set of wheels. We unloaded the groceries, packed our final bottle of Flor de Caña, and settled back on the quad, tossing stones near Marley to discourage him from following us.

We drove straight through Montezuma and up the hill to Cobano, trying to recall the bizarre directions to the waterfall. We did see a nature lodge and bakery in close proximity to one another, but we didn't see a road we felt confident taking, so we decided just to go through Cobano. We turned after the banco and as soon as civilization soon morphed back into rolling jungle hills, I asked Jon if he knew what a corral was. His burst of laughter told me that he did not and I laughed but seriously hoped we would figure it out. I kept my eyes peeled for the "lavish gate with nothing behind it".

Suddenly, there it was. A magnificent portal that seemed to be guarding only vast grasslands. Shortly afterwards, there was a small house to our right, and a livestock pen to the left. The information slammed to the front of my brain, a corral did sound like something from one of my PopPop's Eddie Arnold tapes! I bet that was it. A place to keep cows, etc. I told Jon to turn around and we approached the casa.

I hopped off the ATV, with a cautious *"hola"*, truly hoping we were in the right place. I stood in front of the tiny house amidst its enormous garden, hoping that someone had heard my call. Soon, a smiling woman emerged. I asked if this was La Cascada de Florida and she began talking very fast. I tried to explain that I hablo Español malo. She smiled, insisting my pronunciation was good, and gratefully spoke again, this time slowly, and with more hand gestures. I gathered that we were in the right place while she walked with me towards the road. Once we had reached Jon and the quad, she pointed to a gate tucked next to what I was now confident was a corral. Then, she stuck out her palm, requesting her money, and I found I had no problems passing her four bucks for directions to paradise.

We spun the ATV around, pulled up to the gate, passed through it, and started down the trail, a streak of red dirt transcending the vibrantly green grass.

Vacas were grazing in the pasture and they watched us with bored expressions as we waved at them from our chariot. This was so exciting for us and so typical for them. We did manage to get a rise out of a group of calves whose wobbly legs ran off in an awkward panic as we noisily approached.

We stopped to snap a few photos, reveling in the mountainous countryside. The ocean was beautiful and mysterious, but these vast green pastures possessed an entirely different energy and charm. The perfect spot for a little hobbit hole amongst the cows and staggering arboles. A place to live off the land. To be a short ATV ride away from all sorts of culture. To be alive and appreciate that everything around you is alive. Were we insane to leave this behind to return to civilization, steeped in its own self-replicating culture of consumerism, built in dirty concrete and staggering metal?

Maybe, but this just didn't feel like "ours". We couldn't help but feel like Cabuya didn't need us. We would be better off trying to fight the good fight and live in harmony with Mother Nature somewhere where she was more poorly represented.

We passed through a second gate, then the third, and then the trail led us straight to a tree. La Cascada de Florida had to be around here somewhere.

We turned the key in the ignition and once the motor died, the silence allowed us to hear the sound of rushing water coming from a cluster of trees behind The Tree. We stepped into the forest and I had chills, assuming this must have been what it felt like to walk into Narnia…

It was a different world entirely. We were standing at the edge of a cliff, atop a grooved valley, the only humans in sight. A river ran vertically down the dramatic rock formations, and wild vegetation sprawled, soaking in the abundance of H_2O. We descended through the brush, a few man made blocks and well placed zip-lines providing steps where Nature had provided only a slope. Within moments we were standing on the boulders below, gazing up at one waterfall to our left, and down on another to our right.

The valley seemed to stretch endlessly straight up and down, but its infinite view was occluded by dense jungle, sharp curves, and steep drops of waterfall. Jon tried to take photographs, but it was the depth of the place that was so mind blowing, the two dimensional interpretation unable to capture the magic.

Leaving the backpack under the shade of a tree, we kicked off our shoes, stripped down to our swimsuits, walked to the edge of the rocks, and peered into the large pool. The first few inches of the stone that supported my feet could be seen underwater, its colors distorted by the water and a layer of algae, but the pool showed nothing else. It's surface was calm, black, and bottomless. I gulped, intimidated by the power of the falling water.

Jon dove in gracefully. I crouched and clumsily slid in, mostly worried about losing my bikini to the abyss. The water was shockingly cold but we dunked and swam, our breath short from the combined effort of constantly treading while laughing. We splashed around, giddy with the natural beauty of the place, alive in the present moment, in harmony with everything around us.

We climbed to the top of the fall for a different perspective and sat on a rock, talking about our love for nature and our fears about returning to civilization. We talked about our calling to unite these two things that may be fundamentally divided. Then we kissed, and I wished that everyone could make out at the top of a waterfall, eyes closed, senses bombarded with everything it is to be an Earthling.

We climbed back up to The Tree (a task much more demanding then climbing down had been), and back onto the ATV. I tucked my chin onto Jon's shoulder and we ascended and descended across the countryside. I cringed when I imagined the traffic and road rage I would soon experience behind the wheel. Jon pulled over and snapped some photos, suggesting we take a swig of rum, straight out of the bottle, like pirates.

We continued on and as we neared Santa Teresa we drove past a chalkboard sign advertising craft beer. Jon made an instant u-turn, parked the ATV, and we entered the vacant bar. We ordered a tropical golden ale and a red ale, both of which were new experiments from a Costa Rican brewing company. The hops were simply delicious and we talked candidly and passionately, fueled by a slight buzz, about how Craft Beer, like Cannabis, and MindBody Fitness, could be an Industry designed with Permaculture in mind. We ordered another round and the conversation returned to how much we were going to miss this place. We both agreed that we wanted to come back here in the future. After round three, I was tipsy and hungry. We emerged from the bar still engrossed in our conversation…

Oh Shit! The sky was getting dark! We had missed sunset! The main reason we had wanted to come back once more to Mal Pais! We jumped on the quad and turned towards the ocean, but it was too late, the orb had already sunk out of view. The colors were still incredible, but soon they faded, so we left. Pura Vida. We ate and headed back to Cabuya.

Driving the ATV at night was such a different experience. We stopped a few times, turning off the engine and the headlight, admiring the epic stars in the dark silence of the jungle. As we drove over the final hill before we would descend past The Cabina and into Cabuya, we noticed extraordinarily bright lights coming from the direction of Cabo Blanco. Intrigued, we decided to go check it out.

We drove past The Only Bar, La Panadería, and The Supermercado before slowing down near a soccer field, which was the source of the bright lights. We parked in an alley already crowded with vehicles and walked gingerly towards the game, unsure if we were welcome or not. We smiled with relief when we saw Granjero, who immediately waved us over. We found out the game was Cabuya vs. Cobano, and the score was 5-4, Cobano. There were no bleachers, but fans still surrounded the field, cheering and jeering in Español. Dogs and children ran freely as well, somehow knowing better than to run too close to the action. Players squatted on the sidelines, some with cervezas and cigarettes alternating from hands to lips. The perimeter was lined with giant flood lamps, their glow illuminating the jungle, towering above us on the outskirts of all the frivolity.

Konstnär was there and joined us, switching between English and Español when addressing us and Granjero. It was impressive to see the languages so effortlessly interchanged. I had learned so much from my first days here, but I wasn't leaving nearly as fluent as I had hoped to be. Cabuya scored, tying the game. Before long a referee blew a whistle and the players ran off, smiling, as a new team ran on. No one had won, but it seemed to me The Game was still worth playing.

We decided to skip the second game and go to Lessor's party instead. We waved our rum as we approached the gathering, and were greeted by a couple seated on a bench, and three men seated around a table. Lessor floated between the two groups to kiss us and invite us in. We introduced ourselves, took long swigs from the bottle, and wound up having a great time.

Our plan was to wake up early and use the quad to check out some of the beaches on the way to Montezuma.

Unfortunately, we were a little hungover (the "little" a miracle actually, if you consider we were drinking like pirates all day), so we decided to nurse our headaches instead.

When we eventually embarked, the wind in our hair and the sun on our cheeks was an instant cure, and I tucked my chin onto Jon's shoulder again, relishing our last ATV ride through the jungly hills. We dropped off the vehicle and headed to The Super to buy an onion loaf in hopes that it would soak up the last of the queasiness in our stomachs.

The walk back to Cabuya was hot and exhausting, both of our hip and knee joints already sore from bouncing across so much terrain the day before. Our headaches returned with the effort of lugging ourselves up the hills. It was a lazy Sunday morning, no one seemed to be driving around. We discussed how the seclusion of Época Verde is tranquil, but very bad for hitchhiking.

When we finally made it back to Casa Playa, we were both lacking energy and groaned aloud when we remembered that we had promised the night before to attend Konstnär's potluck this evening. We genuinely did want to go, we just felt so cranky, and had totally forgotten to pick up ingredients at The Super to make something to bring for the potluck. We figured we had all day to decide what to do.

Musico stopped by, with a flash drive full of audio recordings of Jon's Open Mic performances. He and Jon talked about music, both admitting they had learned a lot from each other, and were sad that they met so late in our stay. They discussed their plans for the future. The language barrier that once seemed so insurmountable now barely noticeable, even though neither one was speaking in the other's tongue. I joined the boys outside, and found that their conversation had turned to Konstnär's potluck. Musico assured us our lack of potluck dish would go unnoticed, and that he and Musica were going around 4:00P.M. if we wanted to walk with them. Then, he picked his bicycle out of the dust, bestowed a kiss on my cheek, grasped Jon for a handshake that morphed into a hug, and took off towards the dusty road.

I showered, and Jon shaved his beard, the appearance of his dimples earning him a few extra kisses on his recently smoothed cheeks. The Musicos showed up at 5:00P.M. (which they explained *is* Italian for 4:00P.M.) and we grabbed an unopened bag of peanuts, unable to show up to a potluck empty handed.

The four of us, and the three dogs, headed south on the beach into a beautiful time of day. The clouds were puffy, and the colors magnificent in the ebbing sunlight. Entering Konstnär 's property from the beach, giant palms swayed overhead, and we crossed a tiny river bed, dry now, but certain to be lovely in the middle of Green Season. She had roped off gardens, and horse corrals(!), and the entire scene was dotted by the flickering glow of fireflies. Other than Konstnär and The Musicos, we knew no one, but I recognized a few faces from the organic market.

We started at the food table and were told everything was vegetariano so we dug in. We ate with The Musicos and started to really appreciate their senses of humor, a personality trait that is often lost in translation. We met the rest of the party, a group of mostly expats, including one of the guys who had passed Jon his joint in the pick-up truck. We were kissed by a jovial, long haired surfer, who Musica explained was actually incredibly shy, but tonight was very drunk. We were stunned by the bilingualism of everyone in attendance. I heard the pick-up truck stoner converse fluidly in English, Español, and Français, switching between the languages without any hesitation.

Appetites sufficed, we walked over to Konstnär's art studio, browsing through her work, which was sometimes funny, sometimes haunting, and always beautiful. We took a seat in the gallery on a large, orange sofa, and were startled when a black cat darted from underneath it. Immediately, Luna noticed it, and the cat swelled and growled, darting back to the hiding place. Luna followed as far as she could, tail in the air, snout under the sofa.

Musico and Jon had both brought their guitars so they sat, strumming and tuning, discussing what to play. A small crowd had formed and Konstnär produced cushions for everyone to sit on. The over-served surfer plopped down in front and started requesting songs by insisting, *"play the one that goes 'Da da da Da daaAA'"*. Everyone was entertained and eventually, Jon caught the gist of his request, starting into Bob Marley's *Redemption Song*.

The whole crowd sang along, much more confidently in the chorus than the verse, but no one as loudly as the surfer who had requested it. The sing along continued. Together, the crowd knew enough lyrics and the band enough chords to play for awhile.

The cat escaped from under the couch again, prepared for Luna this time, and on a table before the canine even thought to move. The cat sat still, tail wrapped around legs, studying a painting on the wall. Luna sat in the same fashion on the floor, staring up at the cat. Marley took the opportunity to steal the cat's hiding spot, scooting his scrawny body under the couch and curling up into a tiny ball.

The crowd dispersed, but Jon and Musico played on, more candidly now that they were audience free. The guests continued leaving, until it was just the four of us, Konstnär , and her date for the evening. We would have talked all night, but became distracted when Musico lifted the canvas the cat was still staring at off of the wall. He turned the piece over, and there, a bunch of baby bats were crawling around. Their bodies were tiny, wings awkwardly large, like the paws on a puppy, or the ears on a kitten. They didn't seem able to fly, but experimented with climbing up then sliding down the canvas, to the *"oohing"* and *"ahhing"* of the human party dwellers.

The Fight

THE FOLLOWING DAY, DUE TO the rain, we had to once again cancel our trip to Cabo Blanco. On the bright side, we got an offer from an old friend (the bassist of Jon's high school band) to split the rent on a house in Logan Square.

We had never really considered rooming with someone, we had definitely grown used to our privacy, but it could help us save significantly on rent, and we would have a built in pet-sitter in the event of travel or a tour...

Neighbor came by wondering if we would keep an eye on her f-animales during her border run. We agreed, shocked it had been ninety days since her last trip to Nicaragua. We watched an insightful documentary on *Tetris*, but when it was over it was still only 9:00A.M., so we worked for a bit, then Jon made some beans. After lunch, we hit the beach for a stroll with the dogs.

When we got home we were able to video-chat with Roommate, who had spent the day house hunting. Thanks to Technology, he was able to give us video tours of his favorite places, and then we were able to discuss everything, as if we had all been present. It looked as though we would have a place in Chicago as soon as we got home. Honestly, we couldn't believe how well it had all worked out. Pura Vida.

As the days drew to a close, we relived our favorite moments. We returned to Tortuga Island for a private island adventure, Musico invited Jon to perform a complete set at Organico, and I compulsively checked the weather trying to find a time to hike Cabo Blanco and have a final dinner at The Café.

I had wanted to go to Cabo Blanco since first Googling Costa Rica back at The Townhouse, but Jon wasn't super interested in the long trek, mostly because Marley couldn't come with us. I wanted him to go simply because I wanted to go, but we were leaving Costa Rica in 72 hours, so at this point I was going with or without him.

On a relatively dry day, I told him as much and started packing. He sat rooted in his chair, barely blinking in his resolve. It made me so angry. I went on my way.

I walked slowly and stalled at just about every tree I could touristically stare at, but before long I reached downtown Cabuya and still, he wasn't following. I scowled and kept my slow pace, waving to The Neighbors who passed by on The Moto, blissfully on their way home from La Panadería.

It was with a heavy heart that I paid my admission fee. I took my change with a glum *"muchas gracias."* At the sound of a familiar whistle, I perked up. I turned around to see Jon, sweating, holding a bottle of water in one hand and a box of cereal in the other. I had never been so happy to see him.

I handed back my change to pay for his admission and grabbed the map, heading off in the direction the guide had pointed. I was glad Jon had come, and that we were going to do this hike together.

Almost immediately, he started picking a fight again, and my anger flared. I was so ready to forgive him ten seconds ago…

I say he never wants to do what I want to do. He says nothing is ever enough for me. A screaming fight ensues, and for the first time ever, we mention it. The word. *Divorce.*

He said, *"If you are so unhappy, why don't you just divorce me?"*

I screamed, *"I don't want to divorce you, I just wanted to go to Cabo Blanco with you!"*

We pushed on in a devastating silence, interrupted only by the crackling of the twigs below our sneakers. I stopped to read every sign. I had to admit, the nature was epic: monkeys, foliage, hills almost impossible to trespass. I was incredibly glad I wasn't alone, even if I would have preferred to take this hike with a different version of Jon. I am sure he would have preferred to do it with a different version of me as well…

We continued hiking in this way, fuming, avoiding eye contact. The silence was welcome for the most part, my heart and lungs were already working too hard to be burdened with conversation and laughter, let alone heated arguments.

Finally, what seemed like way longer than the two hours advertised, we reached the beach. I felt equally as exhausted as I had on the walk to Mal Pais.

Things between Jon and I were still awkward so I just laid in the sand and did some yoga. I was sandy so I rinsed off in the ocean, and while I waded I couldn't help but think that this beach didn't seem any more special than Casa Playa's. Then, I donned the backpack and we headed back into the jungle. Jon led the way this time, in his socks, sneakers in hand to relieve a blister on his heel.

I quickly fell behind, panting up the steep hills, heart palpitating, breath too loud in my ears. Jon took the backpack, which made things easier, but I felt bad. It must have been harder for him with his already sore feet. He eventually put his shoes back on, and after what seemed like twice as long as the hike in, we exited the park. The victory of being finished eased the tension between us, slightly.

I wondered aloud about The Café and Jon agreed that we should eat. On route we talked. It was terse, but gradually improving.

When we arrived, Cocinera was glad to see us. I explained that we had come to say goodbye and she sat with us to catch up. We told her about our adventures, how we had been writing, and our experiences practicing Español and English with Granjero. She told us about the bike marathon she completed from Tambor (where we picked up my parents) to Manzanillo (past Santa Teresa!), and we were embarrassed to admit how exhausted and hungry we were from our hike through Cabo Blanco that day.

I was nostalgic for pizza so we ordered it, then Jon and I attempted again to talk about the tension between us.

Within moments, the stiff yet peaceful interaction between us turned sour. The pizza came, but I couldn't stomach it, my insides twisted with anger. Jon ate and I was glad Cocinera wouldn't be insulted, but I couldn't believe that this day had turned into Jon begrudgingly eating cheese, instead of the two of us having a fun date on our last Friday in paradise.

We paid and visited, amicable as long as we didn't have to talk to each other. We headed out before it got too dark, trekking the kilometer back to Casa Playa in complete silence. We showered the sweat and dust from our skin, then got into a terrible fight which ended with me running upstairs at 7:00P.M. and slamming the door.

It was dark and boring up there, and my mind was racing. I do think we are a happy couple, but sometimes I get mad at him. And any time I get mad at him, all of a sudden, he thinks I should leave if things are so bad. I don't want to leave. Would he really rather me leave than fight with me about this thing?

I thought about the implications for my philosophies. If two people who love each other this much can find it so impossible to communicate sometimes, how are we supposed to come together as a species?

I knew I was being mean and unforgiving, but I was mad, madder than I was when this fight had started. I tried to read, but couldn't focus, so I burrowed my head in the pillow and tried to think. I had to throw up. I raced downstairs, passed Jon, and dashed into the baño where I emptied the bile that was the scoop of cereal, banana, and bite of pizza that had been my sustenance today. Why was I so sick? Could I really be that mad at Jon?

I exited the baño and we spoke but it was nasty, so I ran up the stairs again, pounding my feet on the wooden boards above his head to accent my screams of indignation.

Eventually, Jon bravely ascended the stairs and tried yet again. I laid in our bed staring at the ceiling, he crouched in a corner by the screened door. We fought some more, but eventually started articulating our thoughts a little more clearly. At some point we made it down the stairs and to the patio table where we lit a joint to help us calm down. After a few puffs we were no longer enemies. This led to the lucid realization that I was angry at him for dismissing what I want, and he was angry with me for not expressing my wants clearly enough for him to not accidentally dismiss them. That seemed fair.

He hadn't realized going to Cabo Blanco held so much meaning for me. We were both to blame for that.

We also came to the conclusion that our departure from Costa Rica might be a lot more emotional than we had anticipated.

Everything is Moving. There is no perfect solution, no right and wrong, no end goal. There is only an ongoing fight for a delicate balance. We need to work together instead of against each other if we want to hope to survive.

I stood and Jon waved me to him, eyes huge, inviting. I joined him and we kissed, glad we had made it through yet another battle. I told him how nauseous I felt, he suggested I was pregnant. I punched him playfully, but my stomach flipped again.

We were too exhausted to actually consummate the peace agreement, but we headed up to bed together, and intertwined our fingers while we fell asleep.

On Monday, we made café for the last time with the Elephant Condom. I did my last Tico load of laundry, nervous that the cloudy morning would leave our suitcase full of damp garments. We packed and Jon rolled the rest of our cannabis into three joints. We laughed, we had a lot of smoking to do today...

We headed to the hammocks to watch the high tide splash against the rocks, and with that, joint number one was gone.

We both used the inspiration to write, but soon, a recently chewed nut casing fell from the tree tops and onto my stomach. The monkeys had come to say goodbye. They were hanging in the trees directly above us, shaking the branches to sprinkle leaves upon us, and occasionally hurling a stick or nut in our direction. We clutched our electronics and retreated, waving and laughing, noticing a tiny baby swinging in their midst. We relocated to the breakfast nook, but they followed us, so we headed all the way back to the patio table, and Jon made one last casado.

We were only a few puffs into joint number two when Neighbor walked over to tell us that Novio, our ride to the airport tomorrow, had the flu. Jon put out the joint and called the cab driver who had chauffeured us around during my parents visit. In typical Tico fashion, he jovially agreed to give us a ride, across the country, tomorrow morning at dawn. Pura Vida. We were set. We lit the second joint again.

Granjero came to say goodbye, gifting us the jade blanket that lay across the bed in his best bedroom. We were glad to have such a meaningful souvenir from the trip. He explained in his pantomime way that we are now family, and I believed him. Neighbor also came to say goodbye and we laughed as Luna, Buddy and Juniper wrestled, unbeknownst to the fact that they would never see us again.

Neighbor would be taking over Luna's care until someone else moved into Casa Playa, so we gave her the rest of our dog and cat food. With hugs and well wishes she and her f-animales took off past the trees.

We finished packing, then decided to "get throned", a.k.a. smoke joint number three and watch *Game of Thrones*. We only made it through half of the joint and half of the episode before deciding to head up the stairs, one last time, to fall asleep to the sound of the jungle rain.

We awoke to an alarm at 4:00A.M. In the darkness, we stood and gathered the last of our belongings. We put on our traveling clothes, headed downstairs, herded The Cats, and rearranged our luggage one last time.

We walked to the hammocks and stood, looking up at the stars and a crescent moon that shone fuzzily through a haze of wispy clouds. We took in the ocean, inhaling its presence into our sensory memory. It was low tide and the shadows of rock were rising out of silver-black pools of predawn sea. Lightning crackled near Isla Cementerio. We crossed our fingers, hopeful the worst of the storm had passed. Our cab arrived and we started off into the dark morning.

When we passed the bay in Montezuma, a few tears slipped from my eyes as I gazed at the familiar landscape. The growing tide was sleepy in its tumult, and deep in its blue without the presence of the sun. The radio blared a mix of hits in both Español and English, and at one point I was forced to accept that *Every Rose Has Its Thorn* was somehow written about me and Jon leaving Cabuya.

We sped down the green countryside, already running late for our 6:00A.M. ferry.

We arrived in Paquera at 5:51A.M., put Marley on his leash, and boarded. As Jon handed me Dylan's crate he informed me that Dylan had unfortunately had an accident. Poor guy. We walked, his damp crate rubbing against my leg. Seated in the designated pet area, we grabbed a few paper towels that we packed and I soaked up what I could while Jon went in search of more napkins, and a cup of café. We tried to get Dylan as dry as possible, and he seemed like he was comfortable. I didn't think the odor was too bad, but maybe I was just getting used to it.

The ferry ride passed quickly, and soon we were back in the cab, speeding through Puntarenas, and onward towards the Central Valley. Slowly, more civilization began to appear, first billboards, then fast food chains, then suburban strip malls, then crowded city streets, then finally, the airport.

When the cab driver pulled over at our terminal, he mentioned that when we were ready to come back to

Cabuya we should call him and he would pick us up -
and our animals, he added with a laugh, and our babies,
he added with a wink.

Check-in was easy. We waved goodbye to Marley,
headed through security, and trudged along to find our
gate, stopping to eat at a place with free wifi and vegetarian sandwiches. We boarded, positioned The Cats under
the seats in front of us, and then we left Costa Rica.

As soon as we landed in Miami, Jon turned on his cell
phone. We taxied to our gate, then descended into The
States. We followed the signs for passport control, whose
arrows often pointed in contradicting directions, and we
received another stamp in each of our passports. From
there, we followed the masses through customs, and
found ourselves confused, more than once, about which
line we were supposed to be in.

Usually the process is quite self-explanatory, and considering MIA must see many international travelers, their
system seemed flawed, and inefficient. Or maybe, we had
just forgotten what civilization was like.

As I handed my customs form to the man in the uniform, I asked about Marley and the flight connection
process. He explained that I was going to have to get the
dog and physically bring him through customs. We
turned to where he was pointing, and for the first time
noticed Marley's crate, and our little guy sitting silently
inside, wagging away.

We also noticed our suitcases lying nearby....was our
luggage not connecting to our next flight either? We
asked another uniformed person and she assured us that
we needed to collect all of our baggage and bring it

through customs (something that had happened magically the last time we had stopped off in Florida). We grabbed two small luggage carts and loaded everything and everyone on. We showed the animals health certificates, sent the bags through the X-ray, and were told to follow a series of yellow dots along the floor.

At the end of the dots, they took our suitcases, but explained we needed to take the dog upstairs to TSA, pointing us in the direction of the elevator. We had to wait for three elevators before there was one with enough room for all of us and we packed in, pressing the "2" for our airline's check-in. We tried to talk to the employees, but everyone kept pointing us onward explaining pet check was at the next set of check-in counters. Finally, we saw a sign for pets and got in line behind another cat carrying couple. After waiting patiently, even by airport standards, we started getting anxious about not having a long enough layover.

We were both starving and wanted dinner, but now that we were back here at check-in, we were going to have to go through security again. Who knew how long that would take.

At 7:30P.M. (our flight began boarding at 7:45P.M.), I cornered an unsuspecting uniformed employee and explained our situation. He informed me that since we already had our boarding passes we could just drop the dog off (he pointed to a set of huge metal doors) and then go through security. I was so glad we hadn't wasted more time. We followed his directions.

Our boarding passes had no gate info, so as we hiked towards security, I peeked at the information screen and burned "D8" into my memory. The line for security was massive, but Jon had seen a sign that suggested only a fifteen minute wait time, so we stood, anxious, shuffling our bags a few feet in front of us every few minutes.

At 7:57P.M. we knew we weren't going to make our 8:15P.M. flight, so Jon hopped out of line to plead our case, Marley was already on that plane...

They let us cut in line. We booked it for D8. Concourse D had sixty terminals, and of course, we were standing by D30. We knew we had an incredible hike to take in the under ten minutes. We tried to run, but The Cats and the backpack weighed us down. I took the backpack and the suitcase and sped ahead. Jon kept a calmer pace for our furry friends. As soon as I saw the sign for D8, I also saw a clock, it read 8:13P.M.

Holy shit, this was close. I ran up to the gate and slammed our passports on the desk, begging not to be too late for check-in. The employee looked at my boarding pass, and raised his eyebrows. My flight wasn't at this gate, my flight was at D42. The flight to Chicago from D8 left at 9:15P.M. Jon appeared just in time to hear this information and his expression admitted the complete defeat that I felt. We explained that our dog was on the plane, and the attendant said he would call D42 and try to have them stall for us.

So, we started back in the direction we had come from, sweating and panting. When we returned to the security checkpoint, the signs for D42 led us up two escalators and to a sky tram. We were stunned. There was no way we were going to make this flight, but we might as well keep going now, we had already walked this far.

We boarded the tram and had to wait until the third and final stop to jump out. It was down two more escalators, and a brisk walk past another few gates where we found D42 which was, of course, deserted. We stood at the desk and caught our breath. So, Marley was on his way to Chicago without us. Now what? Our buddy back at D8 had made it seem like there was room on the 9:15...

Jon sat with the stuff, I ran over to D44 and explained the situation, pleading with the attendant to get us on the next flight to Chicago. She clicked her nails over the keys and explained that they were about to start boarding, but there were quite a few seats left on the flight. We should be fine if we got back to D8 in a hurry. Well, great. As if we hadn't done that before.

We walked quickly. Up the escalators, took the tram, down the escalators, and all the way back to D8. The attendant immediately recognized us and booked us two seats on the 9:15P.M. It was 8:45P.M. We would start boarding any minute.

I couldn't believe that two hours of airport stress and shenanigans had almost erased the peace that six months in the jungle had brought me. I took a deep breath. Yes, we missed our flight. We also caught one the next hour. Pura Vida.

On the plane, I tried to sleep, but my legs were jumpy from all the running without any stretching, so I wrote. Jon listened to music.

At baggage claim, we found Marley, still in his crate, surrounded by a couple of animal lovers who were arguing over who would get to take him home if he remained unclaimed. We loaded him onto our luggage cart and waited in silence for Dad to pick us up.

On the drive my mind wandered, why is it so cold here? And why are there so many lights on? The closed Chili's does not need to be so illuminated at 1:00A.M...

Almost 24 hours after we left Casa Playa, we arrived at my parent's house. The 60-inch TV was on, even though no one was home. What is that huge thing? Why is advertising so weird?

It was late, but I was full of nervous energy, so I wandered around the house, turning out all of the lights, fighting the urge to shake the decorative throw pillows for scorpions.

Made in the USA
Lexington, KY
15 November 2018